Learning and Teaching Concepts

A STRATEGY FOR TESTING
APPLICATIONS OF THEORY

EDUCATIONAL PSYCHOLOGY

Allen J. Edwards, Series Editor
Department of Psychology
Southwest Missouri State University
Springfield, Missouri

Published

Herbert J. Klausmeier and Thomas S. Sipple. Learning and Teaching Concepts: A Strategy for Testing Applications Theory

James H. McMillan (ed.). The Social Psychology of School Learning

M. C. Wittrock (ed.). The Brain and Psychology

Marvin J. Fine (ed.). Handbook on Parent Education

Dale G. Range, James R. Layton, and Darrell L. Roubinek (eds.). Aspects of Early Childhood Education: Theory to Research to Practice

Jean Stockard, Patricia A. Schmuck, Ken Kempner, Peg Williams, Sakre K. Edson, and Mary Ann Smith. Sex Equity in Education

James R. Layton. The Psychology of Learning to Read

Thomas E. Jordan. Development in the Preschool Years: Birth to Age Five

Gary D. Phye and Daniel J. Reschly (eds.). School Psychology: Perspectives and Issues

Norman Steinaker and M. Robert Bell. The Experiential Taxonomy: A New Approach to Teaching and Learning

J. P. Das, John R. Kirby, and Ronald F. Jarman. Simultaneous and Successive Cognitive Processes

Herbert J. Klausmeier and Patricia S. Allen. Cognitive Development of Children and Youth: A Longitudinal Study

Victor M. Agruso, Jr. Learning in the Later Years: Principles of Educational Gerontology

Thomas R. Kratochwill (ed.). Single Subject Research: Strategies for Evaluating Change

Kay Pomerance Torshen. The Mastery Approach to Competency-Based Education

The list of titles in this series continues on the last page of this volume.

Learning and Teaching Concepts

A STRATEGY FOR TESTING
APPLICATIONS OF THEORY

Herbert J. Klausmeier

Department of Educational Psychology
The University of Wisconsin—Madison
Madison, Wisconsin

with the assistance of

Thomas S. Sipple

Wisconsin Research and Development Center
for Individualized Schooling
The University of Wisconsin—Madison
Madison, Wisconsin

ACADEMIC PRESS   1980

A Subsidiary of Harcourt Brace Jovanovich, Publishers

New York   London   Toronto   Sydney   San Francisco

ACADEMIC PRESS, INC.
111 Fifth Avenue, New York, New York 10003

United Kingdom Edition published by
ACADEMIC PRESS, INC. (LONDON) LTD.
24/28 Oval Road, London NW1   7DX

Library of Congress Cataloging in Publication Data

Klausmeier, Herbert John, Date
    Learning and teaching concepts.

    (Educational psychology series)
    Includes bibliographies.
    1. Teaching. 2. Cognition in children. 3. Concepts.
4. Individualized instruction. I. Sipple, Thomas S.,
joint author. II. Title.
LB1025.2.K563   372.11'02   80–758
ISBN 0–12–411450–4

PRINTED IN THE UNITED STATES OF AMERICA

80 81 82 83   9 8 7 6 5 4 3 2 1

Contents

List of Figures

List of Tables

List of Appendix Tables

Preface

This book presents an overview of a theory of cognitive learning and development and describes a generic model for arranging instruction to provide for differences among students. Applications of the theory and the instructional model were identified and tested in 13 controlled experiments in two paired sets of schools. The research strategy and the results of the experiments are reported and discussed.

Educational researchers and graduate students in courses in research methodology and instructional psychology will be particularly interested in analyzing and evaluating this particular strategy for identifying and testing applications of a learning theory and an instructional model. Scholars and graduate students in courses in learning, development, and curriculum will be interested in the substantive theoretical information and in the verification of the applications through the controlled experimentation.

One primary contribution of the book is that it deals with process concepts, that is, concepts that can be performed as well as understood. For example, the basic science concepts, *observing, inferring,* and *predicting,* can be performed but also understood in the same way as other concepts, for example, *tree, justice,* and *between.* There is a substantial amount of research literature regarding the learning and teaching of the latter kinds of concepts, but none was identified for process concepts.

A second primary contribution is that classroom applications of a theory of cognitive learning and development are identified and tested. Similarly, applications of a generic model of arranging instruction to meet an individual student's entering cognitive behaviors are tested. There is very little literature that reports the testing of applications of theories in on-going educational environments. In general, implications of theory for educational practices are derived logically and are not tested empirically.

A third major contribution is the research strategy that was employed to test the applications. Thirteen experiments were conducted, and each was replicated simultaneously. Furthermore, in each of 10 experiments a different process concept provided the substantive basis for the experiment. This strategy enabled the author to avoid drawing both erroneous and incomplete conclusions of the kind that would have occurred had only a single unreplicated experiment been conducted. The final significant contribution is that the applicability of both the theory of conceptual learning and development and the generic model to educational settings have been verified. This verification will make it easier to identify other applications logically and to test applications in other educational settings.

Acknowledgments

The experimentation reported on in this book was funded for 6 years by the National Institute of Education through the Wisconsin Research and Development (R & D) Center for Individualized Schooling. Monies were provided to support the research activities of the author and his project staff, including full-time employees of the R & D Center and graduate students. Support was given to the following graduate students: Michael E. Bernard, Kay S. Bull, Kathryn V. Feldman, Terence Janicki, Richard M. Gargiulo, Nancy E. McMurray, Gregory K. Mize, Winston E. Rampaul, Joan M. Schilling, James E. Swanson, and Suzanne P. Wiviott. Full-time employees of the R & D Center who contributed significantly on a part-time basis to various aspects of the study were as follows: Michael L. Brumet, Geneva L. DiLuzio, Margaret L. Harris, Linda J. Ingison, and Conrad G. Katzenmeyer.

The assistance of former graduate students and other persons who participated in the research for 1 or more years is deeply appreciated.

The participation of the children, their parents, their teachers, and the school administrators is acknowledged with the deepest gratitude. These persons are not identified in order to protect the privacy of all the participants.

Recognition is due Elizabeth Schwenn Ghatala and Dorothy A. Frayer, coauthors with me of *Conceptual Learning and Development: A Cognitive View,* Academic Press, 1974. The basic elements of the theory of conceptual learning and development are presented in that book. Recognition is also given to Patricia S. Allen, coauthor with me of *Cognitive Development of Children and Youth: A Longitudinal Study,* Academic Press, 1978. In the latter book, the original theory of conceptual learning and development is refined. An overview of that theory is presented in this book, and it is the applications of that theory that were tested.

Elizabeth Schwenn Ghatala and Juanita S. Sorenson are recognized for their assistance in carrying out some of the early research on which the present model of instructional programming for the individual student is based. The refined model is presented in this book.

Anyone familiar with the accounting and reporting requirements of federal and state agencies and also with the practical problems involved in gathering and processing large amounts of data will be aware of the many contributions of individuals whom I have not acknowledged here by name. I do wish to recognize the continuing assistance provided by the administrative and support staff of the Wisconsin R & D Center.

From the beginning to the end of this project, Thomas S. Sipple, project associate, made the arrangements with the participating schools to carry out the experiments and to administer the data-gathering instruments. He coordinated the computer processing of the information and the preparation of the tables and figures appearing in this book. He assisted in writing Chapters 5, 6, and 7, the chapters that deal with the experimentation directly, and he reviewed the other chapters.

My dedicated administrative secretary of many years, Arlene Knudsen, assumed responsibility for typing the several drafts of the book, checking the references for accuracy and completeness, and in general coordinating the preparation of the manuscript.

Learning and Teaching Concepts

A STRATEGY FOR TESTING
APPLICATIONS OF THEORY

1

Introduction

Powerful theories regarding learning, development, and individual differences continue to be formulated. One might expect this to contribute directly to improving education. For this expectation to be realized, applications of the theory either must be understood and used directly by teachers as part of their methodology, or they must be incorporated into instructional materials and procedures that are used by students.

Formulating a theory that may apply to education is aided by moving from the laboratory or other nonschool setting into the schools as soon as possible. Deriving principles of learning or development empirically, or verifying them, can be accomplished readily with school-age students. But these are only the first steps. Either materials of instruction or methods of instruction based on these principles must be developed. In turn, these must be tested in school settings either under existing conditions of teaching and learning or with modifications of existing conditions that can be made without great difficulty.

This book presents the main constructs and principles of a theory of cognitive learning and development (CLD) that have been verified through controlled experiments and longitudinal research in school settings. It also describes how the theory can be applied to preparing printed instructional materials and to designing instruction that provides for differences among students in their entering achievement levels. The materials and the design were used in 13 controlled experiments

1

that were carried out to determine the effects of using the materials and the design.

The experiments were conducted in four elementary schools, two experimental and two control. The experiments had two parts. In the first part of each experiment the students of the experimental schools received the specially prepared instructional material mentioned earlier, namely, a printed lesson to help them understand a process concept of science, for example, *observing, inferring,* or *predicting.* In the second part of each experiment student instruction in the regular science curriculum of the school district dealt with the same concept as a process to be experienced and performed, and the curriculum was adapted to the students' entering achievement levels. The students of the two control schools did not receive the process concept lesson, and their instruction in the regular science curriculum was not adapted to their entering achievement levels. The published science curriculum of the schools was *Science—A Process Approach* (American Association for the Advancement of Science, 1967). This curriculum is usually referred to as SAPA. It focuses on eight basic processes and five integrative processes of science. These 13 processes are regarded as all the processes that scientists employ in their scientific activities.

Each of the 13 experiments had two parts, and in each part, applications of different aspects of CLD theory were tested. The process-concept (PC) lessons used in the first part of each experiment to enable the students to understand the process concepts incorporated applications of CLD theory regarding the internal and external conditions of concept learning. The method used in the second part of each experiment to adapt instruction in the SAPA curriculum to the students' entering achievement levels was formulated to be compatible with CLD theory regarding differences among students in their rates of learning and their within-individual variability to learn concepts from different subject fields. Furthermore, the regular teachers at the experimental schools carried out the experimental instruction as part of the regular science instruction. In this way, the applications of the theory that were embedded in the specially prepared PC lessons and in the adaptive method of teaching the SAPA curriculum were tested under fairly typical instructional conditions.

This book contains the original report of the 13 experiments. The results directly help to extend our knowledge about the learning and teaching of abstract but powerful concepts of science. In addition, the book provides sufficient information about CLD theory and the experimental strategy — procedures, methods, materials, and tests — so that the interested person can test applications of the present theory to other curricular areas or levels of schooling. The strategy also may be used in testing applications of other theories of interest. The CLD theory is discussed in Chapter 2. The applications that were made are given in Chapters 3, 4, and 5. The results are presented in Chapters 6 and 7, and a summary and reflections follow in Chapter 8. The background of the project and the strategy employed are presented in this chapter.

BACKGROUND

The project was part of the activities of the Wisconsin Research and Development Center for Individualized Schooling. The Center was funded initially by the United States Office of Education and later by the National Institute of Education. The program of research and development centers was started by the federal government in 1963 to improve the quality of education. It merits careful attention because long-term funding enables scholars to formulate theories and then to test applications of those theories to educational practices. The importance of testing the applications of a theory is not to be underestimated. For example, Hilgard (1964) stated "we believe that the scientific psychology of learning should go all the way from theory to practice, using criticized data in every step [p. 418]." The "R & D Centers Program" of the United States Office of Education conveyed the same view regarding all kinds of theory.

Research and development centers were established by the United States Office of Education and the participating universities to concentrate human and financial resources on a particular problem area in education over an extended period of time. The objective was that each center would make significant contributions toward an understanding of, and an improvement of educational practice in, the problem area. More specifically, the R & D Centers Program of the United States Office of Education called for the personnel of a center to (a) conduct basic and applied research studies, both of the laboratory and field type; (b) conduct development activities designed to translate research findings systematically into educational materials or procedures, and to field test the developed products; (c) demonstrate and disseminate information about the new programs or procedures that emerge from the research and development efforts; and (d) provide nationwide leadership in the chosen problem area.

As formulated by Klausmeier, codirector for Research from 1964 to 1966, and Center Director from 1966 to 1972, the primary problem area of the Wisconsin R & D Center was the improvement of education through a better understanding of cognitive learning. The importance of this problem area may be inferred from five propositions regarding learning and instruction (Klausmeier, 1968):

1. Concepts provide much of the basic material for thinking. They enable the individual to interpret the physical and social world and to make appropriate responses. Concepts, once learned, serve as symbolic mediators between sensory input and overt behaviors. Without concepts with which to think, human beings, like lower-form animals, would be limited mainly to dealing with sensori-motor and perceptual representations of reality that are closely tied to immediate sensory experiences.

2. Concepts and principles comprise the major outcomes of learning in subject fields, such as English, mathematics, science, and social studies. *Observing, inferring,* and *predicting* represent three process concepts of science. *Set, number,* and *fraction* represent abstract concepts in mathematics. The identification of concepts and their arrangement in a hierarchical order and the identification of principles are concerns of scholars and curriculum workers in the the respective subject fields.

3. Cognitive processes, such as cognizing, hypothesizing, and evaluating, are learned. These and other processes, combined with cognitive contents, are designated cognitive abilities. Children who have learned basic concepts and skills of reading can acquire knowledge in the absence of other persons. When they have mastered mathematical concepts and computational skills, they can find solutions to many problems.

4. The learning of concepts and other cognitive outcomes is related to conditions within the learner and to conditions within the situation. Two conditions within the learner associated with learning concepts and principles are attention, related to motivation, and the current level of cognitive functioning. In school settings, the preceding internal conditions and other external conditions that are related to the content and sequence of instruction and the quality and methods of instruction are paramount.

5. Knowledge about cognitive learning, concepts, cognitive skills, and conditions of learning generated by scholars requires validation in school settings. Although knowledge regarding the teaching and learning of concepts has been generated, and instructional theory has been formulated, the validity of the theory has not been tested in school settings. Similarly, instructional materials for students must also be developed and tested.

Studies Related to the Present Project

A conference was organized and held at the Wisconsin R & D Center in 1965 to gather and synthesize knowledge regarding cognitive learning. Sixteen scholars from the fields of philosophy, psychology, educational research, and various other disciplines shared information regarding schemes for classifying and learning concepts, learning–teaching processes, and the major concepts in various subject fields (Klausmeier & Harris, 1966).

After this conference, many experiments were conducted in laboratories and in schools to extend our knowledge regarding the learning and teaching of concepts. The results were summarized and synthesized in an emerging theory of conceptual learning and development (Klausmeier, 1971; Klausmeier, Ghatala, & Frayer, 1974). The principles of learning included in this theory were used in the present experiments in analyzing the process concepts of science and in preparing the lessons to teach these concepts. The theory also provided the substantive framework for designing two other studies that follow.

Harris and Harris (1973) carried out a large-scale factor-analytic study to identify the interrelationships of concept achievement in four subject fields, as well as the mental abilities related to concept achievement in each subject field. Contrary to a prevalent but false assumption that cognitive development proceeded in a unitary, global manner, such as is predicted by stage theory, they found that the concept achievements of Grade 5 children had already become highly differentiated according to the four subject-matter areas of language arts, mathematics, social studies, and science. In other words, students who achieved at a certain level in one subject did not necessarily achieve at the same level in the other subjects.

In another important area, Harris and Harris (1973) did not find support for the many special abilities identified by Guilford (1967). Rather, they found abilities corresponding to Thurstone's primary mental abilities (1938). They found these primary mental abilities to be associated differentially with the concept achievements in the different subject fields. For example, verbal fluency, inductive reasoning, and memory were found to be associated with the concept achievement of both boys and girls in science and social studies, whereas numerical reasoning, word fluency, and memory were associated with concept achievement in language arts and mathematics. Only minor sex differences in the abilities and related subject fields were observed.

Klausmeier and Allen (1978) reported a longitudinal study carried out from 1973 to 1976, to chart the development of concepts, principles, structures of knowledge, and problem-solving skills of children in Grades 1-12. Normative trends in the development of these outcomes were established. Furthermore, interindividual differences and intraindividual variability in cognitive development were delineated.

As part of the preceding longitudinal study, students in Grades 1-9 were administered 12 tasks that were constructed to measure the operations that characterize the stage of concrete operational thought as defined by Piaget (1970) and 16 other measures constructed by Brainerd (1972) to measure the psychological structures that, according to Piaget (1970), explain the stage of concrete operational thought (Klausmeier & Associates, 1979). The results of this study disconfirm the construct of the stage of concrete operational thought as a reliable description of children's actual cognitive development from ages 6-12 and of the psychological structures proposed by Piaget as an explanation of the stage. Based on these results and those reported earlier by Harris and Harris (1973), no attempt was made in the present project to try to identify the Piagetian stage of development of the participating school children or to employ the stage construct in designing the PC lessons or the method of SAPA instruction. Rather, the relevant empirically derived CLD principles of learning and development were employed.

About the time that the studies by Harris and Harris, and Klausmeier and Allen were being conducted, another area of interest was pursued. CLD theory was formulated initially and refined (Klausmeier, 1971; Klausmeier, Ghatala, & Frayer, 1974). As part of the theory formulation, the external conditions of learning that facilitate students' concept learning were identified through a series of controlled experiments in schools settings. These facilitative conditions were incorporated in the PC lessons used in the present 13 experiments to aid the children in the experimental schools to understand the process concepts of science. Based on the theory, procedures for carrying out a content analysis of concepts were formulated and tried out with concepts from a number of subject fields. In the present 13 experiments, these procedures were employed in analyzing the process concepts of science, and the results of the analyses were used in preparing the lessons to teach the concepts to the participating children.

In another area of interest, the author and other staff members of the Wisconsin R & D Center worked cooperatively with persons in schools of Janesville, Madison, Milwaukee, and Racine, Wisconsin in arranging for instruction to be adapted to meet the wide range of differences found among students of the same age in their ability to learn the same subject matter. After several years of cooperative research with the schools, a generic model of instructional programming for the individual student was formulated (Klausmeier, Sorenson, & Quilling, 1971). It subsequently underwent considerable revision and refinement (Klausmeier, 1977). This model provided the design for adapting the SAPA instruction to the entering achievement levels of the students in the experimental schools of the present study.

Overview of the Project

The present project, from the initial planning to the final draft, took about 6 years. The first 2 years were devoted to planning, developing the PC lessons, and constructing the PC and SAPA tests. The 13 experiments were conducted during the next 2 years. Data processing and writing were carried out during the last 2 years.

Recall that four elementary schools, two experimental and two control, were included in the study. In the two experimental schools (E1 and E2), modifications in the science instruction were made. In the two control schools (C1 and C2), instruction proceeded as usual; however, the children received more tests, and the teachers kept logs, indicating the amount of time spent in instruction and describing their instructional procedures. School E1 was paired with C1, and School E2 was paired with C2, primarily on the basis of whether or not instruction followed an age-graded pattern. In one pair of schools, most instruction was in the familiar age-graded arrangement. In the other pair, children from two or three grades were placed together for instruction. In all four schools, the socioeconomic status of the parents was about the same, with about as many families below as above middle class.

Recall also that there were 13 experiments. In the first year, Grade 4 students participated in experiments 1–5 and Grade 5 students, in experiments 6–10. In the next year, those students who had participated while in Grade 4 participated in experiments 11–13 while in Grade 5. The first year Grade 5 students did not participate the next year.

Science Curriculum of the Schools

The school district in which the experiments were conducted was selected in part because *Science—A Process Approach* (American Association for the Advancement of Science, 1967) was the district-adopted science curriculum. It focused on science processes. Prior research had been done using other categories of concepts, but none had been done with process concepts. A summary of the more important information contained in the published teachers' guide for the SAPA program follows. This will clarify the focus of the science instruction given in the control schools and in the experimental schools before the present project began.

SAPA makes the assumption that children, even in the primary grades, will derive more from the study of science if they learn the behaviors of scientists. In learning to do what scientists do, the children become highly involved in using the processes of science. For the primary grades, the following basic process skills are stressed in SAPA: observing, using space–time relationships, classifying, using numbers, measuring, communicating, predicting, and inferring. These basic processes provide the foundation for the more complex or integrative processes that are emphasized in the intermediate grades. The integrative processes are these: controlling variables, interpreting data, formulating hypotheses, defining operationally, and experimenting.

The publisher indicates that the ability to read is not essential in SAPA, as it is in many other curricula. Thus, inquiry into science can begin as early as kindergarten. Success does not depend on skill in reading, but rather on the ability to use the processes of science. In accordance with the preceding ideas, most of the SAPA printed materials have been prepared for the teacher only. Rather than reading about science, in this curriculum children learn science through the use of their senses, mental involvement, and direct manipulation of objects in their immediate environment. Those children who want to know more about topics they investigate should be encouraged by the teacher to read about the topic.

According to the publisher, the greatest difficulty in teaching the SAPA processes is not likely to be keeping the classwork pupil centered, but rather to remember that the chief objective is not to teach content but to teach process. For example, as children are observing an expanding balloon to learn how to communicate what they see, the teacher should not become concerned about whether or not each child knows what caused the balloon to increase in size. Instead, attention should be focused on how well individual children are able to communicate the changes they have observed.

The publisher indicates that there can be no question that a conscientious teacher of SAPA faces fewer problems if adequate floor space, storage and shelf space, and movable furniture are available. Since the SAPA curriculum stresses active participation by children, each child should have many opportunities to handle materials, to demonstrate the use of simple equipment, and to construct tests of ideas. No single, permanent arrangement of the classroom will meet the learning needs of the children for all science activities. Space requirements for group work change from day to day. Sometimes, maximum clear floor areas are required; at other times, the whole class will need to be able to observe clearly a single operation and discuss it. Most frequently, small groups will be busy at work stations spaced as far apart as possible.

The publisher states that SAPA was designed to take advantage of cumulative learning; therefore, the sets of exercises dealing with each process are arranged in hierarchies. A sequence chart shows the prerequisite relationships among all the sets of SAPA exercises. This chart indicates the earlier sets of exercises dealing with the same process and also with any other process that should be taught to ensure that the children possess the prerequisite skills necessary for success with any particular set of exercises of interest. Teachers are advised to follow the sequence prescribed by the hierarchy for each science process, that is, to teach the sets of exercises in the order in which they are recommended.

New words and phrases are introduced in each exercise. After the pupils have completed an exercise, they should be able to respond to or use these words, but they should not be expected to use the words freely until after they have had many experiences with the objects and ideas which the words name or describe.

Extensive evaluation materials are an essential part of SAPA. Each SAPA exercise contains clearly stated objectives, phrased in terms of observable pupil behavior. Included in each exercise is the means to test pupil achievement in relation to the stated objectives.

The publisher strongly recommends the use of individual competency measures. These measures are based on the teacher's observation of an individual student's performances. However, the performance of a classroom group is also observed. (The schools in which the present experiments were conducted did not use any written SAPA tests prior to the start of the project.)

Each exercise of SAPA begins with a statement of objectives, expressed in terms of children's performances. The objectives are statements of what an individual child is expected to be able to do after successful completion of the exercise. These objectives are called behavioral objectives. The successful attainment of an objective can be demonstrated by having the child do specific things which the teacher can observe.

Some examples of behavioral objectives from the teachers' guide are

> The child should be able to *identify* the following three-dimensional shapes: sphere, cube, cylinder, pyramid, and cone.
> The child should be able to *identify* and *name* numbers in the sequence 11 through 99 as successors of 10, 20, 30, and so on.

The child should be able to *distinguish* between statements that are observations and those that are explanations of observations, and *identify* the explanations as inferences.

The child should be able to *construct* an inference to explain the movement of liquid out of an inverted container when air moves into it.

The child should be able to *describe* and *demonstrate* that the farther an object is located from the center of a revolving disc, the greater is its linear speed, although its rate of revolution is the same.

The child should be able to *construct* predictions from a graph about water loss from plants over a given period of time [American Association for the Advancement of Science, 1967, p. 22].

The reader will properly infer, according to the publisher, that all these objectives deal with experiencing and performing the processes of science. However, students working on the exercises might perceive their task, in part, as having to acquire and remember the SAPA information that was presented in the exercise.

The objectives for the sets of exercises for any particular process comprise the definition of the process and its hierarchy, which is a sequential arrangement. It is a hierarchy in the sense that the sequence has been determined by identifying the dependencies among the objectives, with a top level, an intermediate level, and a bottom level. The most complex performances named by objectives in the exercises are at the top of the hierarchy. Next are those performances or behaviors which are essential for performance of the most complex behaviors. In turn, each subordinate behavior has connections leading down to other behaviors on which the higher behavior depends. This procedure of identifying dependencies is continued until the least complex behaviors for each process are reached. These behaviors comprise the bottom level of the hierarchy.

A hierarchy has been developed in this manner for each of the 13 SAPA processes of science. These hierarchies are the skeleton of the program and constitute the rationale for the order of the sets of exercises.

The 13 separate process hierarchies are not independent of one another. Typically, activities designed to develop capabilities in one process contribute to the child's capability in other processes. Therefore, developing a skill in one process may be dependent on the prior acquisition of skills in other processes. The SAPA sequence chart mentioned earlier shows these dependencies; it is made available to the teachers.

The behavioral hierarchies guide the assessment of SAPA pupil achievement and program evaluation. The competency measures, as mentioned earlier, are performance tests designed to determine whether or not the child has achieved the objectives of the exercise. The child should at least achieve the objectives of the sets of exercises at the bottom of the hierarchy of the particular process and also the prerequisite objectives of other processes.

The publisher reports in the teachers' guide that the SAPA curriculum was pilot tested in many locations and that excellent results were obtained. Although this curriculum has been tested with favorable results, a number of departures from the publisher's recommendations have been made in the schools participating in the project before the start of the present experiment. The most important departures were as follows: First, although the recommended sequencing of the exercises was followed, some of the exercises involving the eight basic processes recommended for the primary grades were used in Grades 4 and 5, because the exercises had been judged to be too difficult for the children of the primary grades in the school district. Second, the individual competency measures and the group competency measures were not used systematically; the students, as a class, moved from one set of exercises in a hierarchy to another without being assessed regularly during the school year; in many cases, the students moved to higher levels without achieving the recommended prerequisite objectives. Third, some of the students seemed to prefer acquiring the interesting scientific information in the exercises rather than experiencing and performing the particular process. Fourth, the students progressed through the sets of exercises as classes, not at different rates appropriate for individual students.

STRATEGY

Many theories have been formulated in the areas of human learning, human development, and individual differences during the last decades. The constructs and principles of many of these theories have been disseminated widely to educators. However, in most instances, possible instructional strategies and materials based on the theory have not been developed, and research to test the effectiveness or lack of effectiveness of the strategies and materials in school settings has not been carried out. Therefore, possible applications of theory to students with different learning abilities in kindergarten through high school, to different curricular areas, and to different instructional conditions have not been identified. Despite the absence of empirically tested strategies and materials, teachers have been urged to base their instructional practices on someone's notions of what the applications of a particular theory should be.

As a result of attempts such as these to move from theory to practice without the intervening development and testing of instructional materials and strategies, many variations of child-centered education based on Dewey's conceptions of the child, the school, and society were introduced, but then disappeared. Many training approaches to instruction following Skinner's principles of operant conditioning also flourished for a while and disappeared. Recently, teachers have been encouraged to apply Piaget's description of learning stages in determining students' readiness, based on the assumption that at a particular point in time a student becomes ready to learn all kinds of subject matter. However, only isolated elements of Piagetian theory have been investigated empirically by individual researchers, and practically no comprehensive research has been done to test the applicability of any one of the four *complete Piagetian stage* descriptions to student readiness for learning. As pointed out earlier in this chapter (Klausmeier & Associates, 1979), children's actual readiness to learn concepts of English, mathematics, and science during the school years does not coincide with the stage of concrete operational thought as described by Piaget (1964, 1970).

Many single, short-term experiments unrelated to theory also have not improved instruction significantly. In this kind of experimentation, students are the experimental subjects who provide information that the experimenter is interested in, but the experimental treatments are not the kind the students would receive as part of a school's instructional program. The experiments are brief, with the data gathering completed in as little as one or two sessions of 30 minutes each. Only initial learning is measured; there is no follow-up to measure retention or transfer. No replication is done. There are no successive experiments to generate knowledge in a cumulative fashion.

An attempt was made to avoid these shortcomings in the present project. Let us review first, how CLD theory was applied to students learning to understand the processes of science as concepts, and then how CLD theory was applied to their attaining the objectives of the SAPA curriculum.

Applications of CLD Theory

Recall that the science program (SAPA) of the experimental and control schools of the present project focused on students' experiencing and performing 13 processes of science. A content analysis, a behavioral analysis, and an instructional analysis were made of these 13 science process concepts. The results of these analyses were used to prepare the process-concept lessons that were used in the experimental schools to help the students understand the processes as concepts. These analyses were based directly on CLD constructs and principles (Klausmeier *et al.,* 1974; Klausmeier & Allen, 1978), as will be discussed in Chapter 3. In turn, the results of these analyses were used by the project staff to prepare the PC lessons (see Chapter 5) and to teach the students of the experimental schools about each process concept before studying the set of SAPA lessons that deal with the same concept as a process to be experienced and performed. It was assumed that if the students of the experimental schools scored significantly higher on the tests measuring understanding of the process concepts than did the students of the control schools, these applications of CLD theory to the learning and teaching of process concepts were made successfully.

Knowledge concerning interindividual differences and intraindividual variability was used in formulating the model of instructional programming for the individual student. The primary application of this model in the present project was that the teachers of the experimental schools adapted the SAPA instruction to the entering achievement levels of the students (see Chapter 4). More specifically, the attempt was made during the first year in the first 10 experiments to use this method while holding constant the amount of time for SAPA instruction in each pair of experimental and control schools. In the second year, both the amount of time and the instructional method were varied systematically so that the SAPA instruction might follow the model more directly. If the students of the experimental schools scored significantly higher on the SAPA tests than did the students of the control schools, it was presumed that this application of CLD theory to science instruction was successful.

Experimental Arrangements

We will now turn to other features of the 13 experiments that are described more fully in later chapters. Table 1.1 provides an overview of the experiments. Each of the 13 experiments was carried out in two paired sets of experimental and control schools, E1–C1 and E2–C2. Thus, there was a simultaneous replication of each experiment. This replication made it possible to determine whether or not the results were the same for two different paired sets of schools.

In the second part of each experiment, the same set of SAPA exercises

TABLE 1.1 Schedule of Experiments

Experiment number	Grade	Year	Semester	Concept	Number of exercises[a]	Process-concept lesson used in E1 and E2	Instructional pattern in E1 and E2
				Sets of SAPA exercises used in E1, E2, C1, and C2 schools			
1	4	1975–1976	1	Classifying	2	Yes	Differentiated instruction; same amount of time for SAPA instruction throughout the year as in C1 and C2.
2			1	Inferring	3	Yes	
3			1	Predicting	2	Yes	
4			2	Using numbers	2	Yes	
5			2	Measuring	5	Yes	
6	5	1975–1976	1	Observing scientifically	3	Yes	Differentiated instruction; same amount of time for SAPA instruction throughout the year as in C1 and C2.
7			1	Inferring	3	Yes	
8			1	Using space–time relationships	2	Yes	

9			2	Controlling variables	2	Yes	
10			2	Communicating	2	Yes	
11	1976–1977	5	1	Observing scientifically	3	Yes	Differentiation as during 1975–1976. Same amount of time for SAPA instruction as in C1, C2. Extended time for PC lesson. Transfer test used.
12			1	Inferring	3	No	Greater differentiation of SAPA instruction. More time for SAPA instruction in E1 and E2. No PC lesson. No transfer test.
13			2	Controlling variables	2	Yes	Greater differentiation of SAPA instruction as in experiment 12. More time for PC lesson as in experiment 11. Transfer test as in experiment 11.

[a] These refer to the number of SAPA exercises, not to daily classroom lessons. Each SAPA exercise was carried out during several class sessions.

dealing with a particular science process was used in the two experimental schools and the two comparison schools. However, a different set of SAPA exercises, each dealing with a different SAPA process, was used in experiments 1–10, except that, in one experiment, a more sophisticated level of a science process used in an earlier experiment was taught. In the first part of each experiment, a process-concept lesson prepared by the project staff was used in the experimental schools. This PC lesson was for the same SAPA process used in the second part of the experiment. In this way, the applications of the theory could be tested for nine different concepts in experiments 1–10.

The Grade 4 students who participated in experiments 1–5 and continued to go to the same schools were the Grade 5 students in experiments 11–13 during the next year. This made it possible to study the cumulative effects of serving as participants in the experimental schools and in the control schools.

The experimental treatments, or instructional procedures, were carried out by the participating school teachers of E1 and E2. This allowed for the testing of theoretical applications under fairly typical conditions for teaching science. However, as will be noted later in this chapter, the start-up costs were considerable, and more time than usually allocated for science instruction was needed by the experimental teachers to teach the process-concept and to carry out the SAPA instruction.

Changes in the experimental arrangements to be carried out in experiments 11–13 were determined on the basis of the results of experiments 1–10. For example, in experiments 1–10, the amount of time spent in SAPA instruction was held constant in the experimental and control schools; in experiments 12 and 13 it was not. Changing these and other experimental conditions permitted a number of important questions to be answered.

Earlier in this chapter it was indicated that a generic model of instructional programming for the individual student had been formulated (Klausmeier, Sorenson, & Quilling, 1971). At the time of this study many schools throughout the United States, including both the experimental and control schools, had applied this model to instruction in reading, mathematics, and spelling. The space, equipment, and materials necessary for applying the model are relatively easy to obtain and manage in these curricular areas. In these experiments, a systematic attempt was made to apply the model to science in schools in which both a science laboratory and a substantial amount of science equipment were shared by the students attending that particular school. A literature search indicated that no prior testing of the application of the model to science instruction had been reported.

Determination of Cost and Work Effort

The strategy of simultaneously replicating experiments and testing applications to many different concepts by conducting a large number of experiments is costly. The approximate cost of the project follows. It includes the additional costs for instructional materials and instructional aides in the experimental schools, the additional time that the school staffs had to give to planning the activities with the project staff in workshops conducted by the project staff, and the amount of project personnel and time involved in developing the PC lessons and tests and the SAPA tests.

In the year before experimentation began, seven workshop sessions were held. These sessions, each 1½ to 2 hours long, involved the teachers in the two experimental and the two control schools, the school principals, the school district science coordinator, and the project staff of the Wisconsin Research and Development Center. In the summer before the first year of experimentation, a workshop was held for 5 consecutive days with the team leaders in the two experimental schools, the principal of one of the schools, and the district science coordinator. Early in the fall, after the first 10 experiments had been conducted, a 2-day workshop was held with the same persons who participated in the preceding summer workshop. The total honoraria paid to the school staff during the entire project amounted to $4450.

The teachers of E1 and E2 devoted a great deal of time to the project as part of their regular teaching load and did not receive additional payment. The teachers of C1 and C2 also kept logs and administered tests, which they did not normally do as part of their regular teaching.

To adapt the SAPA instruction in E1 and E2 to the design of the experiments, two instructional aides, one in each experimental school, were employed. Each aide worked 15 hours during each week of instruction. Also, additional copies of the published SAPA curricular materials were required, and supplementary science texts were provided for enrichment activities. The cost for the aides was $5760, and extra materials came to $1350. Adding the honoraria of $4450, the total expenditure amounted to $11,560.

The project was funded over a 6-year period by the National Institute of Education through the Wisconsin Research and Development Center for Individualized Schooling. The first year was given to planning the study and getting it funded. During the second preparatory year, the SAPA achievement tests used in the experiments were constructed, the PC lessons used to teach process concepts were developed, an exploratory experiment was carried out, and the workshops were held for the participating school staffs.

Final data processing and the writing of this book occurred during the 2 years after the experiments were completed. The number of R & D Center personnel and the amount of time they required to carry out the activities during the 6 years were substantial. Throughout the 6 years, the author devoted from 5 to 10% of his total time to the project; while his project specialist, Thomas Sipple, devoted from 5 to 30% of his time to it. Five other project assistants and one assistant scientist devoted from 20 to 50% of their time to test construction and lesson development in year 2. During that same year, three other persons with expertise in test development and evaluation devoted from 5 to 50% of their time to the project, and a technical specialist in computer analysis devoted 10% of his time. During the third year, when experiments 1–10 were carried out, three project assistants gave 25 to 50% of their time to the project activities, and 15% of a computer programmer's time went to the analysis of data. In the final year that data was collected in the schools, two project assistants were budgeted for 50% of their time to the project and a computer programmer for 15% of his time.

PLAN OF THE BOOK

The major CLD theoretical constructs and principles of learning appear in Klausmeier et al. (1974). The principles of development and the relationships between learning and development are explained in Klausmeier and Allen (1978). A condensation of both of these works is given in Chapter 2 of this book. It is intended to be sufficiently complete so that the reader can understand the theoretical framework for the present series of experiments and also secure an overview of the specific applications that were made.

A content analysis, a behavioral analysis, and an instructional analysis were made of the process concepts used in the present series of experiments. These analyses were based on CLD constructs regarding structures of knowledge and the internal and external conditions of learning that are part of CLD theory. The results of the analyses were used in preparing the PC lessons in the present experiments. The procedures for conducting the analyses are given in Chapter 3, as are the results of the analyses. Considerable attention is given to describing the procedures and to presenting the results of the analyses so that the interested reader may apply the procedures to concepts that are of interest.

The generic model of instructional programming for the individual student that served as the basis for designing the SAPA instruction in the experimental schools is explained in Chapter 4. The model was formulated before the present project began. Therefore, the illustrations and examples used to clarify applications of the model are drawn from several subject fields, rather than being limited to the process concepts of science.

In Chapter 5, the construction and validation of the SAPA tests and the preparation of the PC lessons and PC tests are explained. Excerpts from PC lessons are included. The technical characteristics of the SAPA tests and the PC tests are given. As noted earlier, both the PC lessons and the PC tests are based directly on various CLD constructs and principles.

The activities of the second preparatory year of the project and the results of the 10 experiments carried out during the third year are given in Chapter 6. The results of the last three experiments and the cumulative effects of the experiments are presented in Chapter 7. Chapter 8 is a discussion of the results.

REFERENCES

AAAS Commission on Science Education. *Science — A Process Approach.* Washington, D.C.: American Association for the Advancement of Science/Xerox, 1967.

Brainerd, C. J. *Structures of thought in middle-childhood: Recent research on Piaget's concrete-operational groupements.* Paper presented at the Third Annual Meeting on Structural Learning, Philadelphia, March 1972.

Guilford, J. P. *The nature of human intelligence.* New York: McGraw-Hill, 1967.

Harris, M. L., & Harris, C. W. *A structure of concept attainment abilities.* Madison: Wisconsin Research and Development Center for Cognitive Learning, 1973.

Hilgard, E. R. Postscript: Twenty years of learning theory in relation to education. In E. R. Hilgard (Ed.), *Theories of learning and instruction* (63rd yearbook, Part I. National Society for the Study of Education). Chicago: University of Chicago Press. 1964. Pp. 416–418.

Klausmeier, H. J. The Wisconsin Research and Development Center for Cognitive Learning. In H. J. Klausmeier & G. T. O'Hearn (Eds.), *Research and development toward the improvment of education.* Madison, Wis.: Dembar Educational Research Services, 1968. Pp. 146–156.

Klausmeier, H. J. Cognitive operations in concept learning. *Educational Psychologist,* 1971, 9, 1–8.

Klausmeier, H. J. Instructional programming for the individual student. In H. J. Klausmeier, R. A. Rossmiller, & M. Saily (Eds.), *Individually guided elementary education: Concepts and practices.* New York: Academic Press, 1977. Pp. 55–76.

Klausmeier, H. J., & Allen, P. S. *Cognitive development of children and youth: A longitudinal study.* New York: Academic Press, 1978.

Klausmeier, H. J., & Associates. *Cognitive learning and development: Information-processing and Piagetian perspectives.* Cambridge, MA.: Ballinger Publishing, 1979.

Klausmeier, H. J., Ghatala, E. S., & Frayer, D. A. *Conceptual learning and development: A cognitive view.* New York: Academic Press, 1974.

Klausmeier, H. J., & Harris, C. W. (Eds.). *Analyses of concept learning.* New York: Academic Press, 1966.

Klausmeier, H. J., Sorenson, J. S., & Quilling, M. S. Instructional programming for the individual pupil in the multiunit elementary school. *The Elementary School Journal,* 1971, 72, 88–101.

Piaget, J. Development and learning. In R. E. Ripple & V. N. Rockcastle (Eds.), *Piaget rediscovered.* Ithaca: Cornell University Press, 1964. Pp. 1–12.

Piaget, J. Piaget's theory. In P. H. Mussen (Ed.), *Carmichael's manual of child psychology* (Vol. 1, 3rd ed.). New York: Wiley, 1970. Pp. 703–732.

Thurstone, L. L. *Primary mental abilities* (Psychometric Monograph No. 1). Chicago: University of Chicago Press, 1938.

2

CLD Theory and Applications

The 13 experiments that will be reported in Chapters 6 and 7 of this book were designed to extend knowledge regarding the learning and teaching of concepts and also to test applications of a cognitive theory of learning and development (CLD). CLD theory deals with both learning and development, since a basic assumption of the theory is that cognitive development cannot occur independent of learning. Rather, development is a product of the interaction of learning and maturational factors, and the internal and external conditions of learning necessarily change as the individual achieves successively higher levels of cognitive functioning.

The CLD constructs and principles of learning summarized in this chapter are reported in greater detail in Klausmeier, Ghatala, and Frayer (1974). They are based primarily on a series of experiments, the first of which was carried out in a learning laboratory and the later ones in school settings. The content analyses, behavioral analyses, and instructional analyses made on the process concepts of science (see Chapter 3) are based on these CLD constructs and principles. In turn, the results of these analyses were incorporated in the process-concept (PC) lessons prepared for and used in the present project (see Chapter 5).

The principles of development presented in this chapter are explained in Klausmeier and Allen (1978). The principles were verified empirically in a longitudinal study in which four groups of students from Kinder-

21

garten through Grade 12 participated. Some of these principles were incorporated in the methods that the teachers of the experimental schools used in teaching the SAPA curriculum in the present series of experiments. Some were considered when preparing the PC lessons. This overview of CLD theory is provided so that the reader will be able to understand the specific applications of it in the present set of 13 experiments.

THE COGNITIVE STRUCTURE

The cognitive structure of the individual at any point in time includes everything the individual has learned (Ausubel, 1963, 1966, 1968). The products, or outcomes, of learning may be categorized as perceptual information; verbal information and skills; concepts; principles; structures of knowledge, including taxonomies; and problem-solving skills, including strategies of learning and remembering. These products are learned initially, represented internally, organized, and then stored in the form of images, symbols, meanings, and as the relationships among images, symbols, and meanings. The cognitive structure changes from birth, onward, as a result of learning and maturation, and simultaneously has both molecular and molar features. The representation of the simplest perceptions are included, such as an image of the sun sinking beyond the horizon, as well as the most abstract ideas that may be learned, such as those involved in theorizing about the origin of the sun.

Concepts, principles, structures of knowledge, including taxonomies and other hierarchies, and problem solving are powerful outcomes of learning in the cognitive domain. Development of these outcomes to progressively higher levels is accompanied by a more complete understanding of the physical and social world any by increasing independence in learning. CLD theory deals with these outcomes of learning. Each kind of outcome merits brief review before the mental operations employed in learning concepts are dealt with.

Concepts

A concept is both a mental construct of the individual and the societally accepted meaning of one or more words that express the particular concept. Concepts as mental constructs are the critical components of a maturing individual's continuously changing, enlarging cognitive structure and are the basic tools of thought. Concepts as societally accepted meanings of words comprise much of the subject matter of science, English, mathematics, and social studies which children and youth learn during the school years. Much formal education is directed toward concept learning and the related structures of knowledge into which concepts and principles are organized.

There are a number of different ways to classify concepts. One is in accordance with the six form classes of words: nominals, adjectivals, verbals, adverbials, prepositionals, and conjunctivals. Words and groups of words that can be categorized as belonging in each of these form classes represent concepts.

Another means for classifying concepts is in terms of whether the defining attributes can be perceived. Mussen, Conger, and Kagan (1974) indicate that concepts that have perceptible attributes, for example, *animal, swim, color* are concrete; whereas concepts whose attributes cannot be directly perceived, for example, *nominals, imagine, however* are abstract. Gagné (1974) uses the term *concrete concept* in much the same way as Mussen *et al.,* but he uses the term *defined concepts* to refer to concepts whose attributes cannot be "pointed to." Markle (1977) makes a useful distinction between "generic" and "specific" concepts to take into account inclusiveness. The generic concept *animal* is more inclusive than *cow,* but the examples of animal are as concrete as those of cow — both can be pointed to.

Although it may be useful to think of all concepts as either concrete or abstract or concrete and defined, the approach taken in CLD theory calls for a somewhat more analytical treatment. Thus, the class of learning outcomes called concepts may be considered as mental constructs of individuals and as societally accepted meanings of words and word phrases shared by persons who have similar environmental backgrounds and who speak the same language. Further, the term *concept* itself can be defined in terms of attributes. The eight attributes of concept are learnability, usability, validity, generality, power, structure, instance abstractness, and instance numerousness (Klausmeier *et al.,* 1974). These attributes are presumed to be applicable to any public concept, that is, to the societally accepted meaning of any word that stands for a concept and to concepts as mental constructs of individuals.

As part of the content analysis performed on the process concepts of science employed in the present project, each concept was defined in terms of its attributes. For example, the defining attributes of *inferring* are (a) relating a scientific observation to something which is known; and (b) drawing a conclusion about what was observed. This definition was included in the specially prepared PC lesson on inferring.

Principles

A principle may be defined formally as a relationship between two or more concepts. Understanding the concepts embedded in the principle is necessary but not sufficient for understanding the principle. Like a concept, a principle serves both as a mental construct of the individual and as the societally accepted meaning of the statement that expresses the principle. Principles, like concepts, are powerful tools of thought that are necessary for interpreting phenomena in the physical and social world and for solving problems.

Four basic types of relationships expressed in principles are *cause-and-effect, correlational, probability,* and *axiomatic.* An example of each of the first three follows:

> Tuberculosis is caused by the organism *Myobacterium tuberculosis.* (Cause-and-effect)

> Sample correlations between two sets of scores on standardized reading achievement tests of the same children taken at yearly intervals during the successive elementary school years range from .70 to .90 (Correlational)

> The probability of giving birth to a boy during any one pregnancy is .52. (Probability)

Axioms are universally accepted truths or conditions. They represent the largest class of principles. The class of axiomatic relationships may be divided into five subclasses: fundamentals, laws, rules, theorems, and axioms. What each class of axioms is called and how axioms function vary among disciplines such as mathematics, physics, and psychology.

Principles that were identified through the content analysis performed on each process concept in the present project could be classified as rules. For example, two principles involving the concept, *inferring,* were as follows: (a) Making more accurate and reliable scientific observations permits the drawing of more accurate and reliable inferences; and (b) Inferences based on two or more scientific observations are more reliable than those based on a single observation.

Structures of Knowledge

Persons throughout the recorded history of humanity have been adding to their individual and collective knowledge, organizing it, and putting it into communicable forms, primarily symbolic. Taxonomies, other hierarchies, and theories are three important frameworks for organizing an individual's cognitive structure and the communicable knowledge of a group who share the same language and cultural experiences. Concepts and principles are the building blocks of these structures of organized knowledge.

The structure of knowledge for the process concepts employed in the present series of 13 experiments was a hierarchy involving either prerequisite dependency relationships or parallel relationships among the process concepts. For example, *observing scientifically* is regarded as a prerequisite for *inferring,* and *inferring* is regarded as a prerequisite for both *classifying* and *predicting. Predicting* and *classifying* are treated as having a parallel relationship.

Problem Solving

The ability to solve problems is perhaps the most important product of learning, inasmuch as a person who is capable of solving problems can learn independently. The means of attacking problems and acquiring, processing, and remembering information may be called strategies. Concepts, principles, and strategies are used in solving problems.

The process concept of the present experiments that specifically involves problem solving is *experimenting.* In the school-adopted SAPA curriculum, experimenting is regarded as the most effective means of solving problems.

MENTAL OPERATIONS EMPLOYED IN CONCEPT LEARNING

Scientific methods for identifying the mental operations that are necessary for attaining concepts during short time intervals include the behavioral analysis of concept learning tasks, observation and questioning as the learning tasks are performed, controlled experimentation, computer simulation of learning processes, and factor analysis based on tests of the mental operations. Guilford (1967) employed task analysis and factor analysis in formulating a structure of mature intellect that includes five main operations: cognition, memory, productive thinking convergent, productive thinking divergent, and evaluation. Miller and Johnson-Laird (1976) drew heavily on information processing by computers in formulating their theory of perception and language. They explain all human intellectual functioning in terms of five basic operations: perceiving, intending, remembering, knowing, and feeling.

Neither Guilford nor Miller and Johnson–Laird dealt directly with the changes that occur in mental operations from birth through adolescence. We recognize, however, that the structure of intellect of the

2-year-old child is very different from Guilford's 120-factor structure of the educated adult. There are also great changes in perception and information processing from infancy into adulthood.

The means by which the mental operations involved in learning concepts were identified in CLD theory merit brief attention. Behavioral analyses of concept learning tasks were performed, and controlled experiments with individuals of various ages were carried out to infer the subjects' employment of the processes. Through this approach, four levels of attaining the same concept were identified, and the operations necessary to attain each level were inferred (Klausmeier *et al.,* 1974). Subsequently, tests were constructed to measure students' use of the operations at each level (Klausmeier, Bernard, Katzenmeyer, & Sipple, 1973; Klausmeier, Ingison, Sipple, & Katzenmeyer, 1973a,b; Klausmeier, Marliave, Katzenmeyer, & Sipple, 1974). These tests were used in a longitudinal study of cognitive development during the school years (Klausmeier & Allen, 1978). The test results were analyzed in various ways, including factor analysis (Klausmeier & Associates, 1979). Based on the data from all these sources, it appears that the construct of four levels of attaining the same concept has been verified and that the mental operations necessary for attaining each level have been identified reliably.

The four successive levels at which the same concept is attained are designated *concrete, identity, classificatory,* and *formal* (Figure 2.1). The four successively higher levels apply to the many concepts that (a) have more than one example; (b) have observable three-dimensional examples or examples expressed in the form of drawings, words, or other symbols; and (c) are defined in terms of intrinsic attributes, functional attributes, or both. Not all concepts are of this kind. Some concepts have only one example, for instance, the *earth's moon.* Some concepts do not have observable examples, for instance, *atom, eternity, soul.* Still others are defined in terms of a single dimension or quality—*rough, thin;* or in terms of an invariant relation, including spatial—*south, between, above;*

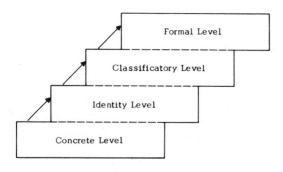

Figure 2.1. Four levels of concept attainment.

temporal — *before, after;* and deictic — *they, whom.* Concepts of these categories cannot be attained at all four successive levels, but all are attained at one, two, or three levels. For example, the attainment of any concept that has only one perceptible example or that has perceptible examples of an identical form may be described in terms of some combination of the concrete, identity, and formal levels, but not the classificatory, inasmuch as the classificatory level is defined as treating two different examples as equivalent. Attainment of some concepts defined by a single perceptible dimension, for example, *rough,* or in terms of an invariant relationship, for example, *before,* may be described primarily in terms of the classificatory and formal levels, but probably not in terms of the concrete or identity level.

In the following pages, the operations necessary for attaining the four successive levels of the same concept are indicated. They apply to concepts whose examples have intrinsic attributes, functional attributes, invariant relations, or some combination of these types of attributes.

Concrete Level

A young child *attends* to a clock on the wall, *discriminates* it from other objects in the environment, represents the image of the clock internally, maintains the image (*remembers*), and then, after a while, attends to the clock and again recognizes it as the same thing attended to earlier. This child has attained a concept of this particular clock at the concrete level, not necessarily as a clock, but as an object. The operations involved in attaining this level, as shown in Figure 2.2, are attending to an object, discriminating it from other objects, representing it internally as an image, and maintaining the representation (remembering).

Identity Level

Attainment of a concept at the identity level is inferred by the individual's recognition of an object as the same one previously encountered when the object is observed in a different situational context, from a different spatiotemporal perspective, or sensed in a different modality, such as hearing or seeing. For example, the child who recognizes the clock as the same one that has been removed from the wall of one room and placed in another room has attained the concept of the particular clock at the identity level. Similarly, the child who recognizes the family poodle whether seen from straight ahead, from the side, or from various angles has attained the concept of the particular poodle at the identity level. As shown in Figure 2.2., the operations of attending, discriminat-

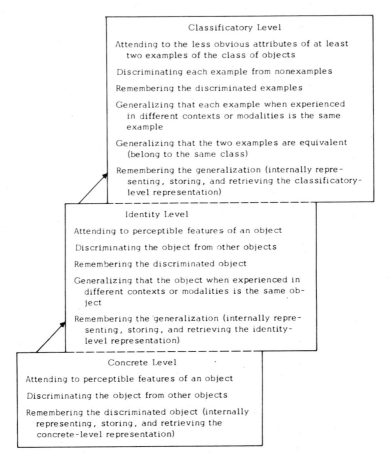

Figure 2.2.   Mental operations in concept attainment at the concrete, identity, and classificatory levels.

ing, and remembering are involved in attainment at the identity level as well as at the concrete level. However, concept attainment at the concrete level involves only the discrimination of an object from other objects, whereas attainment at the identity level involves not only discriminating various forms of the same object from other objects, but also generalizing the forms of the particular object as equivalent, or generalizing across the different contexts in which the same object is experienced. Generalizing is the new operation postulated to emerge as a result of learning and maturation that makes attainment at the identity level possible.

We should recognize that as adults we meet many new and different persons for very short time periods. We are continuously attaining concepts of individual persons at the identity level; however, we already have the concept *person* at both the classificatory and formal levels, so our task is much easier than that of the young child.

Most psychologists treat concepts at the concrete and identity levels as discriminations, not as concepts. Miller and Johnson–Laird (1976) treat them as percepts. Piaget (1970) does not differentiate between the concrete and identity levels but refers to object concepts. Gagné (1977) defines concrete concepts as those that have examples that can be pointed to and that are learned by direct observation of the examples. According to Gagné, children learn about a particular example of a class of objects, qualities, and so on, as a concrete concept by observing it. Children discriminate between particular examples and can generalize to the same example when encountered in other contexts, and to other examples that are equivalent. Thus, Gagné's treatment of learning concrete concepts is somewhat analogous to attaining the identity level and the classificatory level of *the same concept* in CLD theory.

Classificatory Level

As shown earlier in Figure 2.2, the new mental operation that enables us to attain concepts at the classificatory level is generalizing that two or more objects, events, processes, or relations are equivalent. The lowest level of attainment of a concept at a classificatory level is inferred when the individual responds to two or more different examples of the same class of objects, events, or processes or to the invariant relations among objects, events, or processes, as equivalent. For example, the child who treats the clock on the wall and the one on the desk as equivalent in one or more ways, such that both have the same shape, have moving parts, and are used to tell time, has attained a concept of clock at a beginning classificatory level. At this beginning level, children seem to base their classifications on some of the intrinsic and functional attributes of the concept examples that they have experienced; but they cannot state the basis of their classifications.

Individuals are still at the classificatory level when they can correctly identify a large number of things as examples and others as nonexamples, but they cannot use the defining attributes of the concept in evaluating examples and nonexamples. At this higher phase in attaining concepts at the classificatory level, children discriminate some of the less obvious attributes of the concepts and generalize correctly to a greater variety of examples, some of which are very much like the nonexamples. Also, they are able to make the basis of their classification more explicit, but it is still incomplete.

Formal Level

Persons demonstrate a concept of *tree* at the formal level if, when shown some examples of trees, shrubs, and herbs, they properly identify the trees and call them "trees," discriminate and name the defining attributes of tree, give a societally accepted definition of tree, and evaluate how examples of trees differ from examples of shrubs and herbs in terms of the defining attributes of tree. When individuals can do these things, it is inferred that they have learned the concept at the formal level through performing the inductive or the reception operations shown in Figure 2.3.

The inductive pattern involves formulating, remembering, and evaluating hypotheses regarding the attributes of the concept, including invariant relations, and then inferring the concept definition, if the concept has already been attained at the classificatory level, or inferring the concept itself if it has not been previously learned at the classificatory

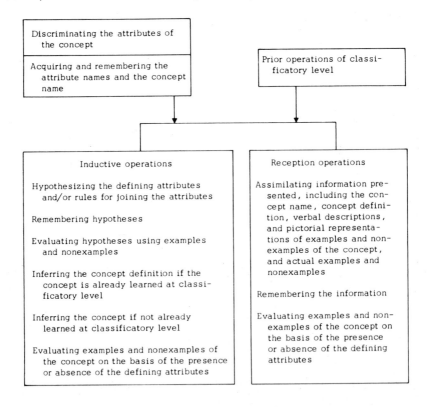

Figure 2.3. Mental operations in concept attainment at the formal level.

level. (A high school student encountering the concepts *participle* or be-*havior modification* for the first time illustrates the latter.) The opera-tions involved in the inductive hypothesis-testing strategy characterize individuals who secure information potentially available to them from both examples and nonexamples of the concept. These individuals ap-parently reason like this: "Thing 1 is land totally surrounded by water. It is a member of the class. Thing 2 is land that is only partially surrounded by water. It is not a member of the class. Therefore, lands totally sur-rounded by water belong to the class, but lands only partially sur-rounded by water do not." The individual has hypothesized a defining attribute, remembered it, evaluated the hypothesis, and is making pro-gress toward inferring a definition of island in terms of its defining at-tributes. As another example from the experimentation of the present study an individual may reason like this: "Mary related a scientific obser-vation to something which was known and drew a conclusion about what was observed. This is an example of the process. John observed the same event and related it to something known but did not draw a con-clusion. This is not an example of the process. Therefore, drawing a con-clusion is a necessary attribute of the process." This individual will prob-ably then infer that the process concept is *inferring.*

A meaningful reception strategy, rather than an inductive one, is often employed in school settings with older students, to enable the students to not only classify examples of concepts, but also to understand the concepts at a mature level. In expository instruction using a meaningful reception strategy, students are given the name of the concept and its defining attributes. Explanations and illustrations are provided by the teacher; information may also be made available in books and visuals. The students' main task is to attend to, receive, and process the informa-tion that is provided and then to retrieve it when needed.

The term *successive levels of attaining the same concept* deserves at-tention. I have found the term *level,* rather than stage, to be useful in indicating the new operations that are necessary to attain the same con-cept with deeper understanding and also to use the concept to interpret new situations, understand principles and hierarchical relationships, and solve problems. Attaining the same concept at the next higher level is qualitatively different from attaining the prior level in that one or more new and more mature operations are necessary; also the operations of the prior level must be carried out using more information. Attaining the same concept at the next higher level is also cumulative in that the prior operations must be performed and the prior level must have been attained. These ideas, however, are very different from an orthodox Piagetian stage account of concept development that proposes not only different psychological structures and different operations for the successive stages of concept learning but also large observable changes between the successive stages (Piaget 1970). Our research suggests that the deeper understanding and greater use of the same concepts at the successively higher levels is more a product of learning and experience than of maturation. It does not appear to be explainable by the emergence and neural integration of new psychological structures (Klausmeier & Associates, 1979) as Piaget has proposed.

In the present series of experiments, each printed PC lesson was prepared to teach the students of the experimental schools the concept at the formal level. When a concept is attained at this level, it is understood, can be defined, and examples and nonexamples can be evaluated reliably. In the main, a meaningful reception strategy was employed when preparing the lessons, except that some exercises within each lesson called for the student to hypothesize and infer the defining attributes of the concept or the concept itself. On the other hand, the school-adopted SAPA curriculum called for students to learn the process by observing teacher demonstrations involving the process and by carrying out activities involving the process, for example, observing scientific phenomena, classifying objects, and experimenting. By these methods, students presumably would learn the process, not as a concept to be understood and to serve as a tool of thought, but as an operation to be performed.

We should clarify what is meant by the terms *attribute* and *defining attribute of a concept*. Bruner, Goodnow, and Austin (1956) defined an attribute narrowly as "any discriminable feature of an event that is susceptible of some discriminable variation from event to event [p. 26]." Some attributes are merely "discriminable features" of events, but others are not. An attribute may be a directly observable or inferable use of an object, event, or process, or an observable or inferable function thereof. Also, it may be an observable or inferable invariant relation between objects, events, or processes. Things that are members of taxonomies, for example, most members of the plant and animal kingdom, have observable or readily inferable intrinsic attributes. The same things that have intrinsic attributes may also have uses, for example, the classes of plants and animals that are used for food by persons of particular cultural or ethnic groups. Also, there are observable or inferable invariant relations between and among members of classes, for example, between dogs and human beings in general or between a particular child and a dog that is the child's pet.

Many valid and powerful concepts, such as the concepts comprising the form classes of the English language, do not have directly observable attributes in the same sense as plants and animals. Here some of the attributes of the classes can be expressed in terms of the functions of each class when used in a sentence. The function of any word in a sentence implies a relationship with the function of other words in the same sentence. The attributes of events and processes in hierarchically organized systems and models, such as the process concepts of science employed in the present project, are expressed in terms of invariant relationships between and among the concepts.

The *defining attributes* of a concept include all the attributes that are necessary to determine whether any instance experienced is or is not an example of a concept. In the content analysis performed on each process concept used in the present project, the following rationale was adopted for determining the defining attributes: The defining attributes of a generic concept (process) are the discrete operations necessary to perform it and the prerequisite operation. The defining attributes of *observing* (which has no prerequisite process) and inferring follow:

Observing: 1. Using one or more of the senses.
             2. Examining critically.
             3. Recording data precisely.

Inferring: 1. Relating a scientific observation to something which is known.
             2. Drawing a conclusion about what was observed.

Attributes that are used in taxonomies are of three kinds: defining, critical, and variable. A more complete discussion of these categories of attributes may be found in Markle (1977) and Tiemann, Kroeker, and Markle (1977).

We digress briefly to indicate that "recording data precisely" does not logically appear to be a defining attribute of *observing;* it seems to be a process that may or may not follow an observation. It was included as a defining attribute in the present project because it was treated as a necessary aspect of observing in the SAPA curriculum.

TRANSFER AND THE USE AND EXTENSION OF CONCEPTS

Concepts are the building blocks of cognitive learning and development, not only because they enable one to understand and relate many otherwise discrete phenomena, but also because they provide the basis for vertical and horizontal transfer. There is vertical transfer from one successive level to the next as individuals attain the successively higher levels of the same concept. There are four directions of horizontal transfer, corresponding to the four categories of uses that may be made of concepts as shown in Figure 2.4.

A concept attained only to the concrete or identity level may be used in solving simple perceptual problems that do not require thinking with the use of symbols. Concepts learned at the classificatory and formal levels can be used to generalize to examples and discriminate nonexamples when encountered, to form structures of knowledge including the understanding of taxonomic and other hierarchical relationships involving the concept, to understand principles, and to solve problems. As a concept is used in any of these ways, the meaning of the concept itself is extended. For example, when a principle or a taxonomy is understood, new relationships among each of the concepts embodied in the principle or the taxonomy are also understood, thus extending the meaning of the concepts. A more complete account of transfer may now be examined.

Historically, three theories have been formulated to account for transfer from one learning situation to another—identical elements, generalization, and transposition (Klausmeier & Davis, 1969). There is no lack of agreement among the theories that transfer occurs; the difference lies in what transfers. According to the identical-elements theory, specific facts, skills, and attitudes transfer from one situation to the next. Principles based on related specifics are assumed to transfer according to the generalization theory. According to transposition theory, the broader

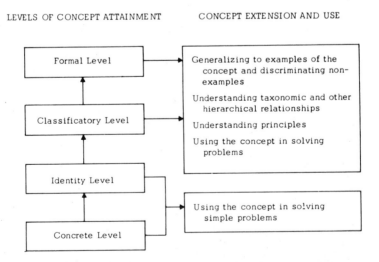

Figure 2.4. Levels of concept attainment and use.

patterns of means–ends relationships between situations provide the basis for transfer.

A more comprehensive model than any of the preceding three (Ferguson, 1956; Klausmeier & Goodwin, 1975) specifies that abilities and information transfer from one situation to the next. The abilities include the ability to generalize across modalities and situational contexts as well as to carry out all of the other mental operations involved in learning concepts, learning principles, and problem-solving techniques. This information–abilities model is shown in Figure 2.5. The model is intended to be applicable to all products of learning in the cognitive domain, in the psychomotor domain, and in the affective domain. Similarly, it accounts for both vertical transfer and horizontal or lateral transfer.

The information and abilities aspects of vertical transfer may be illustrated in connection with an individual having attained the identity level of a concept and then learning the classificatory level. Regarding the information base of transfer, assume that an individual has attained the concept of a tree at the identity level and is now involved in attaining the classificatory level, that is, learning that two different trees are equivalent. We may speculate that, when learning the identity level of each of two trees, the individual acquired perceptual information about each tree related to its form, size, and color. This information acquired when learning to recognize each of two trees as the same ones at the identity level is presumed to transfer to the new task of learning at the classificatory level.

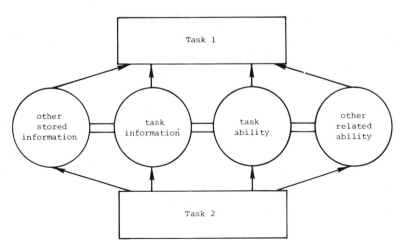

Figure 2.5.   Information and ability bases of transfer.

We may now consider the abilities aspect of vertical transfer. When attaining the identity level of each of the two particular trees, the student demonstrated the ability to attend to and discriminate one tree as different from other treelike objects in the environment and also generalized that each of the two particular trees, when experienced later, was the same one that had been experienced earlier from a different spatiotemporal orientation. These attending, discriminating, and generalizing abilities are presumed to transfer when learning the concept, *tree,* at the classificatory level.

Having the task information and the attending, discriminating, generalizing abilities necessary for the identity level is necessary but not sufficient for attaining the classificatory level. Generalizing that two or more examples are equivalent or, as in this example, that the two trees attained at the identity level are equivalent, is the new and higher-level ability required. Attending to and discriminating more information involving two trees rather than one and more complex information (assume the trees vary in size and are an elm and a maple) are required.

Other information also may transfer from learning at the identity level to learning at the classificatory level. For example, some of the contextual information (the relative position of each tree in the yard) learned at the identity level may also transfer. In addition to the prior specific abilities, generalized conceptualizing abilities involving other objects, events, and processes may also transfer to learning at the classificatory level if the individual has also attained other concepts at the identity level and classificatory level. Similarly, strategies for learning and remembering may also transfer.

We may relate this analysis of vertical transfer regarding *tree* to short-term learning situations and to long-term development. During a short period of time, perhaps in less than a minute, the individual who had attained the identity level of two trees and had become capable of generalizing that they were equivalent moved from the identity level of *tree* to the classificatory level. But this was the very earliest rudimentary classificatory level. That is, only two particular trees were categorized as being equivalent. As more trees and other green things, including shrubs, are experienced during the next months and years, the person will continue to learn to discriminate among different classes of trees, such as coniferous and deciduous. The final mature classificatory level of *tree* will not be attained on the basis of merely adding together the short-term, discrete experiences with individual trees. Instead, as learning continues, the individual will also continuously organize and reorganize the products of these short-term learning experiences into a more highly differentiated and inclusive concept of *tree.* Further, other concepts, including *shrub* and *herb,* will be learned, and the entire set of concepts will be organized and combined into an increasingly inclusive but differentiated conceptual core. One may speculate that this kind of reciprocal interweaving of the products of short-term learning with an ever-increasing information base and more advanced abilities characterizes the relationship between learning across short time intervals and development across longer periods of time.

It may be added that during the developmental years from infancy to adolescence, individuals vary in the mental operations they are capable of performing because of the interaction of maturational factors and learning opportunities. With maturation and practice, individuals become increasingly capable of the higher mental operations that are necessary for attaining the successively higher levels of a concept and for forming more complete and inclusive conceptual cores. This does not imply that the emergence and refinement of the higher mental operations ceases nor that the ability to employ the operations on more content and more complex content ceases when physical maturation is achieved. On the contrary, the producers of new knowledge typically make their significant discoveries long after achieving full physical maturation.

Lateral or horizontal transfer may be illustrated in the relationship between having attained the formal level of the process concept *observing* and using this information to attain other concepts of the hierarchy, understanding the relationships among other concepts of the hierarchy, understanding a principle of which the concept is a part, and solving problems that require use of the concept. Figure 3.1 (p. 63) shows the hierarchy of which observing is a part.

Let us assume that the student has attained the concept *observing* at the formal level. How does the information necessary for attaining the formal level of this concept transfer to learning other concepts of the taxonomy and their relationships, to understanding principles, and to problem solving?

The defining attributes of *observing* are using one or more of the senses, examining critically, and recording data precisely. The defining attributes of *classifying* are identifying how things are different, identifying two or more things that are alike in some way, and grouping together the things that are alike. Having this information, that is, knowing the defining attributes of *observing,* should transfer to discriminating examples of *observing* from examples of *classifying.* Knowing that *observing* is a prerequisite for *classifying* should transfer to an understanding of this relationship between these two concepts of the hierarchy.

A principle involving a relationship between *observing* and other concepts is stated as follows: Using more than one of the senses in observing objects and events increases the probability of gaining more precise information. To understand this principle requires not only understanding the concept *observing* and the transfer of it, but also understanding all the other concepts embedded in the principle.

An illustrative problem for children to solve is given below. It indicates the growth of a root from Day 1 to Day 2.

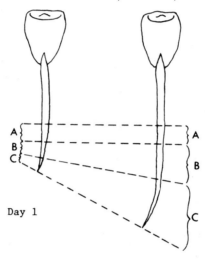

Day 2

The student is asked to observe the drawing and to indicate in which section, A, B, or C the root has grown the least and in which section it has grown the most. Knowing the three attributes of observing should help the student solve the problem, but other knowledge and abilities are also required.

To this point, the successive levels of concept attainment, the mental operations involved in attaining each level, and the uses and extensions of concepts have been indicated as providing a framework for describing some of the internal conditions necessary for learning concepts during short periods of time and for describing conceptual development across long time periods. A similar account of the external conditions that facilitate concept learning is in order; however, this is presented in considerable detail in Chapter 3 which deals with the procedures for conducting an instructional analysis. The brief introduction presented in this chapter and the information in Chapter 3 are intended to be sufficiently complete so that the construction of tests and development of lessons presented in Chpater 5 may be understood. Although not dealt with in any detail in later chapters of this book, ideas regarding motivation are now presented in order to provide a more complete account of CLD theory.

MOTIVATION IN COGNITIVE LEARNING AND DEVELOPMENT

Many psychologists are departing from reinforcement theory to information-processing theory in explaining the motivational aspects of human cognitive behavior. For example, Miller and Johnson–Laird (1976) employ the theoretical construct—executive control—to account for the self-regulation of all behavior, including mental and motor activity. The construct, *intend*, is employed to indicate the operation concerned specifically with the motivational aspects of behavior; the term, *plan*, is used to indicate any set of internal hierarchical processes that control the order in which a sequence of goal-directed instrumental activities is performed. A person's intention to carry out a plan to attain a goal initiates and directs a sequence of instrumental activities. The intention arises from a perceived incongruence or inconsistency between a desired or expected state of affairs or conditions, and a current state of affairs or conditions. This example of one information-processing view regarding the self-regulatory, motivational basis of instrumental mental and motor activity is taken as the starting point for the treatment of motivation that follows.

The human being is an information-processing, stimulus-seeking organism whose thought influences action. Thoughts, particularly in the form of intentions, have a powerful effect on the first three of four phases of a behavioral sequence: its activation or instigation, its direction, its persistence until goal achievement, and finally, the consequences following achievement or nonachievement of the goal. Although thought influences action and thinking is involved throughout an action sequence, not all behavior is intended consciously. Reflex actions and firmly established habitual patterns of behavior are carried out without conscious intent.

The relationships between a goal-directed sequence of observable or inferable instrumental activities and cognitive motivational activities are indicated in Figure 2.6. A sequence of activities may be completed during a very short time interval or it may be carried out over a period of years. The infant's behavior sequences are necessarily of short duration,

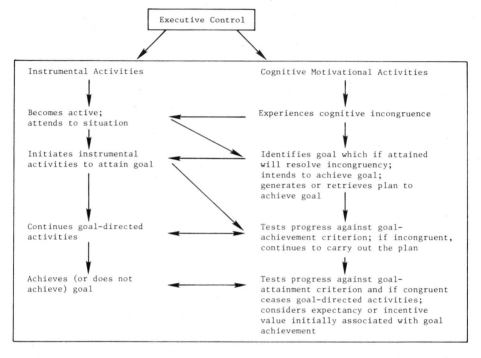

Figure 2.6. Parallel sequences of instrumental goal-directed activities and related cognitive motivational activities.

but those of adults range from very short duration to extending for years. We may further consider the relationships between the instrumental and motivational aspects of the four phases of a behavioral sequence.

1. Let us assume that a person planning a nature walk finds out that there is some poison ivy in the trail area. Being aware of this, the person experiences an incongruency or inconsistency between taking the walk and possibly being poisoned. This cognitive incongruence is accompanied with mental activation, including attention to this particular situation.

2. The cognitive incongruence is followed with two closely related activities—formulating a goal and intending to achieve it. The goal is to learn to identify poison ivy plants.

Goals may take the form of an expectancy, that is, an expected condition or state of affairs to be achieved; a desired incentive, such as a feeling of success accrued from attaining a goal; or a combination of the two. Both function in connection with many goals.

After formulating a goal and intending to attain it, the individual either generates a plan for achieving it or retrieves from memory a plan that has been carried out earlier. Intending to carry out the plan is followed with an executive control instruction to start carrying out the instrumental activities to achieve the goal. Let us assume that in our example the plan calls for studying a particular book to identify poison ivy. The person gets the book and starts studying it.

3. The plan for attaining the goal—study the book until poison ivy can be identified—is used to test progress toward the goal. The intention and the plan serve to direct and sustain the goal-related activities, in that as long as the plan is not completed and the intention remains, the individual continues the instrumental activities. During this phase of the behavioral sequence, the individual tests the progress being made against the goal-achievement criterion. If the goal is not yet attained, and the individual yet intends to attain it, the intention and the initial plan or a refined plan will serve to continue to direct the instrumental activities. In our example, the person studies the book until the criterion of being able to recognize poison ivy is met.

4. Assume that the goal is achieved, that the individual has learned to identify poison ivy plants. More thought may result and influence instrumental actions. For example, if the individual feels confident of being able to recognize poison ivy, no ointment or other remedy may be purchased. If the individual is not certain, another plan may be generated that starts another behavioral sequence, namely, to purchase the ointment.

We may assume that individuals differ in their motivational activities and states as they do in other areas of cognitive functioning. Recent approaches to understanding motivation from a cognitive frame of reference, including attribution theory and locus of control, hold promise for understanding the differences as Wittrock & Lumsdaine (1977) have indicated in their review of motivational research and theory.

There seems to be agreement that earlier S–R (Stimulus–Response) formulations regarding reinforcement as automatically strengthening responses and as reliably and automatically serving as incentives for initiating and directing instrumental activities are inadequate bases for understanding human motivation. The fact that receiving reinforcement tends to strengthen behavior and to serve as an incentive for engaging in the same behavior should be interpreted on the basis of informational feedback as well as the incentive value that the reinforcer may provide. Receiving the reinforcement apparently provides information that is analyzed by the recipient; and this analysis, along with other cognitive variables, determines the effects of the reinforcer.

In the present project, attention-getting devices were used when preparing the printed process-concept lessons, including the use of draw-ings of humorous characters who presented much of the information (see excerpts of lessons in Chapter 5). Early in each lesson, it was made clear that the student would be learning a concept. Feedback was pro-vided by including in the printed lesson the answers to the exercises. The attempt was not made, however, to ascertain whether or not the student carried out the instrumental activities or the cognitive operations specified in Figure 2.6 while studying the lessons. Thus, no applications of these motivational aspects of CLD theory were tested directly in the experiments.

PRINCIPLES OF COGNITIVE DEVELOPMENT

The remainder of this chapter is given to students' development of concepts, principles, structures of knowledge, and problem solving dur-ing the school years. The descriptions of the developmental progressions and related individual differences are stated in the form of principles to summarize and synthesize a large amount of empirical information that was gathered as part of a large-scale longitudinal study. More complete information is presented in Chapters 6, 7, and 8 of Klausmeier and Allen (1978).

Concept Attainment in an Invariant Sequence

Individuals attain four successively higher levels of the same concept in an invariant sequence. Invariance implies that the successive items of a complete sequence appear in a fixed, constant progression. For exam-ple, if A, B, and C are identified as three hypothetical cognitive acquisi-tions in an invariant developmental series, then A must appear before B, and B must occur before C. The sequence in attaining A, B, and C does not vary among individuals; it is invariant. However, the rates at which A, B, and C first emerge and eventually reach full functional maturity may vary among individuals. Invariance of a a developmental progres-sion results from the interaction of biological maturation with the regu-larities that individuals experience in their physical and social en-vironments, rather than as a product of either biological inheritance or environmental conditions independently.

Empirical testing of the invariant sequence in attaining the four suc-cessive levels of *cutting tool, tree, equilateral triangle,* and *noun* was done as part of the longitudinal study (Klausmeier & Allen, 1978). The performance of each student on each test of each level of each concept each year was evaluated for mastery or nonmastery, and the resulting individual student protocols were analyzed. The vast majority of the students were found to have mastered the successively higher levels of the same four concepts in an invariant sequence and also to have maintained mastery after their initial mastery. The small number of exceptions are not regarded as sufficient to invalidate the principle. The empirical basis of the principle is now illustrated with one concept, *equilateral triangle*.

In the three left columns of Table 2.1 are given the routes or patterns of mastery of the four levels for the first, second, and third year of measurement that conform to the principle of invariance. The percentages of each of the four longitudinal groups of students who followed each particular route for the three successive years of measurement are shown, as are the percentages for the four groups combined. The conforming patterns for each concept are presented as follows: in the top rows of the table are given the routes that culminate with mastery of the formal level; in the next rows are the patterns ending with mastery of the classificatory level; and finally, in the bottom rows are those ending with the identity. To illustrate, an individual whose highest attainment in Year 3 was the formal level, might have arrived at that level via a number of different routes, all consistent with the principle of invariance: formal→formal→formal (i.e., starting with and maintaining full attainment of the formal level); classificatory→formal→formal→; identity→classificatory→formal; and so on. In fact, for each concept there are 15 possible Year 1→2→3 routes leading to full attainment of the formal level, which are in accord with an invariant progression; there are 10 possible Year 1→2→3 routes for the classificatory level, 6 for the identity level, and 3 for the concrete. Only those routes that students' actually followed are shown in Table 2.1.

As may be observed, 87% of the students attained the four levels of *equilateral triangle* in an invariant sequence. The percentages of each longitudinal group of students who conformed to an invariant sequence ranged from 83 to 94.

Some exceptions to the invariant sequence were observed. A small percentage of the students who mastered a particular level one year did not do so the following year. Based on post hoc analyses of the students' test scores and their responses to items missed on a later test administration that were not missed at an earlier time, it was concluded that the majority of these exceptions resulted from inevitable error of measurement, the criteria of mastery established for each test, and the tendency of high scores to regress toward the mean. The possibility also remains that a few of the exceptions represent a true exception to an invariant se-

TABLE 2.1 Percentages of Students Whose Patterns of Attaining the Successively Higher Levels of *Equilateral Triangle* Conformed to an Invariant Sequence

Conforming patterns and year of measurement			Longitudinal group, grade in school, and N remaining in each group in Year 3				Combined groups
Year 1 →	Year 2 →	Year 3	A 1-2-3 (N=62)	B 4-5-6 (N=77)	C 7-8-9 (N=80)	D 10-11-12 (N=73)	(N=292)
Fo →	Fo →	Fo	—	3	31	56	23
C1 →	Fo →	Fo	—	13	23	15	13
C1 →	C1 →	Fo	3	22	11	3	10
Id →	Fo[a] →	Fo	—	4	4	—	2
Id →	C1 →	Fo	—	4	3	—	2
Id →	Id →	Fo[a]	—	1	—	—	<1
Co →	C1[a] →	Fo	—	1	—	—	<1
C1 →	C1 →	C1	60	27	13	7	25
Id →	C1 →	C1	24	4	5	3	8
Id →	Id →	C1	—	4	—	1	1
Co →	C1[a] →	C1	2	—	—	—	<1
No levels →	C1[a] →	C1	2	—	—	—	<1
No levels →	Id[a] →	C1	2	—	—	—	<1
Id →	Id →	Id	2	—	—	—	<1
N conforming			58	64	71	62	255
Percentage conforming			94[b]	83	89[b]	85	87

[a] This and the next lower level(s) were mastered for the first time in this year of measurement.
[b] This percentage is based on total conforming N/N and differs from what would be obtained from adding the column because each column entry is rounded.

quence. The biological inheritance of individuals and their environmental interactions vary so widely that we probably should not expect every individual to conform to any invariant sequence in all the dimensions of cognitive development that were studied.

How may the invariant developmental progress be accounted for in terms of internal and external conditions? The five necessary internal conditions for mastering each successively higher level are as follows: (a) mastery of the prior level; (b) functioning of at least one new mental operation in combination with the continuing operations of the prior level; (c) performing the operations of the prior level on content of increasing quantity and complexity experienced in a greater variety of contexts; (d) intending to attain the next higher level; and (e) persisting until it is attained. These internal conditions are controlled by a mechanism called executive control. In addition to the preceding internal conditions, being able to discriminate the defining attributes of the concept and to name the concept and the defining attributes are prerequisite and necessary for carrying out the new operations at the formal level. The necessary external conditions of learning include experience and practice with the content of the particular concept as represented in examples of it and in examples of related concepts. The amount of experience and practice vary among concepts and for the four levels of attainment.

In the present project, each printed PC lesson was prepared to teach the students the formal level of the concept; however, part of the lesson was also directed toward teaching the students to classify examples of the concept correctly. During the lesson preparation, it was assumed that few if any of the Grade 4 and Grade 5 students of the experimental schools would have mastered the classificatory level fully at the time the first experiments were started. And time constraints did not permit the testing of students, the scoring of tests, nor the grouping of students according to the level each had mastered. As we shall see immediately, the assumption that few students had mastered the classificatory level was probably correct inasmuch as students normally begin to attain the formal level of abstract concepts years before fully mastering the classificatory level.

Development of Successively Higher Levels of the Same Concept

Individuals develop the four successively higher levels of the same concept continuously for many years and any three successive levels concurrently for one or more years. In the longitudinal study of cognitive development (Klausmeier & Allen, 1978) seven dimensions, or items, used in the study of cognitive development were identified for each of the four concepts, namely, the four levels of attainment — concrete, identity, classificatory, and formal — and understanding of principles, understanding of taxonomic relations, and problem solving.

The developmental curves for the concrete, identity, classificatory, and formal levels of *noun* are given in Figure 2.7. Curves are not presented for the levels of the other concepts because the children had fully attained the concrete, identity, and classificatory level of *cutting tool* and the concrete and identity level of *tree* and *equilateral triangle* before Grade 1. (These and other curves that are presented in this chapter for groups of students were derived empirically as the best fit of the observed data.)

As shown in Figure 2.7, the children made much progress toward full attainment of the concrete and identity level of *noun* by Grade 3. Functioning at near a chance level in Grade 1, they attained the classificatory level of *noun* at a rapid rate from Grade 1 through Grade 3, however, in Grade 5 the mean percentage correct was only 65 or thereabout. A less rapid but continuous rate of increase was shown by the older groups of students until near full attainment was reached in Grade 12. Functioning at essentially a chance level in Grade 2, the children attained the formal level at a slower rate than the classificatory level, and the mean percentage correct was about 45 in Grade 5 and 72 in Grade 12.

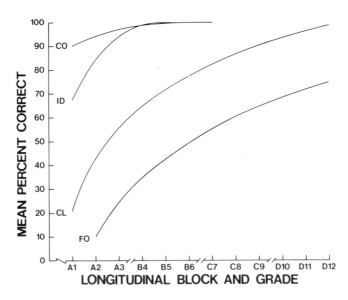

Figure 2.7 Developmental curves for concrete, identity, classificatory, and formal levels of *noun*.

We see in Figure 2.7 that Grade 1 children had attained about 90% correct at the concrete level, whereas the percentage correct at the formal level in Grade 12 was about 72%. Further observation of the curves indicated that there was concurrent attainment of the concrete, identity, and classificatory levels during Grade 1 through Grade 3 and concurrent attainment of the identity, classificatory, and formal levels, from Grade 2 through Grade 4. Development of the classificatory and formal levels proceeded concurrently from Grade 2 through Grade 12. We conclude that progression from one level to another of the same concept may be characterized as gradual and continuous. Development of any three levels is concurrent for 1 or 2 years, whereas development of the classificatory and formal levels is concurrent for many years–in the case of *noun,* for 11 years, from Grade 2 through Grade 12.

We may pause to consider the terms, *concurrent* and *synchronous.* Concurrent implies only that two or more items, such as the levels, are developing at the same time. Synchronous indicates that the items under consideration are developing at the same time and also that (a) their functioning starts in about the same year; (b) their terminal or maximal functioning is reached in about the same year; and (c) the shape of the developmental curves of all the items is similar. Thus, synchronous development of two or more cognitive items is necessarily concurrent, but concurrent development is not necessarily synchronous. In the case of the levels of concept attainment, the development of two or more levels is concurrent for one or more years; but it is clearly not synchronous.

Development of Understanding of Principles, Taxonomic Relations, and Problem Solving

Individuals develop understanding of principles, taxonomic relations, and problem solving skills continuously and concurrently during most of the school years. The developmental curves for understanding principles, understanding taxonomic relations, and problem solving are given in Figures 2.8 a, b, c. Little understanding of principles occurs during the primary school years. Progress in understanding principles increases at about the same rate throughout the intermediate, junior, and senior high school years. In Grade 12, the mean performance is still relatively low.

Understanding taxonomic relations increases rapidly during the primary and the intermediate school years. The rate of increase is quite slow during the junior and senior high school years, and the final performance in Grade 12 is relatively low.

Children have developed considerable proficiency in problem solving by the end of the primary school years. Students continue to develop

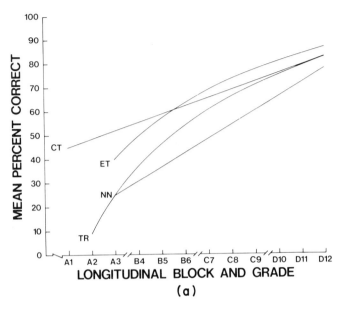

(a)

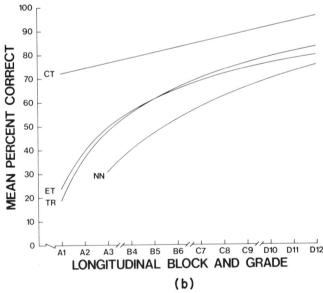

(b)

Figure 2.8   Legend on facing page.

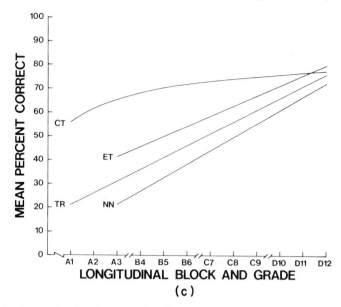

Figure 2.8. Normative development related to: (a) understanding principles; (b) understanding taxonomic relations; and (c) problem solving.

problem-solving skills at a relatively slow rate during the intermediate, junior, and senior high school years. The level of performance throughout the school years is quite low, even in Grade 12.

From the preceding, it is clear that growth in understanding principles, understanding taxonomic relations, and problem solving continues from the primary school years through Grade 12, and there is concurrent development from Grade 3 through Grade 12. The continuous nature of this development may be accounted for primarily in terms of the students' attaining the concepts that are involved at successively higher levels; their ability to attend to, discriminate, and remember more information and more complex information; their increasing language competence; and their more effective strategies for securing, processing, and remembering information.

In the series of experiments to be reported in Chapters 6 and 7, the students' acquisition of principles, taxonomic or other hierarchical relationships, and problem-solving skills involving the process concepts was not included in the objectives of the PC lessons nor the school-adopted SAPA curriculum. Rather, the objectives of each process-concept lesson was attainment of the particular concept at the formal level whereas the primary objective of each set of SAPA lessons was the use of the process in activities that are usually not characterized as problem-solving or understanding principles. The assumption underlying preparation of the PC lesson was that the Grade 4 and Grade 5 students would not readily learn principles or be able to solve problems involving the particular process concept.

Attainment of Different Concepts at Different Ages

Individuals fully attain the same levels of different concepts at different ages. The differences in the percentage of the longitudinal students of each grade who mastered the classificatory level and the formal level of the four concepts were large as is shown in Figure 2.9. For example, the percentge of Grade 1 students who mastered the classificatory level (Klausmeier & Allen, 1978) of *cutting tool, tree, equilateral triangle,* and *noun* was about 90, 60, 65, and 0 respectively. The percentage of

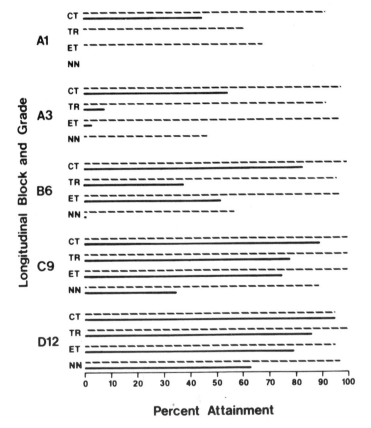

Figure 2.9. Percentage of students in grades 1, 3, 6, 9, and 12 who mastered each concept at the classificatory level (broken line) and at the formal level (solid line).

Grade 6 students who mastered the formal level was 83 for *cutting tool,* 38 for *tree,* 52 for *equilateral triangle,* and 1 for *noun.* There were more Grade 1 students who mastered the formal level of *cutting tool* than Grade 9 students who mastered the formal level of *noun.* Concepts that have many three-dimensional examples widely distributed in the immediate environment and experienced early in life are mastered earlier than are concepts, the examples of which are represented only symbolically and involve semantic content.

Based on the grade at which the levels of these conepts were mastered, we may conclude that the age at which individuals become capable of performing the operations and meeting the other conditions necessary and sufficient to master the successive levels is related to the content domain of the concept and the abstractness of the examples of the concept. Such fundamental operations as discriminating, hypothesizing, and inferring are performed years earlier on three-dimensional examples involving figural content than on examples expressed symbolically that involve semantic content.

Mastery of Concept Levels and Understanding Principles, Taxonomic Relations, and Problem Solving

Mastery of the classificatory and formal levels is accompanied by increasing mastery of understanding principles, taxonomic relations, and problem solving. Information from the longitudinal study (Klausmeier & Allen, 1978) was used to test three predictions: Mastery of the concrete and identity levels will be accompanied only with mastery of simple perceptual problems; mastery of the classificatory level will be accompanied with some mastery of understanding principles, taxonomic relations, and problem solving; mastery of the formal level will be accompanied with most mastery of principles, taxonomic relations, and problem solving.

In accordance with the predictions, many students of the longitudinal study who, when in the primary and intermediate grades, mastered the concrete or identity levels of different concepts as their highest performance rarely mastered understanding of the related principles and taxonomic relations, or the problem-solving exercises (Table 2.2). The proportion of the total instances of mastery of the uses to the number of students of the longitudinal study who mastered either the concrete or the identity level was .08. (The highest proportion possible was 3.0; each student who mastered a level of a concept could also have mastered its three uses.)

Substantial numbers of students at all grade levels mastered the classificatory level of one or more concepts as their highest achievement.

TABLE 2.2 Total Number of Students Fully Attaining Each Concept Level and Total Instances of Mastery of Understanding Principles, Understanding Taxonomic Relations, and Problem Solving

Group and grade		Concrete/Identity combined	Classificatory	Formal
A1	N attained level	90	112	28
	Instances of mastery of uses	2	27	29
A3	N attained level	38	167	41
	Instances of mastery of uses	0	60	47
B6	N attained level	38	136	134
	Instances of mastery of uses	7	76	254
C9	N attained level	9	90	221
	Instances of mastery of uses	4	71	473
D12	N attained level	1	55	236
	Instances of mastery of uses	1	43	539
Total	N attained level	176	560	660
	Instances of mastery of uses	14	277	1342
	Ratio of mastery of level to instances of uses	.08	.49	2.03

The instances of uses mastered in relation to the number of students mastering the classificatory level increased across the grades. The proportion of the total instances of mastery of the uses to the total number of students who mastered the classificatory level was found to be .49.

Few students during the primary school years fully attained the formal level of any concept except *cutting tool,* and in Grade 6, only one had fully attained the formal level of *noun.* Unlike mastery of the other levels, mastery of the formal level is accompanied with far greater mastery of understanding taxonomic relations, understanding principles, and problem solving at all grade levels. The proportion of the total instances of mastery of the uses to the number of students who mastered the formal level of one or more concepts was found to be 2.03.

Interindividual Differences

Individuals of the same age vary greatly in attainment of the four levels and mastery of principles, taxonomic relations, and problem solving. Interindividual differences among individuals of about the same age in Grades 3–12 may be illustrated with mastery of the formal level and mastery of understanding principles. Development of these two cognitive items is concurrent from Grade 3 through Grade 12. The number of students who did and did not master the formal level of the four concepts and the understanding of principles varied greatly within each

TABLE 2.3 Percentages of Students Who Did and Did Not Fully Attain the Formal Level of Each Concept and Who Did and Did Not Master the Related Principles

Group and grade	Formal level								Principle							
	CT		TR		ET		NN		CT		TR		ET		NN	
	A	NA	A	NA	A	NA	A	NA	A	NA	A	NA	A	NA	A	NA
A1	45	55	0	100	0	100	0	100	2	98						
A3	55	45	8	92	3	97	1	99	3	97	2	98	0	100	2	98
B6	83	17	38	62	52	48	35	65	49	51	6	94	38	62	1	99
C9	89	11	78	22	75	25	63	37	50	50	31	69	51	49	25	75
D12	95	5	86	14	79	21			60	40	47	53	73	27	49	51

Note: A = fully attained; NA = not fully attained.

grade and across the grades (Table 2.3). For example, 52% of the students in Grade 6 were found to have mastered the formal level of *equilateral triangle,* whereas 48% had not. The magnitude of the difference between grades was very great. For example, 3% of the children in Grade 3 mastered the formal level of *equilateral triangle* whereas 21% of the students in Grade 12 did not. The percentage of the students in Grade 6 who mastered understanding of principles related to *equilateral triangle* was 38, but 27% of the twelfth graders failed to reach the mastery criterion. Similar differences were found in understanding taxonomic relations and problem solving. Most teachers and theorists would probably not expect the differences to be so large.

Large differences such as these clearly call for adapting instruction to the learning characteristics of the individual student, including varying the amount of time given students to achieve the same objectives and permitting students to achieve a set of objectives at different rates when they are given about the same amount of time daily for instruction. The model of instructional programming for the individual student, to be described in Chapter 4, was formulated to take into account interindividual differences of the magnitude reported above. In turn, the model was applied to the methods employed by the experimental teachers in the present series of experiments, but there were time constraints and school-discrict policies to be accounted for also. It was not until the second year of experimentation that the amount of time could be varied appropriately, and even then district policy did not allow students to proceed at different rates through the school-adopted SAPA curriculum. Enrichment rather than acceleration was employed with rapid achievers, whereas slow achievers proceeded to new objectives without mastering the previous ones.

Intraindividual Variability

Intraindividual variability becomes increasingly differentiated according to content fields from age 6 to 12. This principle is inferred from the results of factor analyses that were performed on the longitudinal data, Grades 1–12; the analyses are reported in Klausmeier and Associates (1979). Here, only the primary conclusions are considered. In Grade 6, a separate factor was identified for each of the four concepts measured in the longitudinal study: *cutting tool, tree, equilateral triangle,* and *noun.* These were the only factors identified. Moreover, in each grade, from 6 through 12, only four or five factors were identified, and generally the same four factors were identified as in Grade 6, but with somewhat different loadings of the various tests. The differentiation had started to emerge in Grade 1 during the primary school years and progressed very rapidly from Grade 4 to Grade 6.

From these results, we infer that the individual's cognitive functioning is not unitary or global, characterized by equally high or low performance across all concepts. Rather, individual students typically vary within themselves in their performance relative to attainment of the different concepts and the related principles, taxonomic relations, and problem-solving skills. Other investigators have found intraindividual variability in concept achievement to be closely related to the subject fields of English, mathematics, science, and social studies (Harris & Harris, 1973; Shaycoft, 1967).

These early results regarding intraindividual variability were confirmed by the longitudinal study (Klausmeier & Allen, 1978). The additional significant findings were that, from about age 10 to 12, intraindividual variability in achievement of different subject matters increases markedly; the pattern of intraindividual variability is essentially stable by age 12; and the pattern remains unusually stable thereafter through Grade 12. In the present project, no attempt was made to verify these conclusions or to test their application to science. But the implication of this variability for applying the model of instructional programming for the individual student to different curricular areas warrants mention. Assessment of the students' entering achievement levels in each curricular area must be done. One should not use the results of a single test, such as IQ or reading, to estimate the entering achievement levels of students in science, mathematics, English, or social studies. As we shall see in Chapter 5, objective-referenced achievement tests were used in assessing the experimental students' entering achievement levels relative to the SAPA curriculum.

In the preceding pages we have seen how CLD theory influenced many decisions regarding the present series of experiments, including the substantive area, namely concepts, and the age of the participating students, from age 10 to 12. It may be appropriate now to summarize the primary constructs and principles that are most directly related to each of the two major parts of the experiments; first, that part dealing with teaching the students the formal level of each of the process concepts through use of the specially prepared PC lessons, and second, that part dealing with teaching the school-adopted curriculum, the SAPA processes of science.

What major applications of CLD theory related to the internal conditions of concept learning were incorporated in the PC lessons? First, each lesson, in accordance with the behavioral analysis described in Chapter 3, was designed and later used by the teachers in such a way that the student would learn the formal level of the particular process concept by using the meaningful reception operations specified in the theory (see Figure 2.3 to identify these operations). Second, the principle that the formal level of the same concept is mastered in an invariant sequence after the classificatory level is mastered and that the classificatory and the formal levels develop concurrently for many years were applied in the PC lessons by providing material from which the students would learn not only the formal level but also how to classify examples of the process concepts.

Each PC lesson incorporated the seven external conditions of learning of CLD theory in line with the content and the instructional analyses that were performed on the concepts (see Chapter 3 for a description of these analyses and Chapter 5 for an explanation and illustration of their application). Earlier experimentation had fully established the validity of these principles when applied to a student's learning of nonprocess concepts such as *tree* (Klausmeier, Schilling, & Feldman, 1976), *equilateral triangle* (McMurray, Bernard, & Klausmeier, 1975), and *behavior management procedures* (Bernard, 1975). Furthermore, other experimenters have also verified one or more of the principles in various experiments, but again not with process concepts and not under regular conditions of schooling extending for a long period of time. The lessons were also prepared to conform to the CLD approach to motivation and the information and abilities account of vertical transfer.

We see that each PC lesson incorporated all the preceding CLD applications into the learning of process concepts. If the students of the experimental schools consistently achieved at significantly higher levels than the students of the control schools, we may infer that the applications were made. We should be aware that in the experimentation no attempt was made to determine whether the students carried out one mental operation more or less successfully than another, whether one aspect of meaningful reception learning functioned more or less effectively than another, or whether one external condition of learning or another was incorporated more or less effectively into the lesson.

A vast amount of information regarding the nature and extent of interindividual differences and of intraindividual variability led to the formulation of the model of instructional programming for the individual student that is presented in Chapter 4. The CLD theory, as noted earlier in this chapter, extends this information base in the area of concept learning and development during the school years by identifying the range of differences among individuals in developing the same concept and by identifying the within-individual variability in learning concepts from different subject fields. This new information, as we shall see in Chapter 4, was incorporated in the specific applications of the model made by the experimental teachers in teaching the school-adopted SAPA science curriculum. As is readily inferred, these experiments were not carried out to verify these descriptive principles regarding individual differences. However, from the results of the experiments and the related account of the instructional methods employed, we are able to infer how instruction in science may be adapted to take into account differences in cognitive development of students from about age 10 to 12.

REFERENCES

Ausubel, D. P. *The psychology of meaningful verbal learning.* New York: Grune & Stratton, 1963.

Ausubel, D. P. Meaningful reception learning and the acquisition of concepts. In H. J. Klausmeier & C. W. Harris (Eds.), *Analyses of concept learning.* New York: Academic Press, 1966. Pp. 157–175.

Ausubel, D. P. *Educational psychology: A cognitive view.* New York: Holt, Rinehart & Winston, 1968.

Bernard, M. E. *The effects of advance organizers and within-text questions on the learning of a taxonomy of concepts* (Technical Report No. 357). Madison: Wisconsin Research and Development Center for Cognitive Learning, 1975.

Bruner, J. S., Goodnow, J. J., & Austin, G. A. *A study of thinking.* New York: Wiley, 1956.

Ferguson, G. A. On transfer and the abilities of man. *Canadian Journal of Psychology,* 1956, *10,* 121–131.

Gagné, R. M. *Essentials of learning for instruction.* Hinsdale, Ill.: The Dryden Press, 1974.

Gagné, R. M. *The conditions of learning* (3rd ed.). New York: Holt, Rinehart & Winston, 1977.

Guilford, J. P. *The nature of human intelligence.* New York: McGraw-Hill, 1967.

Harris, M. L., & Harris, C. W. *A structure of concept attainment abilities.* Madison: Wisconsin Research and Development Center for Cognitive Learning, 1973.

Klausmeier, H. J., & Allen, P. S. *Cognitive development of children and youth: A longitudinal study.* New York: Academic Press, 1978.

Klausmeier, H. J., and Associates. *Cognitive learning and development: Information-processing and Piagetian perspectives.* Cambridge, Mass.: Ballinger, 1979.

Klausmeier, H. J., Bernard, M., Katzenmeyer, C., & Sipple, T. S. *Development of conceptual learning and development assessment series II: Cutting tool* (Technical Report No. 431). Madison: Wisconsin Research and Development Center for Cognitive Learning, 1973.

Klausmeier, H. J., & Davis, J. K. Transfer of learning. In R. L. Ebel (Ed.), *Encyclopedia of educational research.* New York: Macmillan, 1969. Pp. 1483–1493.

Klausmeier, H. J., Ghatala, E. S., & Frayer, D. A. *Conceptual learning and development: A cognitive view.* New York: Academic Press, 1974.

Klausmeier, H. J., & Goodwin, W. *Learning and human abilities: Educational psychology* (4th ed.). New York: Harper & Row, 1975.

Klausmeier, H. J., Ingison, L. J., Sipple, T. S., & Katzenmeyer, C. G. *Development of conceptual learning and development assessment series I: Equilateral triangle* (Technical Report No. 430). Madison: Wisconsin Research and Development Center of Cognitive Learning, 1973(a).

Klausmeier, H. J., Ingison, L. J., Sipple, T. S., & Katzenmeyer, C. G. *Development of conceptual learning and development assessment series noun* (Technical Report No. 432). Madison: Wisconsin Research and Development Center for Cognitive Learning, 1973(b).

Klausmeier, H. J., Marliave, R. S., Katzenmeyer, C. G., & Sipple, T. S. *Development of conceptual learning and development assessment series IV: Tree (Technical Report No. 433). Madison: Wisconsin Research and Development Center for Cognitive Learning, 1974.

Klausmeier, H. J., Schilling, J. M., & Feldman, K. V. The effectiveness of experimental lessons in accelerating children's attainment of the concept tree (Technical Report No. 372). Madison: Wisconsin Research and Development Center for Cognitive Learning, 1976.

Markle, S. M. Teaching conceptual networks. Journal of instructional development, 1977, 1, 137–17.

McMurray, N. E., Bernard, M. E., & Klausmeier, H. J. An instructional design for accelerating children's concept learning (Technical Report No. 321). Madison: Wisconsin Research and Development Center for Cognitive Learning, 1975.

Miller, G. A., Galanter, E., & Pribram, K. H. Plans and the structure of behavior. New York: Holt, Rinehart & Winston, 1960.

Miller, G. A., & Johnson–Laird, P. N. Language and perception. Cambridge, Mass.: Harvard University Press, 1976.

Mussen, P. H., Conger, J. J., & Kagan, J. Child development and personality (4th ed.). New York: Harper & Row, 1974.

Piaget, J. Piaget's theory. In P. H. Mussen (Ed.), Carmichael's manual of child psychology (Vol. 1, 3rd ed.). New York: Wiley, 1970. Pp. 703–732.

Shaycoft, M. F. The high school years: Growth in cognitive skills. Pittsburgh: American Institutes of Research, 1967.

Tiemann, P. W., Kroeker, L. P., & Markle, S. M. Teaching verbally-mediated coordinate concepts in an ongoing college course. Presentation at the annual meeting of the American Educational Research Association, New York, 1977.

Wittrock, M. C., & Lumsdaine, A. A. Instructional psychology. Annual Review of Psychology, 1977, 28, 417–459.

3

Analyses Performed on
the Science Process Concepts

Knowledge from many sources was used in formulating the procedural guidelines for conducting the content, behavioral, and instructional analyses that are reported in this chapter. CLD theory supplied the substantive information. More specifically, CLD theory regarding the nature of concepts, their organization into structures of knowledge, their transfer to understanding principles and structural relationships and to solving problems, supplied the substantive information for carrying out the content analysis. Identifying and specifying the mental operations and other internal conditions necessary to attain each of the four successive levels in an invariant sequence provided the basis for the behavioral analysis. Specifying the external conditions that facilitate concept learning at each of the four successively higher levels provided the substantive information of the instructional analysis.

In the present project, the results of these analyses were used to prepare a printed lesson to be used in each experiment by the students of the experimental schools to attain the particular process concept at the formal level. In this way, the applicability of the preceding elements of CLD theory were tested in each experiment.

The analysis procedures are described in this chapter, and the results of the three analyses are presented. Results of earlier analyses and experiments contributed to the formulating of CLD theory, but not those of the present series. Therefore, the examples that are presented to clarify the procedures are not limited to the process concepts of science employed in the present experiments.

CONTENT ANALYSIS

CLD theory specifies that the same concepts are attained at four successively higher levels. Attaining concepts at the classificatory and formal levels is essential for understanding principles, acquiring structures of knowledge, and solving problems. This suggests that the teacher, curriculum designer, and developer of instructional materials should identify the target concepts that the target students are to learn, the level at which the concepts are to be learned, principles that require understanding of the target concepts, problems that require understanding of the concepts, and the taxonomy, other hierarchy, or theory of which the target concepts are a part. The main steps in conducting a content analysis, which were performed in the present project, are as follows:

1. Outline the taxonomy, other hierarchy, or theory of which the target concepts are a part.
2. Define each concept in terms of its attributes.
3. Specify the defining attributes and some of the variable attributes of each concept.
4. Identify illustrative examples and nonexamples of each concept.
5. Identify illustrative principles in which each concept is incorporated.
6. Formulate illustrative problem-solving exercises involving use of each concept.
7. Develop a list of the key vocabulary associated with each concept and its defining attributes.

Steps 2, 3, and 4 of the analysis were formulated by Markle and Tiemann (1969), whereas the others follow directly from CLD theory. The first one follows from the definition of the cognitive structure and how it develops, and the last three follow from the ideas regarding horizontal transfer of concept learning.

Our experience regarding content analysis was gained in preparing lessons for experiments conducted in elementary and high schools. This experience indicates that the analysis should be directed toward the formal level of attaining the concept and that the complete analysis should be expressed in terminology appropriate for teaching senior high school students. The concept analyzer needs to know the subject matter and terminology, at least at this level of schooling, even though the instruction may subsequently be directed to a lower level. Some persons may prefer to use the more exacting terminology of the experts in the field. What eventually is included in a particular set of instructional materials or oral instructional activities must be related to the level of concept attainment desired and to the level of vocabulary and other characteristics of the target population of students. A description of the preceding seven steps of a content analysis follows with illustrative examples pertaining to the concepts *tree* (Klausmeier, Marliave, Katzenmeyer, & Sipple, 1974) and *observing scientifically* (Klausmeier, Swanson & Sipple, 1976). The results pertaining to observing scientifically were used to prepare a concept lesson and to construct the related tests that were used in one of the present experiments. The results related to tree are given to show the great difference between an analysis involving nonprocess concepts that are part of taxonomies and an analysis involving process concepts that are part of other hierarchies. A literature search indicated that this was the first such analysis of process concepts.

Outline a Taxonomy or a Hierarchy

The starting point for the complete analysis of any concept of interest is to identify the taxonomy, other hierarchy, or theory of which the concept is a part. As we are aware, a taxonomy involves inclusive–exclusive relationships among classes of things, whereas a hierarchy implies relationships among things ordered by some principle, such as importance, priority, or dependency. Illustrative inclusive–exclusive relationships included in taxonomies are that some members of a supraordinate class are members of a subordinate class, the sum of the members of all the subordinate classes is equal to the total number of the members of the supraordinate class, and no member of one coordinate class is a member of another coordinate class.

One kind of hierarchy involving prerequisite dependency relationships is the learning hierarchy, as identified and elaborated by Gagné (1968, 1977). Gagné states that a learning hierarchy for an intellectual skill and its subordinate skills can be defined through task analysis directed toward answering the question: "What [skill] should the learner already know how to do and be able to recall, when faced with the task of learning the new rule; the absence of which would make it impossible to learn the new rule? [Gagné, 1977, p. 272]."

According to Gagné, the learning hierarchy for a set of skills provides the basic information needed to sequence instruction, either in instructional materials or by a teacher. Throughout an instructional sequence, one hierarchical skill is built successively upon another. Assumptions underlying the concept of learning hierarchy are that the learning tasks involving skills can be analyzed into hierarchical sets of skills, and that the prerequisite skills must be learned in order to learn the next successively higher skill. Gagné's early ideas regarding performance objectives, task analysis, and learning sets were used by the developers of the SAPA curriculum that was used in the elementary schools participating in the present project (Gagné, 1962, 1964, 1965a,b; Gagné & Bassler, 1963; Gagné, Mayor, Garstens, & Paradise, 1962; Gagné and staff, 1965).

The structure of the 13 process concepts used in the present project is primarily a hierarchy involving dependency relationships among some of the concepts, but there are also parallel relationships among some of them. The rationale employed in developing the structure follows (Klausmeier, Swanson, & Sipple, 1976).

We first identified the 13 processes included in the SAPA curriculum. Next, we examined the published sequence chart that outlines the sets of exercises that were designed to teach the processes (AAAS Commission on Science Education, 1967). We related this chart to the processes and to the sets of SAPA exercises being used in the schools participating in the project. The published sequence chart and the related information did not provide a sufficient rationale for carrying out a content analysis of the 13 processes by our procedures. From the chart we could not infer the prerequisite and parallel relationships among the 13 processes that are necessary to identify the defining attributes of each process as a process concept. Therefore, we took a more general approach and related the processes to scientific inquiry more globally. We postulated the following relationships among the 13 SAPA processes:

- *Observing* is a basic process that is essential for other scientific processes.
- *Observing* is essential for *inferring* and *classifying;* however, one may infer without classifying and one may classify without inferring; therefore, inferring and classifying are treated as parallel.
- Inferences are used in *predicting* specific future events and in *formulating hypotheses,* that is, formulating more generalizable statements that apply to classes of events. Predicting and hypothesizing are parallel processes; one is not dependent on the other.
- To test predictions or hypotheses, the scientist controls experimental variables and defines operationally. *Defining operationally* and *controlling variables* are related in a parallel manner but are prerequisite to carrying out an experiment. As a result of *experimenting,* the scientist will have the needed information to verify a prediction or to accept or reject a hypothesis.

- *Communicating* the results of performing a process may be linked to any process.
- *Using space–time relationships* is a process that involves spatial relationships and their change over time.
- *Using numbers* is a process that is necessary for precise *measuring* and *interpreting data.*
- *Using space–time relationships, using numbers, measuring,* and *interpreting data* are linked to numerous other science processes, and whether the linkage involves a prerequisite dependent relationship or a parallel relationship depends on situational conditions.

The preceding relationships are shown in Figure 3.1. The arrows in the figure indicate prerequisite dependency relationships among the processes; solid lines connect parallel processes; and the dotted lines indicate that communicating the results of performing a process can be with any other process.

Although there are prerequisite dependency relations among certain processes, they are not all sequenced invariantly as are the skills of a single learning hierarchy. Furthermore, the parallel relationships are not the same as are the relationships among the defining attributes of the coordinate concepts of a taxonomy. Finally, notice that in the SAPA curriculum, the 13 items are treated as processes to be experienced and per-

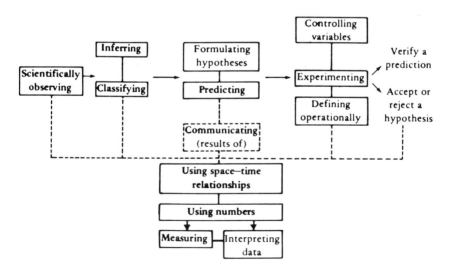

FIGURE 3.1. Hierarchy of process concepts of science. (From Klausmeier, Swanson, & Sipple, 1976.)

formed. In the present content analysis, we treated them as concepts to be learned and understood, as well as processes to be performed.

In relation to the learning of structures and relationships among the parts thereof, Bruner (1960) made a useful distinction between subject-matter structures, such as that of Figure 3.1, and structures that can be learned by students. This is a useful distinction. However, concepts that may be learned by a target group of students, such as those of the present project, cannot be inferred by a concept analyzer without generating the more complete structure, as shown in Figure 3.1. As we shall see, the structure in Figure 3.1 provided much of the information necessary for carrying out the other steps of the content analysis.

At present, the taxonomies, hierarchies, or other structures into which much of school subject matter could be organized are not given in the textbooks or other materials used in the schools, in college courses to prepare teachers, nor in college courses such as history or English. In the absence of this kind of information, the content analyzer develops these structures by using the best available printed materials and secures assistance from persons with expertise in the particular subject matter. The hierarchy for the science processes presented in Figure 3.1 was formulated in this manner.

Define the Concepts

The person conducting a content analysis of a set of concepts must know or arrive at a societally accepted definition of the word representing each of the concepts, even though it may be inappropriate to teach the definition to younger children. Further, so that examples and nonexamples may be identified for use in teaching the concept, the meaning of the word is stated in terms of the defining attributes of the concept. It will be recalled from Chapter 2 that a defining attribute may be an intrinsic property of the concept examples, a function performed on or by the concept examples, an invariant relation between the intrinsic properties or the functions, or a relation between concepts, such as dependency. As we saw in Figure 3.1, there are dependency, parallel, and other less clearly delineated relationships among the 13 process concepts of science. We may examine the differences between definitions of concepts that are included in taxonomies and those that are parts of other hierarchies.

An acceptable definition of a process concept gives the subprocesses that are necessary for performing it, the prerequisite process or processes that may be necessary, or some combination of these. An acceptable definition of a concept that is part of a taxonomy states (*a*) either the name of the supraordinate generic concept or the defining attributes of the generic concept; and (*b*) the intrinsic and/or functional attributes that are common to all examples of the concept and that distinguish its examples from those of other concepts. In most cases, the name of the concept immediately supraordinate is included as part of the definition.

Definitions of *tree* and *inferring* follow. The functional and intrinsic attributes of *tree* are italicized, as are the operations that together make possible the process of *inferring*.

> Tree: A plant that *lives for many years* and has a *single main stem that is woody.*
>
> Inferring: *Relating a scientific observation to something that is known,* and *drawing a conclusion about what was observed.*

The reader will recognize that *inferring* might be treated as a concept that can be understood by a person without being performed, a process that can be performed, or both. *Inferring* and all the other process concepts of science were treated as both in the present project; however, each process–concept (PC) lesson that was prepared was directed toward helping students to understand the process as a concept, not to perform it.

We should recognize that the defining attributes of concepts frequently are not given in the definitions of the words contained in dictionaries. Definitions of words given in abridged dictionaries are usually synonyms, examples, or uses of the words in context. These have limited value in determining the defining attributes of concepts (Markle, 1975). In arriving at the defining attributes of most concepts, the content analyzer, if not expert in the particular subject matter, uses authoritative printed material and also may seek the assistance of subject-matter experts.

Specify the Defining Attributes

The content analyzer specifies the defining attributes of the concept in order to identify sets of examples and nonexamples that will be used in teaching the concept (Markle & Tiemann, 1969) and to teach the students an algorithmic strategy for evaluating instances that are encountered as examples and nonexamples of the concept (to be explained and illustrated later). Those attributes that are present in every example of a concept and essential for distinguishing the concept examples from examples of all other coordinate concepts in taxonomies and parallel concepts in hierarchies are called the *critical attributes*. Other attributes of the generic concept together with the critical attributes comprise the *defining attributes*. Establishing the defining attributes of the concept and arriving at a definition of the word representing the concept proceed simultaneously during the content analysis.

In the content analysis performed on each process concept in the present project, the following rule was adopted for determining defining attributes: The defining attributes of a process concept are the subprocesses that are used in performing the global process, the prerequisite prior processes, or both. Since there are no processes prerequisite to observing scientifically, the defining attributes of this process concept were identified as using one or more of the senses, examining critically, and recording data precisely.

Specify the Variable Attributes

The variable attributes of a concept are identified by the concept analyzer to facilitate the later selection of examples and nonexamples. The variable attributes of coordinate classes of a taxonomy can be identified quite systematically. For example, reptiles are of different colors and sizes; fish also vary in some of the same colors as reptiles, and in size. The variable attributes enable us to discriminate among members of the same class, for example, between our larger goldfish and the smaller ones of a neighbor. However, the variable attributes that members of the reptile class and members of the fish class have in common may hinder persons in discriminating between the members of the two classes, for example, between snakes and eels. (In much previous literature, starting with Bruner, Goodnow, and Austin [1956], variable attributes have been treated as irrelevant attributes.)

The rule used in the present analysis for specifying variable attributes was to identify a nondefining attribute that was present in examples of the particular process concept, a nondefining attribute that was present in nonexamples of the particular process concept, or a defining attribute of another concept. Often, the variable attributes identified for a particular process concept were the defining attributes of other process concepts.

Examples of variable attributes identified for two concepts follow:

Variable attributes for *tree:* (a) height—short, tall; (b) shape.

Variable attributes for *inferring* (a) the kinds of objects or events being observed; (b) the knowledge that is used for the inference; and (c) the kind of relationship inferred (probability, cause-and-effect, correlational, axiomatic).

Select Examples and Nonexamples

Examples and nonexamples of the concept are needed in teaching the concept and in assessing students' attainment of the concept. At least one set (a rational set, as will be described later) of examples and nonexamples is identified during the content analysis. The reason for using rational sets of examples and nonexamples is to ensure that errors of undergeneralization, overgeneralization, and misconception by the learner will be avoided (Markle, 1975; Markle & Tiemann, 1969). Undergeneralization occurs when examples of a concept are encountered but are not identified as examples. Undergeneralization results when the examples of the concept provided in instruction are not sufficiently different from one another in the variable attributes. For example, the child who has experienced only large dogs such as collies may not identify miniature poodles and other small dogs as dogs.

Overgeneralization occurs when examples of other concepts are treated as members of the target concept. For example, an example of *observing* is treated as an example of *inferring*. The primary cause of overgeneralization is that the learner does not experience a sufficient number of appropriate nonexamples.

Misconceptions occur when both kinds of errors are made; some examples are treated as nonexamples and some nonexamples are treated as examples. For example, a misconception of chickens occurs when brown chickens are classified as chickens, white chickens are classified as turkeys, and brown pheasants are treated as chickens. Here, the brown color is treated incorrectly as a defining attribute rather than a variable attribute.

When a set of concepts of the same taxonomy or of the same hierarchy are taught, the examples of any one concept are, in reality, nonexamples of the other concepts. Using examples of concepts of coordinate classes of a taxonomy or examples of concepts of a hierarchy as nonexamples of the target concept permits the critical and variable attributes to be included meaningfully in both the examples and the nonexamples.

It will be recalled that there is no supraordinate concept in the hierarchy of the process concepts and there are no clearly delineated coordinate concepts. Thus, an intuitive approach was followed in the present content analysis, and in general, the attempt was not made to select examples that varied systematically in variable attributes nor to select nonexamples that differed in the number of defining and nondefining attributes. In general, a nonexample had one or more of the defining attributes missing or it was an example of another process concept.

Indications of possible examples and nonexamples of *tree* and *inferring* follow:

> Examples of *tree:* drawings of trees of various heights and various shapes.
>
> Nonexamples of *tree:* drawings of shrubs or herbs of various heights and various shapes.
>
> Examples of *inferring* (a verbal description in which both defining attributes are included): Two children saw a footprint while they were walking on a forest trail. One of the children had observed many wild ducks in the area on past occasions. After examining the webbed footprint, the child inferred that the track was left by one of the wild ducks.
>
> Nonexamples of *inferring* (a verbal description in which one of the two defining attributes is not included): Mary saw some duck tracks on her lawn. She said, "I remember seeing ducks here before. I know that some ducks flew over here yesterday."

Identify Principles

One especially important use of concepts (horizontal transfer) is in understanding the principles that incorporate the concepts. Understanding principles involving cause-and-effect, correlations, and other relationships among the concepts in turn makes it possible to understand and explain many events and, in some cases, to predict and to control. Understanding principles facilitates the solution of problems. It is useful, therefore, to identify illustrative principles of which the target concept is a part and subsequently to teach the principle, in order to promote transfer of concept learning to the understanding of principles. Furthermore, understanding the principle enables the learner to learn a new relationship among the concepts, thereby extending understanding of the component concepts. Illustrative principles related to *tree* and *inferring* follow.

Illustrative Principles Involving *Tree:*

1. The water and minerals that a tree needs to grow and make food are collected by its roots.

2. Water, minerals, and organic materials are transported by the tree's trunk.
3. The food that a tree uses is usually produced by its leaves.
4. The seeds of a tree are formed from special cells in the tree's flowers.
5. New trees develop from seeds.
6. To grow and produce food, a tree requires air, light, water, and minerals.

Illustrative Principles Involving *Inferring*:

1. Making more accurate and reliable scientific observations permits the drawing of more accurate and reliable inferences.
2. Inferences based on two or more scientific observations are more reliable than those based on a single observation.
3. Quantitative observations allow more precision and accuracy in drawing inferences than do qualitative observations.
4. Scientific observing and inferring are essential for predicting the outcomes of scientific events.

There appear to be no rules for generating principles that are applicable to all concepts. The rules for formulating the preceding principles for *inferring* and those for the other process concepts follow: use relationships (cause and effect, correlational, probability, or axiomatic) between the target process concept and other process concepts of the hierarchy; use relationships between the defining attributes of the target process concept; or use relationships between the target process concept and another related concept not in the hierarchy.

Formulate Problem-Solving Exercises

As part of a content analysis, problem-solving exercises are formulated; the solutions are presumably facilitated by understanding the target concept and applying knowledge of a principle or a combination of principles. No attempt is made to make the problem-solving exercises of equal difficulty. On the contrary, a range of difficulty is preferable in the analysis so that additional examples of an appropriate level of difficulty can later be prepared for a particular target population of students. The only rule followed in the present content analysis of the process concepts was to generate a problem that required understanding and use of the target concept and one or more prerequisite processes.

Illustrative Problem for *Tree:*

Suppose that it is spring. You want to find an apple tree that will grow many seeds before winter. You can pick one of many trees growing in an orchard. You should choose a tree that has many _____.

  a. leaves
  b. roots
  c. flowers
  d. branches
  e. I don't know

Illustrative Problem for *Inferring:*

A kitchen baster full of water was put into a beaker of water and squeezed.

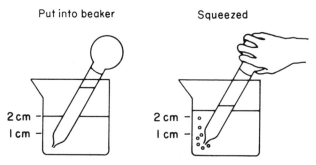

What *inference* can you make from this experiment?

  a. The water in the baster was displaced by air.
  b. The water level in the baster went down.
  c. The air in the baster was displaced by water.
  d. The water level in the beaker went down when the baster was squeezed.

Develop a Vocabulary List

The rule for generating a vocabulary list is to include the name of the concept and the key terms of the defining attributes. The extent to which the terms will be used in teaching a particular concept varies according to the level of attainment desired. None of the vocabulary may be used at the concrete level; all of it, according to CLD theory, must be used at the formal level. Students' knowledge of the name of the concept and the names of its defining attributes has shown a high, positive correlation with the level of concept attainment and with the uses of concepts (Klausmeier, Sipple, & Allen, 1974a,b). The lists for *tree* and *inferring* follow:

> Vocabulary for *tree:* tree, green plant, stem, woody stem, perennial, roots, seeds, leaves, broad leaves, needles, flowers, cones, deciduous, coniferous.
>
> Vocabulary for *inferring:* inferring, relate, observe, scientifically, accurately, conclusion.

BEHAVIORAL ANALYSIS

A behavioral analysis specifies the mental operations that an individual must be capable of to attain the same concept at four successively higher levels. It also specifies the other necessary internal conditions.

The mental operations necesary for attaining concepts at each of four successively higher levels were given in Chapter 2. They were identified initially through a behavioral analysis of concept learning tasks and a review and synthesis of research related to the learning of concepts. Results from subsequent controlled experiments and a longitudinal study confirm the results of the behavioral analysis (Klausmeier & Allen, 1978).

The operations are presumed to be the same for all concepts; however, the age at which the same individuals are able to perform the operations on different concepts varies markedly. Students were found to be able to perform the operations earlier on concepts for which there are concrete examples in the environment—for example, *cutting tool* and *tree*—and later for concepts with examples that are represented by words—for example, *noun* (Klausmeier & Allen, 1978).

The internal conditions of learning regarded as necessary and possibly sufficient for attaining the successively higher levels of a concept are as follows: (a) mastery of the prior level; (b) functioning of at least one new mental operation in combination with the continuing operations of the prior level; (c) functioning of the operations of the prior level with content of increasing quantity and complexity experienced in a greater variety of contexts; (d) intending to attain the next higher level; and (e) persisting until it is attained. In addition, being able to discriminate the defining attributes of the concept and to name the concept and the defining attributes is necessary for carrying out the new operations at the formal level.

The 10 lessons of the present project were prepared to help the students attain each of 10 process concepts at the formal level. It was presumed that the students would employ the operations specified for this level; however, the lessons did not call for the students to have mastered the classificatory level. The mental operations for the formal level and each other level are given in the next section of this chapter, which presents the instructional analysis, so that the operations pertaining to each level may be related to the external conditions of learning for the same level.

INSTRUCTIONAL ANALYSIS

An instructional analysis is conducted to identify the instructional conditions that will help the target learners attain the target concepts at the desired level. In the analysis, the main variables considered are the characteristics of the learners, the level at which the concept is to be attained, the instructional media that will be used, and the amount of teacher guidance to be provided. In the present project, the learners were enrolled in Grades 4 and 5; the desired level of attainment was the formal; printed lessons to teach the process concepts were prepared and used; and the teachers were encouraged to provide guidance to the students to attain the concept. These are dealt with in more detail in later chapters.

In this section, the instructional conditions that facilitate student attainment of concepts at a beginning classificatory level and a combined mature classificatory level and formal level are described. Although the PC lessons were prepared to help the students attain the formal level, being able to perform the operations of the classificatory level and to classify are prerequisites for attaining the formal level. Therefore, the beginning classificatory level is included here also.

Beginning Classificatory Level

The lowest attainment of a concept at the classificatory level is inferred when a person recognizes two different things as being equivalent in some way. Persons are still at the classificatory level when they can properly identify many instances as examples and nonexamples but cannot state explicitly the basis of their categorizing in terms of the presence of the defining attributes in the examples and the absence of one or more of the defining attributes in the nonexamples. The new operation involved in attainment at the classificatory level is generalizing that two or more different instances are equivalent in some way. Students attain the classificatory level of many concepts for which there are concrete examples before they enter the first grade. But the beginning classificatory level of some abstract concepts, such as *noun,* for which there are no concrete examples, is not attained by many students until Grade 3.

The following procedures are presumed in CLD theory to facilitate students' attainment of concepts at the beginning classificatory level:

1. Assure that the concept has been attained at the identity level and that the student is capable of attaining it at the classificatory level.
2. Present at least two examples and one or two nonexamples of the concept.
3. Give the name of the concept along with the concept examples and help the learner associate the name of the concept with the examples. (This applies only to concept names that the learner already has in the speaking vocabulary or can learn to pronounce readily.)
4. Using an inductive method supplemented with an expository method as necessary, help the learner discriminate and name some of the defining attributes of the concept. (This applies only if the attribute names can be learned readily or are already in the speaking vocabulary.)
5. Using an inductive method supplemented with an expository method as necessary, help the learner define the concept. Being able to define the concept is not essential, but it is helpful to the extent that the words used are comprehended. Committing a definition to memory in a rote fashion probably hinders rather than helps the learner attain the classificatory level.
6. Provide for informative feedback.
7. Arrange to use the concept in recognizing newly encountered things as examples or nonexamples.

8. Repeat the preceding sequence as necessary.

With many concepts, several years elapse between the time children first attain a concept at the beginning classificatory level and the time when they are capable of all the operations essential to attaining the same concept at the formal level. The kind of instruction that helps students move from the immature to the more mature phase of the classificatory level through use of printed instructional materials, oral instruction, and other techniques is described next.

Mature Classificatory Level and Formal Level

Printed instructional materials for teaching concepts can be prepared and used effectively with students who can read and who have already attained the target concepts at the beginning classificatory level. The materials may be used to help students classify more correctly and extensively at the classificatory level, attain a beginning formal level, and then attain a mature formal level. To reach these objectives, the materials should take into account the external conditions of learning that have been identified through much empirical research. These learning conditions were taken into account in preparing the PC lessons used in the present project, and results were expected to be similar to those obtained in earlier experiments with other concepts (see, for example, Bernard [1975], Klausmeier, Schilling, & Feldman [1976], McMurray, Bernard, & Klausmeier [1975]).

Chapter 5 gives a description and examples of how the guidelines were followed in preparing the PC lessons; therefore, the remainder of this chapter is given to clarifying the guidelines and to describing experiments on which those guidelines are based, not to lesson preparation.

1. *Establish an intention to learn concepts.* An intention to learn concepts is developed before the student tries to learn a particular concept. This is done by means such as telling the students that they will be learning concepts, by pointing out important features of concept learning, or by describing the concept population comprising the taxonomy or hierarchy. Amster (1966), Frederick and Klausmeier (1968), Kalish (1966), Laughlin, Doherty, and Dunn (1968), and Osler and Weiss (1962) have all reported facilitative effects from instructions to students designed to establish an intent to learn concepts.

Establishing an intention to learn concepts (as opposed to, for example, establishing a set to memorize a definition) activates several operations essential to attaining concepts at the classificatory and formal levels. First, such instructions may alert the learners that they should attend to and discriminate the attributes of examples. Second, such instructions may engage the learners in an active search for the attributes that distinguish examples from nonexamples. At the outset, then, the learner is actively engaged in searching behaviors directed toward learning the particular concept or concepts at a higher level of attainment.

2. *Elicit student verbalization of the concept name and the defining attributes.* To accomplish this, a vocabulary list is presented at the beginning of a series of lessons, and the students are taught to recognize the words. Having the names of the concept and the attributes greatly facilitates carrying out inductive operations at the formal level of attainment, including formulating, remembering, and evaluating hypotheses; and meaningful reception operations, including assimilating and processing information that is presented. Linguistic codes are maximally efficient for carrying out the sequential information processing that is involved in inferring concepts from examples and nonexamples inductively and also for assimilating the information as presented in a definition, a set of verbal examples and nonexamples of the concepts, and verbal explanations or descriptions. Clark (1971) reported facilitation of concept attainment by giving the label of the concept and/or the labels of its defining attributes. When printed material is used, the students must not only be able to use the terms orally but also to read them.

3. *Present a definition of the concept in terms of defining attributes, stated in vocabulary appropriate to the target population.* Providing students with the concept definition eliminates the operations involved in identifying the defining attributes of the concept and inferring the concept from experiences with examples and nonexamples of the concept. However, simply presenting students with the concept definition does not ensure concept attainment, as the students may merely acquire a string of words memorized by rote, not a concept. To ensure that the students acquire a concept and not a string of words, at a minimum they must also be presented with concept examples and nonexamples to classify. Correct classification requires the student to differentiate examples from nonexamples on the basis of the defining attributes contained in the concept definition. Thus, both discriminating the attributes of examples and evaluating examples and nonexamples to determine whether or not they exhibit the defining attributes contained in the definition are operations that the students should perform after they are given the concept definition.

The facilitative effect of a definition is related to several variables, including the number of rational sets of examples and nonexamples that are presented along with the definition. In a controlled experiment with fourth-grade students, Klausmeier and Feldman (1975) found that a definition had about the same amount of facilitation as one rational set of examples and nonexamples. A definition combined with one rational set was more effective than a definition or a rational set alone; and a definition combined with three rational sets showed greatest facilitation.

A definition must be stated in appropriate terminology. Feldman and Klausmeier (1974) found that with fourth-graders a common-usage definition was more effective than a technically stated definition, whereas the technically stated definition was more effective with eighth-graders. Markle (1975) and Merrill and Tennyson (1971) also reported a facilitative effect for definitions.

4. *Present at least one set of examples and nonexamples.* Markle and Tiemann (1969) identified the importance of using both examples and nonexamples in teaching concepts. They devised a procedure for selecting a set of examples and nonexamples to be used in a lesson to teach an individual concept. Their procedure involved selecting the examples and nonexamples, based on matching the defining attributes and variable attributes, to generate a complete rational set of examples and nonexamples. Our research group developed a slightly different procedure for selecting examples and nonexamples for use in teaching individual concepts (Klausmeier & Feldman, 1975). Furthermore, when a set of concepts was to be taught, the complex matching strategy was no longer necessary, since examples of any one concept are nonexamples of each other. The nonexamples are selected intuitively for teaching any one of the concepts of the set (Bernard, 1975). The use of rational sets has been demonstrated repeatedly to reduce errors of undergeneralization, overgeneralization, and misconception (Feldman, 1972; Klausmeier & Feldman, 1975; Markle & Tiemann, 1969; Merrill & Tennyson, 1971; Rothen & Tennyson, 1978; Swanson, 1972; Tennyson, 1973; Tennyson & Rothen, 1977; Tennyson, Woolley, & Merrill, 1972).

In the PC lessons prepared for the present project, either examples of the other concepts of the hierarchy were used as nonexamples in the lesson on a particular concept, or a defining attribute of the particular concept was not included in the nonexample. Using examples and real nonexamples in this manner greatly eased the identification of rational sets to be used in preparing the lessons.

The matter of how many sets to include in any PC lesson had not been determined empirically in the present project. Therefore, the teachers using the PC lessons were instructed to supplement the material included in the PC lesson if the students appeared to need more examples and nonexamples.

5. *Emphasize the defining attributes of the concept by drawing the stu-*

dents' attention to them. Giving students the names of the defining attributes of the concept in the concept definition is insufficient for teaching them how to discriminate the defining attributes and then how to use them to differentiate examples from nonexamples of the concept. Frayer (1970) found that emphasizing the defining attributes by verbal cues improved immediate concept learning and later transfer and retention.

Merrill and Tennyson (1971) compared the effects of a concept definition, a definition that gave the attributes of the concept, a rational set of examples and nonexamples, and attribute prompting singly and in various combinations. Attribute prompting was found to be more facilitative than a definition of the concept or definitions of the attributes. The most effective condition included all four variables. Clark (1971) reported that a large majority of researchers obtained beneficial effects by directing the students' attention to the concept attributes and/or the conceptual rule; also, pointing out the attributes and rules to the students yielded better results than permitting the students to discover them themselves.

As will be seen in the excerpts of a PC lesson included in Chapter 5, each defining attribute of the target concept was taught. The defining attributes were introduced early in the lesson as part of the definition of the concept.

6. *Provide a strategy for differentiating examples and nonexamples.* Bruner, Goodnow, and Austin (1956) identified various focusing and scanning strategies that are used in learning concepts. The experimental subjects were presumed to have learned these strategies incidentally, without specific instruction concerning the strategies.

Frederick and Klausmeier (1968) and Klausmeier and Meinke (1968) developed a strategy for teaching students a conservative focusing strategy. This strategy reduces the demands on memory and inferring effectively and promotes economical learning of concepts. Bernard (1975); Klausmeier, Schilling, and Feldman (1976) and McMurray, Bernard, and Klausmeier (1975) incorporated the same strategy in their experimental lessons. Students as young as age 9 were found to be able to use the strategy effectively.

Incorporating the strategy in the printed material and teaching students to use it ensures that the strategy is learned, and it also eliminates unguided, trial-and-error learning. Furthermore, teaching the students to use the strategy in evaluating instances as examples or nonexamples of the target concept and providing feedback promotes active learning of the strategy and the target concept. These techniques were incorporated in each PC lesson prepared in the present project. An example of the techniques is given in Chapter 5.

7. Provide for feedback concerning the correctness and incorrectness of the responses. Clark (1971), Frayer and Klausmeier (1971), Markle (1975), and Sweet (1966) reported the desirable effects of feedback to students. Clark, for example, reported that concept attainment improved as the frequency of feedback increased. Frayer and Klausmeier, in their survey of research, found that feedback should be provided after every response, but that it is most important after an incorrect response. Feedback that not only tells the students that a response or hypothesis is wrong but also enables them to infer how or why it is wrong and how to correct it is particularly helpful. Illustrations of the use of feedback in the PC lessons prepared in the present project are given in Chapter 5.

In closing, it may be appropriate to review the relationships between CLD theory and each of the three analyses performed on the process concepts and also the use of the results of each of the three analyses in preparing the PC lessons. The substantive aspect of the *content analysis* performed on the process concepts is based on the CLD constructs regarding the attainment of successively higher levels of the same concept in an invariant sequence, the construct regarding the emergence and development of the individual learner's cognitive structure, and the transfer of concept attainment to the learning of principles and taxonomies and to solving problems. The results of each content analysis that was performed were used in preparing a PC lesson to teach each process concept to the students of the experimental schools. The objective of each PC lesson was to teach understanding at the formal level of the concept.

The *behavioral analysis* performed on the process concepts indicates the mental operations specified in CLD theory as necessary for attaining a concept at successively higher levels and also other internal conditions of learning, including attaining the concept at the prior level and intending to learn the concept. The results of the behavioral analysis were applied in preparing the PC lessons. Each PC lesson was prepared so that the students would employ the meaningful reception operations specified for the formal level of attainment, would already have attained the concept at the classificatory level, or would attain it as part of the lesson, and would intend to learn the target concept of the lesson.

The *instructional analysis* indicates the external conditions of learning that are identified in CLD theory as helping students attain concepts at the formal level through a meaningful reception process. All of these conditions were incorporated in each PC lesson that was prepared.

Recall that the first part of each experiment was designed to help the Grade 4 and Grade 5 students of the two experimental schools attain a process concept at the formal level, before teaching the SAPA exercises. The specially prepared PC lessons were used for this purpose. The students of the two control schools did not receive the PC lessons. By this experimental arrangement, it was possible to determine the effectiveness of the PC lessons directly. From these results the effectiveness of the applications of CLD theory that appear in this chapter was inferred.

REFERENCES

AAAS Commission on Science Education. *Science — A Process Approach.* Washington, DC: American Association for the Advancement of Science-Xerox, 1967.

Amster, H. Effect of instructional set and variety of instances on children's learning. *Journal of Educational Psychology,* 1966, *57,* 74–85.

Bernard, M. E. *The effect of advance organizers and within-text questions on the learning of a taxonomy of concepts* (Technical Report No. 357). Madison: Wisconsin Research and Development Center for Cognitive Learning, 1975.

Bruner, J. S. *The process of education.* Cambridge: Harvard University Press. 1960.

Bruner, J. S., Goodnow, J. J., & Austin, G. A. *A study of thinking.* New York: Wiley, 1956.

Clark, D. C. Teaching concepts in the classroom: A set of prescriptions derived from experimental research. *Journal of Educational Psychology Monograph,* 1971, *62* 253–278.

Feldman, K. V. *The effects of number of positive and negative instances, concept definition, and emphasis of relevant attributes on the attainment of mathematical concepts* (Technical Report No. 243). Madison: Wisconsin Research and Development Center for Cognitive Learning, 1972.

Feldman, K. V., & Klausmeier, H. J. Effects of two kinds of definition on the concept attainment of fourth and eighth graders. *Journal of Educational Research,* 1974, *67(5),* 219–223.

Frayer, D. A. *Effects of number of instances and emphasis of relevant attribute values on mastery of geometric concepts by fourth- and sixth-grade children* (Technical Report No. 116). Madison: Wisconsin Research and Development Center for Cognitive Learning, 1970.

Frayer, D. A., & Klausmeier, H. J. *Variables in concept learning: Task variables* (Theoretical Paper No. 28). Madison: Wisconsin Research and Development Center for Cognitive Learning, 1971.

Fredrick, W. C., & Klausmeier, H. J. Instructions and labels in a concept attainment task. *Psychological Reports,* 1968, *23,* 1339–1342.

Gagné, R. M. The acquisition of knowledge. *Psychological Review,* 1962, *69,* 355–356.

Gagné, R. M. The implication of instructional objectives for learning. In C. Lindvall (Ed.), *Defining educational objectives.* Pittsburgh, Pa.: University of Pittsburgh Press, 1964.

Gagné, R. M. *The conditions of learning.* New York: Holt, Rinehart & Winston, 1965(a).

Gagné, R. M. *The psychological bases of science — A process approach.* Washington, D.C.: American Association for the Advancement of Science, AAAS Misc. Pub. 65–68, 1965(b).

Gagné, R. M. Learning hierarchies. *Educational psychologist,* 1968, *6,* 1–9.

Gagné, R. M. *The conditions of learning* (3rd ed.). New York: Holt, Rinehart & Winston, 1977.

Gagné, R. M., & Bassler, O. C. Study of retention of some topics of elementary non-metric geometry. *Journal of Educational Psychology,* 1963, *54,* 123–131.

Gagné, R. M., Mayor, J., Garstens, H., & Paradise, N. Factors in acquiring knowledge of a mathematical task. *Psychological Monographs,* 1962, *76*(7) (Whole No. 525).

Gagné, R. M., and staff. Some factors in learning non-metric geometry. *Society for Research in Child Development,* 1965, 30(1), Serial 99.

Kalish, P. W. *Concept attainment as a function of monetary incentives, competition, and instructions* (Technical Report No. 8). Madison: Wisconsin Research and Development Center for Cognitive Learning, 1966.

Klausmeier, H. J., & Allen, P. S. *Cognitive development of children and youth: A longitudinal study.* New York: Academic Press, 1978.

Klausmeier, H. J., & Feldman, K. V. Effects of a definition and a varying number of examples and nonexamples on concept attainment. *Journal of Educational Psychology,* 1975, *67,* 174–178.

Klausmeier, H. J., Marliave, R. S., Katzenmeyer, C. G., & Sipple, T. S. *Development of conceptual learning and development assessment series IV: Tree* (Working Paper No. 126). Madison: Wisconsin Research and Development Center for Cognitive Learning, 1974.

Klausmeier, H. J., & Meinke, D. L. Concept attainment as a function of instructions concerning the stimulus material, a strategy, and a principle for securing information. *Journal of Educational Psychology,* 1968, 59, 215–222.

Klausmeier, H. J., Schilling, J. M., & Feldman, K. V. *The effectiveness of experimental lessons in accelerating children's attainment of the concept tree* (Technical Report No. 372). Madison: Wisconsin Research and Development Center for Cognitive Learning, 1976.

Klausmeier, H. J., Sipple, T. S., & Allen, P. S. *First cross sectional study of attainment of the concepts equilateral triangle, cutting tool, and noun by children age 5 to 16 of city A* (Technical Report No. 287). Madison: Wisconsin Research and Development Center for Cognitive Learning, 1974(a).

Klausmeier, H. J., Sipple, T. S., & Allen, P. S. *First cross sectional study of attainment of the concepts equilateral triangle and cutting tool by children age 5 to 16 of city B* (Technical Report No. 288). Madison: Wisconsin Research and Development Center for Cognitive Learning, 1974(b).

Klausmeier, H. J., Swanson, J. E., & Sipple, T. S. *The analysis of nine process-concepts in elementary science* (Technical Report No. 428). Madison: Wisconsin Research and Development Center for Cognitive Learning, 1976.

Laughlin, P. R., Doherty, M. A., & Dunn, R. F. Intentional and incidental concept formation as a function of motivation, creativity, intelligence and sex. *Journal of Personality and Social Psychology,* 1968, *8,* 401–409.

Mager, R. F. *Preparing instructional objectives.* Palo Alto, CA.: Fearon, 1962.

Markle, S. M. They teach concepts, don't they? *Educational Researcher,* 1975, *4*(6), 3–9.

Markle, S. M., & Tiemann, P. W. *Really understanding concepts.* Champaign, Ill.: Stipes, 1969.

McMurray, N. E., Bernard, M. E., & Klausmeier, H. J. *An instructional design for accelerating children's concept learning* (Technical Report No. 321). Madison: Wisconsin Research and Development Center for Cognitive Learning, 1975.

Merrill, M. D., & Tennyson, R. D. *The effect of types ot positive and negative examples on learning concepts in the classroom.* Washington, D.C.: U.S. Department of Health, Education and Welfare, Office of Education, Bureau of Research, 1971.

Osler, S. F., & Weiss, S. R. Studies in concept attainment: III. Effect of instructions at two levels of intelligence. *Journal of Experimental Psychology,* 1962, *63,* 528–533.

Rothen, W., & Tennyson, R. D. Application of Bayes' theory in designing computer-based adaptive instructional strategies. *Educational Psychologist,* 1978, *12*(3), 317–323.

Swanson, J. E. *The effects of number of positive and negative instances, concept definition, and emphasis of relevant attributes on the attainment of three environmental concepts by sixth-grade children* (Technical Report No. 244). Madison: Wisconsin Research and Development Center for Cognitive Learning, 1972.

Sweet, R. C. *Educational attainment and attitudes toward school as a function of feedback in the form of teachers' written comments* (Technical Report No. 15). Madison: Wisconsin Research and Development Center for Cognitive Learning, 1966.

Tennyson, R. D. Effect of negative instances in concept acquisition using a verbal-learning task. *Journal of Educational Psychology,* 1973, *64*, 247–260.

Tennyson, R. D., & Rothen, W. Pretask and on-task adaptive design strategies for selecting number of instances in concept acquisition. *Journal of Educational Psychology,* 1977, *69*(5), 586–592.

Tennyson, R. D., Woolley, F. R., & Merrill, M. D. Exemplar and nonexemplar variables which produce correct concept classification behavior and specified classification errors. *Journal of Educational Psychology,* 1972, *63*, 144–152.

4

Instructional Design Employed in Teaching the SAPA Curriculum

The second part of each experiment of this project involved students of Grades 4 and 5 learning the processes of science included in the school-adopted SAPA curriculum. In the two experimental schools, the teachers used applications of a generic model of instructional programming for the individual student in adapting instruction to the entering achievement levels of the students. Although the model was formulated well in advance of the present experimentation (Klausmeier, 1977a; Klausmeier, Sorenson, & Quilling, 1971), knowledge about learning and individual differences related to other concepts was incorporated in the adaptations made in these experiments. The CLD principles incorporated in the applications were indicated in Chapter 2 and are again summarized here.

One principle is that different concepts are mastered by the same students at different ages. For example, the concepts, *cutting tool* and *tree,* which have examples that are directly observable as objects in the environment, were attained by the same student years earlier than was the concept, *noun,* whose examples in visual form are words that can be identified only by reading. We should expect the same student to attain concepts such as *tree* and *frog,* much earlier than the process concepts included in the SAPA curriculum, such as *inferring* and *predicting.*

Another principle: Within-individual variability in cognitive development related to the fields of science, language arts, mathematics, and

83

social studies becomes stable from age 10 to 12 and remains constant thereafter throughout the school years. Most students do not acquire knowledge in these different areas at the same rate. The same student may be a high achiever in science or English and a low achiever in social studies or math. Therefore, to provide properly for intraindividual variability, preassessment must be carried out in each subject, including science, to adapt instruction properly to the entering achievement levels of the students.

A final principle: Interindividual differences in the rate of attaining concepts, in understanding principles and taxonomic relations, and in solving problems are exceedingly large. Some 9-year-old school children are more advanced in these areas of cognitive functioning than are some 18-year-old high school seniors. The differences are so large that we should not expect all the individuals of any age group to master the same level of any particular set of concepts, even when a mastery approach to instruction is employed. More specifically, we should not expect very slow developing students to master abstract process concepts that are appropriately attained only by the rapid developers during any given year of schooling, regardless of how much time may be devoted to the instruction of the slow developing students. In other words, there are real limits beyond which we cannot accelerate a child's learning of abstract concepts through guided practice, or instruction. Similarly, we should not hold back the rapid developers by using too much teacher time and effort with the slow developers.

These principles reaffirm two views that have been expressed repeatedly regarding provisions for individual differences. First, the individual student, rather than an age-graded, class-size group, should be the focus of instruction. Second, it is very difficult or impossible to make the individual student the focus of instruction in age-graded schools as most schools are currently organized and staffed.

In this chapter, a generic model of instructional programming for the individual student is presented along with its application to teaching the school-adopted SAPA curriculum in the two experimental schools. The application takes into account the preceding principles from CLD theory.

Before dealing with the model further, we need to be aware that both the experimental schools and the comparison schools were selected because they practiced a form of education called Individually Guided Education (IGE). In this form of schooling, age-graded group instruction is eliminated in each of the various subject fields as quickly as the teachers are capable of doing so. Just before the present experimentation was begun, the experimental and control schools were using their application of the generic model of instructional programming for the individual student in mathematics and reading, but not in science. Instruction was continuing as class-size group instruction in science. Instructional programming for the individual student is a major feature of IGE, to which we now turn.

FORM OF SCHOOLING IN WHICH EXPERIMENTS WERE CONDUCTED

Individually Guided Education is a form of schooling that focuses on the individual student. It evolved during the 1960s as part of the activities of the Wisconsin Research and Development Center for Individualized Schooling (Klausmeier 1971, 1975); and according to Talmage (1975), it had risen above faddism. It is an alternative to undifferentiated age-graded group instruction, classical individualized instruction, and unstructured open education. Its major aim is to enable school staffs to arrange a complete instructional program appropriate for each individual student each semester and year.

The first elementary schools following the IGE pattern started in 1968, and by 1976 there were about 2500 (Klausmeier, 1977b). A much smaller number of secondary schools practicing some aspects of IGE was functioning in 1979 (Klausmeier, 1979). By 1979, many local schools were treating IGE both as a form of schooling and as a theoretical design for guiding their educational improvement and renewal efforts. Clearly, IGE is neither a finally formulated design nor a static form of schooling. It is dynamic and changes as societal conditions change and as further knowledge about learning and teaching accrue.

Individually Guided Education started and has continued as a product of cooperative problem solving by local schools and staff members of the Wisconsin R & D Center for Individualized Schooling under the leadership of the author of this book. Much research has been conducted in IGE schools. The present design of IGE that follows stems from a synthesis of the accruing research knowledge and a continuing analysis of the conditions of learning and teaching in IGE and other schools. The main components of the IGE design at the elementary school level follow. Both the experimental and the control schools that participated in the present project were carrying out their own applications of each component. Since there was substantial similarity among the schools in all the components, only instructional programming for the individual student will be elaborated on in some detail later in this chapter.

Organizational-Administrative Arrangements

Arrangements to organize the teachers and students into instructional and research units and to involve representative teachers in the administration of the school's educational activities have been conceptualized. These arrangements are aimed at producing an environment and other necessary conditions in the school that make it possible to plan and carry out instructional programming for the individual student (Klausmeier, 1975; Klausmeier & Pellegrin, 1971). Lipham and Daresh (1980), in a review of the research carried out in IGE elementary schools, report that the arrangements had proven effective in promoting communication among teachers and between teachers and administrators, promoting shared decision making, building staff morale, facilitating immediate and long-range planning of individual students' educational programs, and contributing to students' attainment of desired curricular objectives in both the cognitive and affective domains. One important feature of the arrangements is that teachers share in making the decisions that they are responsible for carrying out. Another is that time, space, and other conditions are worked out so that teachers can plan and confer with one another and can then arrange instruction that is adapted to the individual student's characteristics.

The organizational and administrative arrangements at the elementary school level are shown in Figure 4.1. They consist of interrelated groups at three distinct levels of operation: the Instruction and Research Unit at the child-teacher level, the Instructional Improvement Committee at the building level, and the Systemwide Program Committee or a similar administrative arrangement at the school district level. As we shall see, cooperative planning and shared decision making are necessary for any of these groups to function effectively.

The Instruction and Research Unit includes from 60 to 150 students and a cooperative team of teachers and aides. It replaces the age-graded, self-contained classroom, the departmentalized approach to instruction, and self-contained open education. Each instructional team is headed by a unit leader who is a teacher.

The main function of each cooperative team of teachers is to plan, carry out, and evaluate the instructional programs of the individual students of the unit. Teachers in IGE schools spend less time teaching class-size groups and more time teaching small groups of 8–20 students. Students spend less time listening to a teacher and more time in individual activity, including independent study, and in small group activities. The flexibility associated with teaming and the use of paid and volunteer instructional aides permits the more effective use of small-group instruction and of adult-supervised individual study and small-group work.

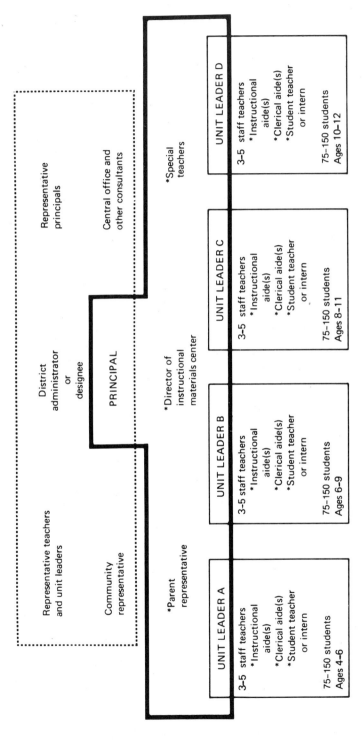

Figure 4.1 Multiunit organization of an IGE school of 400–600 students. (Adapted from Klausmeier, Morrow, & Walter, 1968, p. 19.) _____ Instruction and Research Unit; - - - - - Systemwide Program Committee. Asterisks indicate that inclusion of these persons will vary according to particular school settings.

The Instructional Improvement Committee is a new administrative arrangement that became possible for the first time in American elementary education when the teachers of the first IGE schools organized into I & R units, and the unit leaders then joined with the principals to form the Instructional Improvement Committee. This is the new educational decision-making group in the school that enables teachers, who are also the unit leaders, to participate with the principal in planning and decision making regarding the school's objectives, curriculum, instructional arrangements, evaluation tools and procedures, home–school relations, and other matters. It is a primary strength of IGE compared to other forms of schooling in which teachers do not share decision making with their principal and other school administrators. Not all principals and teachers prefer this kind of approach, and many more are not sufficiently skilled in small-group processes either to get it started or to make it work effectively in their schools.

The Systemwide Program Committee is chaired by the superintendent of the school district and includes consultants and other central office staff, and representative principals, unit leaders, and teachers of IGE schools. Decision-making and facilitative responsibilities for which the Systemwide Program Committee takes primary initiative include formulating district objectives and programs, recruiting personnel for IGE schools and arranging for their inservice education, providing instructional materials and other material resources, and disseminating information about IGE within the district and the community. An arrangement other than Systemwide Program Committee is used in some larger school districts. The primary strength of the arrangement is that principals, unit leaders, and teachers share in decision making and program development at the district level.

Unlike some differentiated staffing programs that call for a proliferation of new roles and titles for personnel, the IGE organizational–administrative pattern establishes only one new position–that of unit leader. Basic changes are made, however, in the roles of the principal, department head, teacher, and counselor. Also, other personnel, such as the special teacher for students with learning disabilities, the teacher aide, the instructional secretary, the student teacher, the teaching intern, and the parent volunteer, become part of the staff of each cooperative instructional team. The unit leader leads the unit staff, is a teacher in the unit, and is a member of the Instructional Improvement Committee. The role is that of a career teacher.[1] This role has great appeal to many excel-

---

[1] The roles and relationships of personnel in IGE elementary and middle schools are described in books as follows: the role of teachers by Nussel, Inglis, and Wiersma (1976); unit leaders by Sorenson, Poole, and Joyal (1976); principals by Lipham and Fruth (1976).

lent teachers who prefer to remain teachers, rather than moving to administration, counseling, or other nonteaching activities.

Be aware that the organizational–administrative arrangements shown in Figure 4.1 are prototypic. Depending on the school enrollment, the philosophy of the principal and teachers, and other local conditions, there are many variations of the prototype. The arrangements of the four schools participating in this project were quite close to the prototype. However, as we shall make clear in Chapter 6, how the teachers were organized for the science instruction varied considerably between the two sets of paired experimental and control schools.

Evaluation

A model to guide the evaluation process in the IGE design of schooling involves five steps directly related to instructional programming for the individual student: (1) Formulate objectives and set criteria of attainment → (2) Measure → (3) Relate measurement to criteria → (4) Judge → and (5) Act on judgment (Klausmeier & Goodwin, 1975). Evaluation in accord with these steps is carried out to facilitate student learning, not for the purpose of grading, selecting, or classifying. As we shall see later in the explanation of instructional programming for the individual student, evaluation is carried out before, during, and after instructional sequences.

The evaluation model is applied to objectives in the cognitive, psychomotor, and affective domains. It also is appropriate for short instructional sequences, such as a unit of instruction, and for completing curricular sequences extending for a year, or even throughout the elementary school years. The evaluation of the student's characteristics and achievements is aimed at providing information at three points in time: before instruction begins, during the instructional sequence, and at the end of the sequence. In the experimental schools of the present project, data on students' achievement in the SAPA curriculum were gathered at these three times. However, objective tests for this purpose were prepared inasmuch as the teachers felt they did not have time to carry out the publisher's recommended individual student evaluations.

Curricular Arrangements and Materials

The school's curriculum must be arranged to meet each individual student's educational needs and also school, district, and state requirements. The curriculum must be sufficiently comprehensive so that an educational program can be planned and carried out with each individual student. This not only calls for statements of curriculum objectives and mimeographed guides, but also high quality materials for students.

To adapt instruction to the developmental and other characteristics of the individual student, including those with learning disabilities and the gifted and talented, instructional materials are needed that meet several criteria. They have clearly stated objectives that may be used to indicate to students what is to be learned and to teachers what is to be taught. There are accompanying evaluation tools and procedures directly related to the objectives to help the teachers evaluate student learning and to help students evaluate themselves. There are multisensory materials that help students with various learning styles and capabilities attain their objectives. Finally, suggestions concerning instructional activities are provided in a curriculum manual or guide to enable teachers to vary the activities for individual students.

Many high quality multisensory materials are needed to take into account differences among students in their rates of learning, styles of learning, and other characteristics. Fortunately, many publishers and other agencies are now preparing excellent multisensory curricular programs. Budget constraints prevent the widespread use of many of these excellent materials.

In the present project, materials to supplement the school-adopted SAPA curriculum were given to the experimental schools. These were regarded by the teachers as essential for adapting their instruction to the different entering achievement levels of the students and to the different rates at which the students achieved the same objectives. Recall also that the project prepared and provided the experimental schools the process-concept lessons.

Home-School-Community Relations

We are all aware of the rapidly changing conditions in our neighborhoods and family environments. The traditional family of father, mother, and one or two children living in the same home may no longer be the prevalent family unit. New patterns in family and home life, and more movement from one neighborhood and school to another will probably continue. These patterns will probably be accompanied with less emotional stability and less intellectual stimulation and guidance of the children. The school in its present form or some other form will be expected to provide more. This calls for cooperative efforts and effective communication between the teacher and the parents or guardian and between the school, the home, and the larger community. School boards may be required to place greater demands on parents and guardians to cooperate in the education of the child.

The key to better home–school–community relations is involvement of parents in the education of their children. Teachers and parents learn to cooperate when school leadership and other conditions exist. We have found that children's cognitive devlopment is nurtured more effectively when there are more interactions and favorable attitudes among the teachers, the parents, and the child (Mize & Klausmeier, 1977). In the present project, differences among the schools in school-community relations were not identified by the project staff or the school staffs as influencing the students' achievements.

INSTRUCTIONAL PROGRAMMING FOR THE INDIVIDUAL STUDENT

A generic seven-step model of instructional programming for the individual student, the primary component of the IGE design, provides a theoretical framework for adapting instruction to meet individual student needs (Klausmeier,1977b; Klausmeier, Sorenson, & Quilling, 1971). It should not be confused with programmed instruction of the 1960s or with Skinnerian principles of operant conditioning. However, knowledge accruing from studies of aptitude–treatment interactions (Cronbach & Snow, 1977) and learning styles (Dunn & Dunn, 1978) can be incorporated into it.

The model is designed to enable teachers to take into account each student's entering level of achievement in each curricular area, learning styles, motivation, and other characteristics. Each student's program in each curricular area and affective domain is to be planned, carried out, and evaluated. The model requires the use of developmental objectives, that is, one or more detailed objectives for each unit of instruction, more general course or curricular objectives for a semester or a year, and program objectives that students work toward achieving throughout the elementary school years or even throughout Kindergarten–Grade 12. Most important, it suggests that an instructional program appropriate for each individual student should be arranged rather than prescribing the same program for all students to attain, but at different rates. After the main features of the model are explained, applications to teaching the SAPA curriculum in the experimental schools are indicated.

Steps in Instructional Programming

The seven phases, or steps, in instructional programming are shown in Figure 4.2. Step 1 involves setting general educational objectives to be attained by the student population of a school within a period of a year or longer. The initiative for setting these objectives is taken by the Instructional Improvement Committee of each school, with appropriate input from unit staff members, central office personnel, parents, and others concerned with the educational priorities of the school.

Step 2 in instructional programming for the individual student requires identifying the instructional objectives that may be attainable by the students of each instructional unit. The initiative for this step is taken by the unit leader and staff teachers of each Instruction and Research Unit. Each unit staff must decide which objectives may be appropriate for the students of their unit so that they can measure their students' achievements and then identify appropriate objectives for each individual student.

In Step 3 the teachers of the unit evaluate each student's level of understanding, skill, or attitudinal development by observing the student's performance or by administering tests. As an integral part of Step 3, an attempt is made to understand each student as an individual. Evaluative information is needed before starting each unit of instruction, but this may not always require *pretesting* the student. For example, when instructional programming is carried out in science, pretesting is done only at the beginning of each semester. Thereafter, evaluative information is gathered during each unit of instruction and at the end of the units.

Step 4 deals with setting instructional objectives for each student to attain during the next instructional sequence or unit of instruction. The objectives that the student has not yet mastered nor attained at some other criterion set by the teachers become that student's instructional objectives and are used in planning the student's instructional program.

Step 5 involves planning and carrying out an instructional program through which the student attains the objectives. To provide for differences among students, the following are varied: (a) the total amount of time for instruction given to each student; (b) the amount of attention and guidance given to each student by the teacher; (c) the amount of time spent by the teacher in interaction with each student; (d) the use of printed materials, audiovisual materials, and direct experiences, particularly to take into account the interests and learning styles of each student; (e) the use of space and equipment, particularly as different kinds of activities suitable for the individual may require them; and (f) perhaps most important, the amount of time spent by each student in one-to-one interactions with the teacher, another student, or the media, in in-

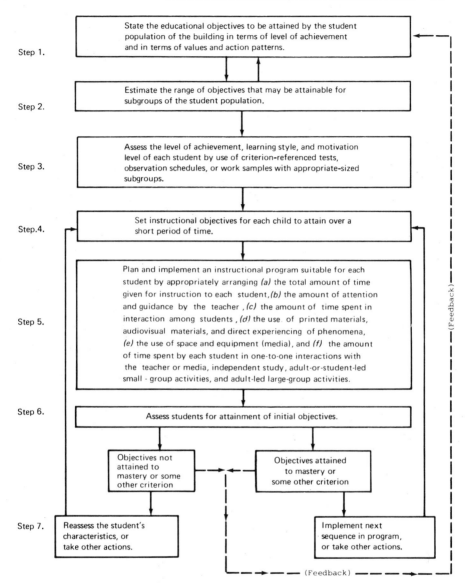

Figure 4.2 Instructional Programming Model in IGE. (Adapted from Klausmeier, Quilling, Sorenson, Way, & Glasrud, 1971, p. 19.)

dividual activity including independent study, in small–group activities, and in large–group activities.

Step 6 involves the teacher's assessment of the student's attainment of objectives.

Step 7 deals with decision making. When a student fails to attain an objective to the criterion that has been set, the appropriateness of the objective for the student, along with readiness to attain it, must be evaluated. Students who attain the instructional objectives move ahead to the next objectives in the sequence or to objectives in another area.

In the present project, the SAPA curriculum called for students to master the objectives of closely related units in a fixed sequence. However, it was district policy not to require mastery. This district policy was followed in carrying out the experiments, although a systematic attempt was made in the experimental schools to get more students to achieve the mastery level.

Patterns of Instructional Programming

Instruction dealing with closely related sets of objectives often is carried out for short period, such as 3–6 weeks. It is convenient to designate the objectives, the materials and activities for attaining the objectives, and the tools and procedures for evaluating students' attainment of the objectives as a unit of instruction. A unit of instruction is defined as a grouping of objectives and related instructional materials and activities for which there is a beginning point and a terminal point.

Three critical matters dealing with units of instruction are (a) whether the objectives are to be attained by all students enrolled in the school, (b) whether the desired level of attainment of the objectives is the same for all the students who are pursuing them, and (c) whether the units of instruction are to be taken in a fixed sequence. These three matters are handled differently both among various curricula and within the same curricular field. For example, in one strand of mathematics, namely arithmetic skills, attaining the same identical objectives may be required of all students; in another strand, namely probability and statistics, only some students may elect to attain the objectives. In the same way, the criteria that are established for attaining certain objectives in a curricular field may be identical for all students (for example, 80% correct on a test). The criteria for other objectives in the same curricular field may be stated variably in terms of each student's characteristics, for example, each student will participate successfully from 1 to 10 times monthly in activities related to the set of objectives; or each student will achieve a level judged appropriate for the student by the teacher. In a certain curricular field, the units of instruction covering one or more years of schooling may be invariantly sequenced, either because mastering each unit is prerequisite to starting the next one or because it is convenient to teach the units in an invariant sequence. In another curricular field, or in a different strand of the same curricular field, any unit of instruction may be started at any point in time during a given semester or school year, and starting one unit may not depend on completing other units.

There are eight possible patterns of common or variable objectives, full mastery or variable attainment of objectives, and an invariant or variable sequence of instructional units, as shown in Figure 4.3. The staff of a school, taking into account state and school district policies and the needs of the students, should decide which of these patterns their students will pursue with regard to the various curricular areas and the areas of instruction within the same curricular areas.

The SAPA curriculum *recommendation,* not the policy carried out in this study, followed the pattern of common objectives, full mastery, and an invariant sequence of proceeding through the units dealing with each science process. The actual pattern followed in this project was common objectives, variable attainment, and an invariant sequence across the units dealing with the same science process. According to this pattern, all the students of the district pursued a particular unit of instruction to attain the same objectives to a level of achievement appropriate for each student. In general, the teachers did not have students proceed through the science units at different rates as they did in math and reading. Rather, they encouraged and helped each student, including those with learning disabilities, achieve as high as possible, and these students moved ahead with all the others to the next unit. In the experimental schools, however, the attempt was made to get a high percentage of mastery of the SAPA objectives.

We may digress briefly to relate the mastery of the SAPA unit objectives to CLD theory. Recall from Chapter 2 that concurrent development of the classificatory and formal levels of the same concept, *noun,* occurred throughout most of the school years. The implication of this finding is that it is not wise to demand mastery of the classificatory level before starting instruction dealing with the formal level.

Specific Applications of the Instructional Programming Design

The application of the seven steps and the pattern of instructional programming for the individual student to the processes of science is different from its application to basic skills in reading and arithmetic. Reading and arithmetic do not require the use of the same equipment and space by many students. On the other hand, the teaching of science usually requires the students of each school building to share a science

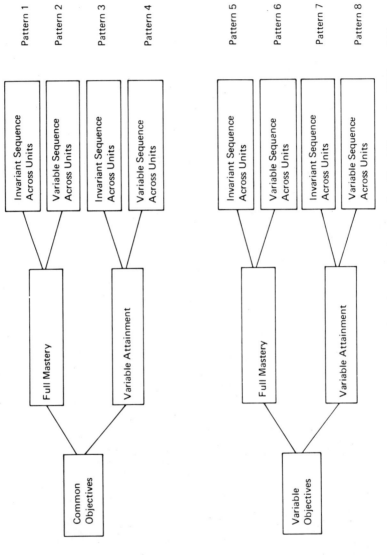

Figure 4.3 Patterns of objectives, criteria of attainment, and sequencing. (From Klausmeier, 1977a, p. 61.)

laboratory and also expensive equipment. In order to use the space and equipment advantageously, much of the instruction occurs in a science laboratory that is arranged to accommodate about 30–40 students. Within this laboratory arrangement, individual work, pairing of students, and small-group work may be carried out, as well as teacher demonstrations and other teacher-led activities directed toward the larger group.

It was in this kind of setting that the application of the design of instructional programming for the individual student was carried out in the present project. We may now deal more explicitly with the applications of each of the 7 steps that were made *in the experimental schools* during the first 10 experiments. Recall that the amount of time for the SAPA instruction was planned to be equal in the experimental and control schools in these experiments.

Step 1. Science objectives were specified for the student population of the building. The objectives for the students of the experimental and control schools were the objectives of the SAPA curriculum except that, before the start of the study, the school district had modified the grade placement of some of the objectives for all of the elementary schools of the district. Mastery of the objectives of the successive sets of SAPA exercises dealing with the same science process was not required, although the sets of exercises were taken in the same invariant sequence in all four schools.

Step 2. The science objectives that might be attainable for subgroups of the student population were determined. The subgroups of interest in each experimental school were all the students enrolled in Grade 4 and Grade 5. The objectives for these groups of students enrolled in the experimental schools and the control schools were identical; they were the objectives of the 17 sets of SAPA exercises allocated by the district office for each grade. The number of objectives for each individual SAPA exercise varied from as few as one to as many as four.

Step 3. An assessment was made of each child's entering level of science achievement. In both the experimental and control schools, each student's entering achievement level related to each set of SAPA exercises studied during each semester was determined by pretesting the students at the beginning of each semester. As we shall see in Step 5, the results of these pretests were used for carrying out instruction in the experimental schools, not in the control schools. Learning styles of the students and motivational levels were not assessed systematically as part of the study. Instead, the team of teachers at each school continued as they had before the experimentation regarding learning styles, motivation, and other student variables.

Step 4. Science objectives were set for each student for a specified period of time. The identical objectives of each individual SAPA exercise were set for every child in the experimental and control schools for the time during which the particular SAPA exercise was taught in each Grade 4 and Grade 5. Furthermore, school policies required that the same sets of 17 exercises assigned to each Grade 4 and Grade 5 should be studied each school year by all the students. (A SAPA exercise was not completed in a single classroom session of 25–30 minutes. Rather, two or three of these sessions were required for each exercise. In turn, 1–5 exercises were included in each set of exercises dealing with each of the SAPA science processes.)

Step 5. An instructional program for each student was planned and implemented. In the experimental schools, an instructional program for each student, based on the student's entering achievement level, was planned and carried out only partially in experiments 1–11, because of time and other constraints imposed by the experimental design. Instead, the students in each experimental school whose scores on the SAPA pretest were in the upper, middle, or lower one-third of the distribution of the scores were put into three corresponding instructional groups before starting the first SAPA exercise of the semester. The content and methods of instruction were differentiated for each of the three groups, and within each group the experimental teachers made further attempts to adapt their instruction for their individual students.

Each of the three groups included from 18 to 24 students. The SAPA posttest scores of the prior exercise were available for reforming groups for the next SAPA exercise. However, relatively few changes in groupings were made during the semester, and most of the same students remained in each of the three achievement-level instructional groups for the entire semester.

Step 6. Students' attainment of the SAPA objectives was assessed. When the students of the experimental schools had completed their study of each successive SAPA exercise, a 10-item posttest directly related to the objectives of the exercise was administered and scored immediately by an instructional aide.

Step 7. Instructional decisions were made on the basis of the assessment. In the first 11 experiments all the students in all four schools started the first SAPA exercise of a set, regardless of how they had scored on the prior SAPA posttest. This was done to keep the amount of time for the SAPA instruction the same in the experimental and control schools. However, in experiments 12 and 13, three new groups were formed in the experimental schools before completing the instruction on each SAPA exercise for the purpose of reteaching and/or enriching. The three groups were reformed on the basis of the rank order of scores obtained on the posttest for each group: The students who attained a post-test score of 8, 9, or 10 (mastery), those who achieved a score of 6 or 7 (near mastery), and the remainder of the students who scored in the 0–5 range. Thus, only in experiments 12 and 13 was the amount of time for instruction varied for the students, depending on their rate of achieving the objectives.

The preceding description has focused more on the experimental schools than on the control schools. In experiments 1–11, one difference between the experimental and the control schools, with regard to their SAPA instruction, was that the students were in three achievement-level groups in the experimental schools and in heterogeneous groups in the control schools. In the experimental schools the teachers used more individual and small-group activities and pitched their instruction to the level of each group. More whole-class demonstrations and instruction were carried out in the control schools, and the instruction was not pitched to three different levels of achievement. Also, the teachers of the experimental schools had the posttest scores of their students for each separate SAPA exercise, but the control teachers did not. Furthermore, the PC lessons were used in the experimental schools but not in the control schools, except in experiment 12, when a PC lesson was not used in any school.

More detailed information is presented in Chapters 6 and 7 regarding all elements of the experimental designs, including the patterns of teaching and testing employed by the teachers in the experimental and control schools for each experiment.

A NOTE ON INSTRUCTIONAL PROGRAMMING FOR THE INDIVIDUAL STUDENT AND MASTERY LEARNING

As we saw earlier in Figure 4.3, four patterns of instructional programming for the individual student involve mastery of objectives and four do not. The idea of mastery learning is not unique to this instructional design.

Morrison (1926) developed and applied a "mastery formula" to guide instruction in the Laboratory School of the University of Chicago and described the system in a widely used methods textbook. Washburne (1932) implemented a plan of differentiated instruction in Winnetka, Illinois, involving mastery and self-pacing by which each student, through individual activity, mastered successive units of work at his or her own rate. Other approaches to mastery learning, including individual contracting, were also formulated during the first half of this century. However, Carroll (1963) formulated an explicit theory of mastery learning. The main assumption of this theory is that, given enough time, every student can master any learning task. This assumption yielded the following equation:

$$\text{Degree of School Learning} = f \left(\frac{\text{Time Spent}}{\text{Time Needed}} \right)$$

That is, the degree of learning a school task is a function of the time spent in learning relative to the time needed to master the task. If the time spent is sufficient for mastery, then the degree of learning is 100%, or mastery.

Carroll hypothesized that the time spent and the time needed were influenced not only by learner characteristics but also by the characteristics of instruction. The time spent in learning is influenced by two factors: perseverance, defined as the amount of time a student is willing to spend actively engaged in learning, and opportunity to learn, defined as the classroom time allotted to learning. Three factors influence the time needed to learn: the student's aptitude for learning the task, the quality of instruction, and the student's ability to understand the instruction. The preceding equation restated in terms of the determinants of the amount of time spent and the amount of time needed follows:

$$\begin{array}{l}\text{Degree of}\\\text{School Learning}\end{array} = f \left(\frac{\text{1. Perseverance 2. Opportunity to learn}}{\begin{array}{c}\text{3. Aptitude 4. Quality of instruction}\\\text{5. Ability to understand instruction}\end{array}} \right)$$

The extent to which a student masters a learning task is a function of perseverance and opportunity to learn relative to aptitude for the learning task, the quality of instruction, and the ability to understand this instruction. Caroll defined a learning task as going from ignorance of some specified fact or concept to knowledge or understanding of it, or as proceeding from incapability of performing some specified act to capability of performing it. The undefined element of the theory is the determination of the differential amounts of time—across short time periods, such as a few lessons, and long time periods, such as the elementary school years—that different students might need to master the same tasks, such as learning to read at a level of functional literacy. It is also not clear whether every student could master understanding of some abstract principles, such as relativity, or learn to solve complex problems, such as in astronomy or philosophy.

Bloom's (1968, 1976) theory of Learning-for-Mastery is an elaboration of Carroll's formulation. Bloom hypothesized that if aptitude was predictive of the amount of time needed to learn, but not of the level of achievement (degree of learning), it should be possible to set the expected level of achievement as mastery. Then, by matching the opportunity to learn (time) and the quality of instruction, teachers should be able to ensure mastery by each student. When these two are matched properly, three variables, according to Bloom, should account for most of the variation among students in achievement: (a) their cognitive entry behaviors, that is, the extent to which the student has already mastered prerequisite knowledge and skills; (b) affective entry behaviors, that is, the extent to which the student is willing to engage actively in the learning process; and (c) the quality of instruction, the extent to which instruction is appropriate to the learner. Bloom's approach presumes that teachers in familiar age-graded, self-contained schools and in departmentalized instructional arrangements will be able to employ the mastery learning strategy to deal with these three variables effectively. Moreover, students can master the learning tasks, and the variability among students in levels of achievement will be diminished greatly.

Block (1974) and Block and Anderson (1975) set forth extensive elaborations of Bloom's mastery strategy. Their sequential steps, similar to those in the mastery patterns of instructional programming for the individual student, are to identify objectives, designate the criterion of mastery, teach, test, arrange for enrichment and other activities for those who master the unit, arrange for corrective and remedial teaching of those who do not master, test, repeat if there are still nonmastery students, and start the next unit of instruction. They do not deal with objectives for which a mastery criterion is inappropriate, nor do they indicate how the self-contained teacher can manage to provide for both the students who master early and those who experience continuing difficulty in achieving mastery.

Peterson (1972) found support for the hypothesis that student achievement would be higher under a mastery approach than under nonmastery approaches in several research studies, all of which were carried out over very short periods of time, usually less than 4 weeks. However, the percentage of students who mastered the age-graded learning tasks varied considerably across the studies. The hypothesis that there would be less variability among the students in achievement was supported by the analysis of the posttests employed in the studies. Did this lower variability result from the higher achievements of the less rapid learners or from not permitting the more rapid learners to move ahead and attain more advanced objectives? These questions were not addressed in the experiments.

Block and Burns (1977) also found that mastery-taught groups achieved higher on posttests than did nonmastery groups in the large majority of the 24 studies reviewed. Likewise, the mastery-taught students performed better on retention measures. In fact, in every study where retention measures were gathered, the mastery-taught students did as well or better than the nonmastery students. The mastery-taught students also exhibited less variability than other students.

The majority of the studies reviewed by Block and Burns (1977) were conducted at the college level; however, 11 involved elementary school children. In only 1 of the 11 studies was the duration of instruction longer than 4 weeks, and in 9 of them, the experimental instruction was only of 1–2 weeks duration. Block and Burns also found that the mastery approach to learning had a positive effect on students' interest in and attitude toward the subject matter learned, as well as on academic self-confidence, attitudes toward cooperation, attitudes toward instruction, and self-concept. Studies by Anderson (1976), Lee *et al.* (cited in Bloom, 1976), and Poggio, Glasnapp, and Ory (1975) support this conclusion.

Although the mastery-learning strategy of instruction has been shown to attain desirable results in terms of higher mean achievement and desirable affective outcomes over *short periods* of time, usually involving only one unit of instruction, it probably cannot be implemented successfully over long time periods in age-graded classrooms. Lower-aptitude students cannot be brought up to mastery by being given more time during the day or week without holding back higher-aptitude students who need less time to master the same objectives and who must then wait, even though engaged in enrichment activities, to start the next set of more advanced objectives. Mueller (1976) evaluated Bloom's contention that mastery learning over long periods of time will maximize learning for individual students enrolled in our familiar age-graded schools as follows:

> In traditionally organized schools, where learning is divided into grade levels and semesters, and where students are advanced together through these fixed-time instructional units, the mastery model cannot be used to maximize learning for all students. Since students learn at different rates, it is not legitimate for an instructor to expect all students to achieve the same level of performance (mastery) over the same amount of material in the same amount of time [p. 44].

The preceding conditions pointed out by Mueller coincide with those identified in the 1960s that led to the formulation of the model of instructional programming for the individual student and also to IGE as an alternative to age-graded group instruction. Mastery of the same objectives by all students, as portrayed in Patterns 1 and 2 of the instructional programming model, is facilitated when students are permitted and aided to proceed at rates suitable to the student across long time periods. This has been found for prereading (Venezky & Pittelman, 1977), reading skills (Otto, 1977), and mathematics (Romberg, 1977). It has also been found, however, that the students in the same grade are working on a wide range of objectives and that this range tends to increase during successive grades.

It is appropriate to pause to recognize that much resistance is still found among school staffs to permit rapid learners to be accelerated, that is, to proceed through successive units as rapidly as they can. To test the hypothesis that mastery learning will reduce the difference among students of the same age in achievement, it is necessary to find schools which will follow the acceleration mode. The initial plan of the present project included this provision in the experimental schools during Grade 6, the last year of elementary schooling. Lack of funding, however, and some unwillingness on the part of the school district to proceed in this manner did not permit implementing this aspect of the plan.

REFERENCES

Anderson, L. W. An empirical investigation of individual differences in time to learn. *Journal of Educational Psychology,* 1976, *68,* 226–233.

Block, J. H. (Ed.). *Schools, society, and mastery learning.* New York: Holt, Rinehart and Winston, 1974.

Block, J. H., & Anderson, L. W. *Mastery learning in classroom instruction.* New York: Macmillan, 1975.

Block, J. H., & Burns, R. B. Mastery learning. In L. S. Shulman (Ed.), *Review of research in education, 4.* Itasca, Ill.: F. E. Peacock, 1977.

Bloom, B. S. Learning for mastery. *UCLA Evaluation Comment,* 1968, 1(2), 1–11.

Bloom, B. S. *Human characteristics and school learning.* New York: McGraw-Hill, 1976.

Carroll, J. B. A model of school learning. *Teachers College Record,* 1963, *64,* 723–733.

Cronbach, L. J., & Snow, R. E. *Aptitudes and instructional methods: A handbook for research on interactions.* New York: Wiley, 1977.

Dunn, R., & Dunn, K. *Teaching students through their individual learning styles: A practical approach.* Reston, Va.: Reston Publishing, 1978.

Klausmeier, H. J. The multi-unit elementary school and individually guided education. *Phi Delta Kappan,* 1971, *53*(3), 181–184.

Klausmeier, H. J. IGE: An alternative form of schooling. In H. Talmage (Ed.), *Systems of individualized education.* Berkeley, CA.: McCutchan Publishing, 1975. Pp. 48–83.

Klausmeier, H. J. Instructional programming for the individual student. In H. J. Klausmeier, R. A. Rossmiller, & M. Saily (Eds.), *Individually guided elementary education: Concepts and practices* New York: Academic Press, 1977 Pp. 55–76 (a).

Klausmeier, H. J. Origin and overview of IGE. In H. J. Klausmeier, R. A. Rossmiller, & M.

Saily (Eds.), *Individually guided elementary education: Concepts and practices.* New York: Academic Press, 1977. Pp. 1–24 (b).

Klausmeier, H. J. *Profiles of selected innovating secondary schools* (Working Paper No. 259). Madison: Wisconsin Research and Development Center for Individualized Schooling, 1979.

Klausmeier, H. J., & Goodwin, W. *Learning and human abilities: Educational psychology* (4th ed.). New York: Harper & Row, 1975.

Klausmeier, H. J., Morrow, R. G., & Walter, J. E. *Individually guided education in the multiunit elementary school: Guidelines for implementation.* Madison: Wisconsin Research and Development Center for Cognitive Learning, 1968.

Klausmeier, H. J., & Pellegrin, R. J. The multiunit school: A differentiated staffing approach. In D. S. Bushnell & D. Rappaport (Eds.), *Planned change in education: A systems approach.* New York: Harcourt Brace Jovanovich, 1971. Pp. 107–127.

Klausmeier, H. J., Quilling, M. R., Sorenson, J. S., Way, R. S., & Glasrud, G. R. *Individually guided education and the multiunit elementary school: Guidelines for implementation.* Madison: Wisconsin Research and Development Center for Cognitive Learning, 1971.

Klausmeier, H. J., Sorenson, J. S., & Quilling, M. R. Instructional programming for the individual pupil in the multiunit elementary school. *The Elementary School Journal,* 1971, *72*(2), 88–101.

Lee, Y. D. *et al.* Interaction improvement studies on the mastery learning project. *Final Report on Mastery Learning Program.* Educational Research Center, Seoul National University, November 1971.

Lipham, J. M., & Daresh, J. C. (Eds.) *Administrative and staff relationships in education: Research and practice in IGE schools* (Monograph Series). Madison: Wisconsin Research and Development Center for Individualized Schooling, 1980.

Lipham, J. M., & Fruth, M. J. *The principal and individually guided education.* Reading, MA.: Addison-Wesley Publishing, 1976.

Mize, G. K., & Klausmeier, H. J. *Factors contributing to rapid and slow cognitive development among elementary and high school children* (Working Paper No. 201). Madison: Wisconsin Research and Development Center for Cognitive Learning, 1977.

Morrison, H. C. *The practice of teaching in the secondary school.* Chicago: University of Chicago Press, 1926.

Mueller, D. J. Mastery learning: Partly boon, partly boondoggle. *Teachers College Record,* 1976, *78*(1), 41–52.

Nussel, E. J., Inglis, J. D., & Wiersma, W. *The teacher and individually guided education.* Reading, MA.: Addison-Wesley Publishing, 1976.

Otto, W. The Wisconsin design: A reading program for Individually Guided Education. In H. J. Klausmeier, R. A. Rossmiller, & M. Saily (Eds.), *Individually guided elementary education: Concepts and practices.* New York: Academic Press, 1977. Pp. 137–149.

Peterson, P. L. *A review of the research on mastery-learning strategies.* Unpublished manuscript, International Association for the Evaluation of Educational Achievement, Stockholm, Sweden, 1972.

Poggio, J. P., Glasnapp, D. R., & Ory, J. C. The impact of test anxiety on formative and summative exam performance in the mastery-learning model. Paper presented at the annual meeting of the National Council on Measurement in Education, Washington, D.C., 1975.

Romberg, T. A. Developing mathematical processes: The elementary mathematics program for Individually Guided Education. In H. J. Klausmeier, R. A. Rossmiller, & M. Saily (Eds.), *Individually guided elementary education: Concepts and practices.* New York: Academic Press, 1977. Pp. 77–109.

Sorenson, J. S., Poole, M., & Joyal, L. H. *The unit leader and individually guided education.* Reading, MA.: Addison-Wesley Publishing, 1976.

Talmage, H. (Ed.). Systems of individualized education. Berkeley, CA.: McCutchan Publishing Company, 1975.

Venezky, R. L., & Pittelman, S. D. PRS: A pre-reading skills program for Individually Guided Education. In H. J. Klausmeier, R. A. Rossmiller, & M. Saily (Eds.), *Individually guided elementary education: Concepts and practices.* New York: Academic Press, 1977. Pp. 111–135.

Washburne, C. *Adjusting the school to the child.* New York: World Book Company, 1932.

5

Test Construction and Development
of Process-Concept Lessons

In each of 12 of the 13 controlled experiments carried out in this project, two kinds of instructional materials were used: Exercises that were part of a published science curriculum, namely, *Science—A Process Approach* (SAPA) (American Association for the Advancement of Science, 1967), and a process-concept (PC) lesson prepared by the project staff. Tests for each SAPA exercise and PC lesson were also constucted by the project staff. (In one experiment a PC lesson was not used in order to have the additional instructional time needed for testing a particular hypothesis.) The primary aim of each set of SAPA exercises was to enable students to experience and perform a process of science. The primary aim of each PC lesson was to help the student understand the same SAPA science process as a concept.

The reader may wish to review the introductions of Chapters 2 and 3 to identify the aspects of CLD theory that were either tested or used in carrying out that part of each experiment involving the use of the PC lesson and that part associated with adapting the SAPA instruction to the entering achievement levels of the students. Recall from Chapter 3 that a content analysis, a behavioral analysis, and an instructional analysis were performed on the SAPA processes before preparing the PC lessons that were designed to promote understanding of the processes as concepts. The substance of these analyses were based directly on CLD theory; thus, the use of the PC lessons in the experimental schools permitted testing of specified applications of CLD theory related to students' learning the process concepts of science.

In this chapter, a brief description of the schools involved in the experimentation and a review of the SAPA science curriculum (see Chapter 1) are given. Then the construction of the SAPA tests is explained. This is followed with a description of the development of the PC lessons and the construction of the related tests. The purposes, experimental procedures, instructional methods, materials, and other conditions of instruction and learning for each experiment are given in Chapters 6 and 7, where the results of the experiments are also presented.

SELECTION OF SCHOOLS

Students from two paired sets of experimental and control schools participated in the experiments. The identification of the two experimental and two control schools was made by the chief administrative officer of the school district and the district science coordinator in consultation with the project staff who indicated desired conditions for carrying out the study. Meetings were held with the school staff to secure their approval and support.

The two pairs of schools were selected to be representative of the socioeconomic, ethnic, and general demographic classifications of the adult population of the school district. Eighty percent of the population of each of the four schools was of middle and higher-than-middle socioeconomic status.

Two schools in which nongraded instruction was carried out with multiaged groups of students in most curricular areas were selected; one was assigned to the experimental condition (E1) and the other to the control condition (C1). A second pair of schools in which instruction in most curriculum areas was carried out with students in age-graded groups was selected; one school was assigned to the experimental condition (E2) and the other to the control condition (C2). All four schools implemented a form of schooling called Individually Guided Education, which is described in Chapter 4. They carried out instructional programming for the individual student in reading and mathematics, but not in science.

In 1975–1976, experiments 1–5 were carried out with Grade 4 students and experiments 6–10 with Grade 5 students. Experiments 11, 12 and 13 were carried out in the following year, 1976–1977, in Grade 5 only.

Grade 4 students of school E1 and E2 who participated in experiments 1–5 in 1975–1976, also participated in experiments 11–13 in 1976–1977, when in Grade 5, and took all the related tests. These students of E1 and E2 who received the instruction and testing both years were used to determine the cumulative effects of one and two years of receiving the experimental instruction.

PUBLISHED SCIENCE CURRICULUM

The first commercial edition of *Science—A Process Approach* was used in both the experimental and control schools (American Association for the Advancement of Science, 1967). (A second edition was published in 1975.) According to the 1967 edition of SAPA, students are to learn processes of science by participating in science activities. The general objective is to teach science as enquiry by having the students experience and perform the intellectual behaviors of scientists. These intellectual behaviors of scientists are called the "processes of science." The teaching and learning of organized knowledge regarding natural phenomena is of secondary concern.

The eight "basic processes" to be developed during the primary school years are observing, classifying, using space–time relations, using numbers, communicating, measuring, inferring, and predicting. The following five "integrated processes" are suggested for development in the intermediate grades: formulating hypotheses, controlling variables, interpreting data, defining operationally, and experimenting.

One feature of SAPA is the hierarchical order in which the students are to learn the processes. There are sets of exercises that concentrate on each process at successively higher levels throughout the elementary school years. Each separate set of exercises dealing with any particular process concentrates on that particular process at at a given level of difficulty or sophistication. Student performance of the process at this level purportedly requires use of the prerequisite knowledge and skills developed in a set of exercises at a lower level in the hierarchy. Achieving the objectives of each set of lessons lower in the hierarchy is required to proceed successfully to the next set of lessons. Teachers are to observe the performances of a sample of the students to evaluate attainment of the objectives by the whole class. These observations are not paper-and-pencil tests to be used with a group; rather, they are observations of the performances of individual students as they carry out certain activities of the lessons.

The schools of the participating school district made some significant departures from the recommendations of the publisher before the start of the study. First, some of the sets of SAPA exercises recommended by the publisher for use in a lower grade were used in a higher grade. Second, observation to assess students' attainment of the objectives was not followed systematically because of lack of time to do so. Finally, this published program calls for students to attain the objectives of the successive sets of exercises within the various strands dealing with a particular science process, such as observing or inferring. Also, certain exercises from a strand, such as using numbers, must be attained before other exercises, such as those dealing with measuring, are started. The elementary schools of the district, including the experimental and control schools, followed most of the recommendations regarding sequence. However, students were not required to master the objectives of any set of exercises before proceeding to the next set of exercises in the hierarchy.

CONSTRUCTION OF SAPA ACHIEVEMENT TESTS

Before the start of the project, the participating schools did not use any paper-and-pencil tests to measure students' achievements of the SAPA objectives, and they generally did not carry out the publishers' recommended observation procedures. Therefore, the project personnel constructed paper-and-pencil tests to measure students' attainment of the objectives of the SAPA exercises. The purpose and use of these tests follow. Also, the test construction process is outlined and the technical characteristics of the tests are given.

Purpose of the SAPA Tests

The tests were constructed to measure achievement of the specific objectives of each SAPA exercise. The design of the experiments called for the tests to be given as pretests at the beginning of each semester and as posttests at the end of each semester in both the experimental and control schools. In addition, the pretest results were used during each semester in each experimental school to arrange the students of each grade into a high, middle, and low entering-achievement level group.

Construction of the SAPA Tests

In the preparatory year of the study, project personnel drafted preliminary versions of the SAPA tests. Seventeen tests using from 7 to 15 items each were constructed in paper-and-pencil format to correspond to the 17 SAPA exercises taught at each Grade 4 and 5. The items were constructed to measure the student's achievement of the objectives of the SAPA exercise and the key vocabulary of the exercise. The "appraisal" and "competency-measure" parts of the teacher's guide that were recommended by the publisher to be administered to a sample of students after the teaching of a SAPA exercise served as the prototype for constructing the items to measure achievement of the SAPA exercise objectives.

The prototype for the vocabulary items was the "key words" section of the published teacher's guide. In addition, some words that teachers in the experimental schools judged to be important were included as vocabulary test items.

Throughout the development of the tests, all the items were reviewed for clarity and format and revised by test construction specialists. The tests were also reviewed by a professor of science education, and from the participating school district, a science teacher of Grades 4 and 5, a science consultant, and a reading consultant. The paper-and-pencil items were constructed to measure use of the process in connection with the science information that appeared in the particular SAPA exercise, rather than to measure the students' use of the process on scientific phenomena and events not included in the exercise. Thus, the items did not test the student's understanding of the process as a concept, independent of particular content, nor the ability to use the process with content not in the SAPA exercise. (As we shall see, the PC tests were designed to measure these abilities.) Illustrative items to measure objectives and vocabulary from the test of the science process, *inferring*, follow.

Objectives items for the SAPA exercise, *Inferring Loss of Water from Plants:*

Look at the drawings below. Plant A and Plant B are the same kind. They are alike, except Plant A has only *half* as many leaves as Plant B.

Here is the way the experiment looked when it was begun.

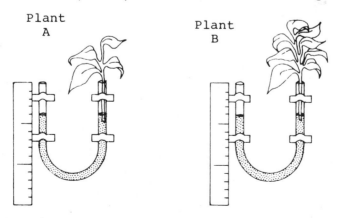

Plant
A

Plant
B

The drop in water level was recorded for each plant over a 10-hr period.

What would you infer about the rate at which the water level dropped?

a. It dropped about twice as fast for Plant A.

b. It dropped about twice as fast for Plant B.

c. It dropped at about the same rate for both plants.

How could you test someone's inference that "a plant does not transpire as much water at night as it does during the day?"

a. Measure the height of a certain plant every morning and evening for 1 week.

b. For a period of 1 week, water one plant only at night and another plant only during the day.

c. Measure the growth rate for two different plants: one kept in the dark and one kept in the daylight.

d. Measure how much water is taken up by a certain plant each hour for 24 hr.

Vocabulary item for the SAPA exercise, *Inferring Loss of Water from Plants:*

"The process by which plants give off moisture." This is a definition of:

a. respiration

b. photosynthesis

c. synthesis

d. transpiration

Objectives items for the SAPA exercise, *Inferring Connection Patterns in Electric Circuits:*

A hidden circuit board was tested, and the following connection pattern was inferred.

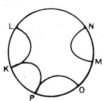

The chart below is only partly completed.

Pair	K-L	K-P	K-O	P-L	O-N
Closed	X	X	X		
Open					X

How would you complete the chart to show the correct connection patterns for P-L?

a. Mark P-L as "Open."

b. Mark P-L as "Closed."

Sue was given a circuit board, a dry cell, a lamp, and some wires. She tested the hidden circuits and drew the following connection pattern to show her results.

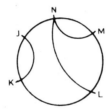

What would happen if Sue connected wires to M and L?

a. The circuit would be open.

b. The circuit would be closed.

Vocabulary item for the SAPA exercise, *Inferring Connection Patterns in Electric Circuits:*

"The complete pathway through which an electric current flows." This is a definition of:

a. switch

b. tube

c. circuit

d. cell

Objectives item for the SAPA exercise, *Inferring the Shape of Cut Things:*

The drawing below shows a solid cone sliced exactly down the middle.

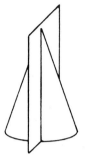

What is the shape of the *cut* surfaces?

a.

b.

c.

d.

Vocabulary items for the SAPA exercise, *Inferring the Shape of Cut Things:*

Look at drawings A, B, and C to answer the next two questions.

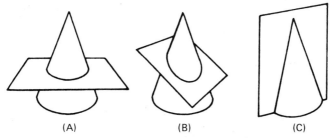

(A)   (B)   (C)

Which of the three ways of slicing the cone would make a *transverse* section?

a. A

b. B

c. C

Which of the three ways of slicing the cone would make a *slant* section?

a. A

b. B

c. C

Tryout of the SAPA Tests

The tests were constructed, tried out, and revised during the two years preceding the start of the first experiments. In the first year, the preliminary versions of the tests were tried with groups of students in Grades 4 and 5. Tests with low reliability coefficients were examined, and the items contributing to the low reliabilities were identified and either modified or omitted from further versions of the tests. In the next year, the tests were tried out again with groups of Grade 4 and 5 students. The students who participated were chosen to represent low, medium, and high levels of educational achievement. Results from this tryout were examined by the project personnel, teachers from the schools, and the science coordinator of the school district. Items showing poor discrimination values were reviewed, and when probable causes for this could be identified, the items were rewritten to alleviate the problems. All items were also reviewed to ensure that the objectives of the SAPA exercise were being measured. So that time schedules could be planned effectively in the experimental and control schools, it was decided that the final version of the tests would contain 10 items for each SAPA exercise. The 17 tests for each Grade 4 and Grade 5 were for the 17 SAPA exercises used each year; the names of the exercises are given in Tables 6.1 and 6.4 of Chapter 6.

Reliability of the Tests

Five tests, one corresponding to each of the five sets of SAPA exercises (each set had two or more exercises) that were used in experiments 1–5 were administered to the Grade 4 students; in experiments 6–10, five were administered to the Grade 5 students. They were administered both as pretests and as posttests to the experimental and control students. Each test had 10 items for each exercise in the set of exercises that was used in the experiments. In Grade 4, three tests had 20 items each (i.e., Classifying—experiment 1, Predicting—experiment 3, and Using Numbers—experiment 4); the Inferring test (experiment 2) contained 30 items; and the test for Measuring (experiment 5) had 50 items. Three tests used in Grade 5 had 20 items (Using Space–Time Relationships—experiment 8, Controlling Variables—experiment 9, and Communicating— experiment 10), and each of the other two had 30 items (Observing—experiment 11 and Inferring—experiment 12). In the second year, the experimentation was carried out for Grade 5 only, and involved three of the same sets of exercises and related tests used in the preceding year, namely, Observing (experiment 11), Inferring (experiment 12), and Controlling Variables (experiment 13).

The reliabilities of the SAPA tests given as pretests and posttests in each school were assessed by means of Hoyt reliability coefficients. These coefficients, the standard errors of measurement, and the numbers of students on which each coefficient is based in each of the 13 experiments are given in Table 5.1. The means and standard deviations will be given in Chapters 6 and 7 when the results of the various experiments are reported. Inspection of Table 5.1 reveals that the reliability coefficients for the posttests in the 13 experiments ranged from .46 to .89 in E1 and E2 and from .02 to .87 in C1 and C2. Only 3 of the 52 coefficients were below .53. In all except three instances the reliability coefficient based on the posttest data was greater than that based on the pretest data. Two of three exceptions occurred for C1 in experiments 4 and 8, and the other for E2 in experiment 1. It may also be observed that both the pretest and the posttest coefficients were generally higher for the experimental school than for its paired control school.

Tests used in 5 of the 13 experiments had reliability coefficients of .50 or higher for both the pretests and the posttests in all the four schools.

TABLE 5.1 Hoyt Reliability Coefficients and Standard Errors of Measurement for Students of the Experimental and Control Schools: SAPA Tests

Experiment	E1		C1		E2		C2	
	Pre	Post	Pre	Post	Pre	Post	Pre	Post
1: Classifying (20 items)								
Hoyt	.44	.74	.15	.59	.49	.46	.00	.31
SEM	1.93	1.75	1.96	1.89	1.91	1.33	1.87	1.81
2: Inferring (30 items)								
Hoyt	.67	.81	.48	.72	.58	.81	.57	.65
SEM	2.42	2.16	2.35	2.29	2.42	2.11	2.37	2.27
3: Predicting (20 items)								
Hoyt	.75	.79	.58	.69	.65	.74	.46	.61
SEM	1.88	1.55	1.96	1.87	1.93	1.53	1.95	1.62
4: Using numbers (20 items)								
Hoyt	.50	.74	.74	.65	.50	.71	.51	.63
SEM	1.97	1.87	1.89	1.94	1.82	1.85	1.90	1.94
5: Measuring (50 items)								
Hoyt	.83	.89	.77	.87	.72	.87	.62	.82
SEM	3.08	2.78	3.10	3.02	3.12	2.74	3.10	2.93
6: Observing (30 items)								
Hoyt	.69	.83	.59	.65	.70	.76	.31	.65
SEM	2.42	2.03	2.38	2.28	2.37	1.96	2.41	2.17
7: Inferring (30 items)								
Hoyt	.45	.74	.18	.71	.33	.69	.48	.55
SEM	2.46	2.25	2.46	2.28	2.48	2.13	2.38	2.36
8: Using space–time relationships (20 items)								
Hoyt	.18	.65	.11	.02	.56	.69	.42	.63
SEM	1.97	1.88	1.96	1.90	1.97	1.59	2.01	1.93
9: Controlling variables (20 items)								
Hoyt	.63	.79	.55	.64	.64	.76	.69	.77
SEM	2.01	1.79	2.04	1.79	1.98	1.55	1.98	1.81
10: Communicating (20 items)								
Hoyt	.65	.76	.57	.78	.64	.77	.67	.75
SEM	1.92	1.83	1.96	1.82	1.93	1.54	1.93	1.83
11: Observing (30 items)								
Hoyt	.66	.74	.50	.70	.73	.83	.54	.56
SEM	2.39	1.92	2.42	2.23	2.41	1.99	2.40	2.21
12: Inferring (30 items)								
Hoyt	.42	.78	.48	.66	.61	.84	.26	.53
SEM	2.45	1.90	2.45	2.19	2.47	1.98	2.47	2.24
13: Controlling variables 20 items)								
Hoyt	.67	.75	.54	.64	.65	.83	.42	.66
SEM	1.95	1.44	1.97	1.79	2.01	1.58	2.02	1.87

Coefficients in the highest range were for the Measuring test (i.e., .62 to .89). This 50-item test, used in experiment 5 with Grade 4 students, also contained the greatest number of items. Only 10 of the 104 reliability coefficients given in Table 5.1 fell below .40, and 8 of them occurred in the control schools. The Classifying tests used in experiment 1 and Using Space–Time Relationships used in experiment 8 contributed most of these low coefficients.

DEVELOPMENT OF PROCESS-CONCEPT LESSONS

Six lessons were developed during the preparatory year of the study as follows: classifying (Schilling & Klausmeier, 1975a), inferring (Schilling & Klausmeier, 1975c), and predicting (Swanson & Klausmeier, 1975) for use with Grade 4 students in experiments 1, 2, and 3; and observing scientifically (Schilling & Klausmeier, 1975d), inferring (Schilling & Klausmeier, 1975b), and using space-time relationships (Sipple, Katz, & Klausmeier, 1975) for use with Grade 5 students in experiments 6, 7, 8. The other four lessons were developed while the earlier experiments were being conducted: using numbers scientifically (Bull & Klausmeier, 1976b), and measuring scientifically (Swanson, Schilling, & Klausmeier, 1975) for use in experiments 4 and 5 with Grade 4 students, and controlling variables (Schilling & Klausmeier, 1976) and communicating scientific information (Bull & Klausmeier, 1976a) for use in experiments 9 and 10 with Grade 5 students.

Rationale for the Lessons

CLD theory as presented in Chapter 2 provided the substantive information for performing the content, behavioral, and instructional analyses performed on the SAPA processes of science. These were presented in Chapter 3. The results of these analyses were used in preparing the 10 PC lessons.

Recall that CLD theoretical constructs regarding the nature of concepts and their relationship to other outcomes of learning were employed in carrying out the content analysis by which, among other things, the concepts were arranged in a hierarchy. The hierarchical relationship among the concepts provided the basis for determining the defining attributes of each concept. The defining attributes were taught as part of the lesson.

The behavioral analysis identified the prerequisite mental operations and the meaningful reception operations that the student had to be capable of to attain the concept at the mature classificatory and the formal level through studying the lesson. The operations are restated here: having the names of the concept and the defining attributes, discriminating the defining attributes of the concept, generalizing that two or more examples of the concept are equivalent and thereby attaining the concept at the classificatory level, and carrying out meaningful reception operations necessary for attaining the formal level. These reception operations include: assimilating the information presented in the PC lesson, including the concept name, the concept definition, the verbal descriptions, and pictorial representations of examples and nonexamples of the concept; remembering the information; and evaluating examples and nonexamples of the concept on the basis of the presence or absence of the defining attributes. The substance and activities of each lesson were arranged to involve student use of all these operations. The seven external conditions of learning that facilitate learning concepts at the mature classificatory level and the formal level included in the instructional analysis guide the preparation of the various parts of the lesson directly. These conditions are stated as headings in the description of the PC lessons that follow.

Description of the PC Lessons

Each of the five PC lessons used in experiments 1–5 at Grade 4 contained from 50 to 63 pages; at Grade 5 in experiments 6–10, each lesson had from 47 to 66 pages. Excerpts from the lesson on inferring used at Grade 5 and the accompanying narrative follow to make clear how the instructional principles expressed in Chapter 3 were used in preparing the PC lessons.

Elicit student verbalization of the name of the concept and the defining attributes. A list of key words was presented at the beginning of each printed PC lesson. The students were taught to recognize the words. This vocabulary list included the concept name, *infer,* and names of the key words included in the defining attributes: inference, observe, scientific observation, relate, relationships, draw, conclusion, conclude, knows.

Establish an intention to learn concepts. As a means of focusing and holding attention, the lesson followed a story format in which cartoon characters presented information and directions to the students. In the introduction of the lesson, the story characters were introduced and an intention to learn the concept was established as follows:

One summer, Tom and Betty decided to learn more about science and what scientists do. They found out that one of the things that scientists do is to

Tom and Betty read everything they could about inferring. They found out that to infer, a person must do two things.

You will learn about these two things by looking at pictures and reading about them. You will be asked to do things and to answer questions about what you are learnng. After you answer the questions, you will see the right answers. As you are reading this lesson, *remember* the two things that we do when we *infer*. Copy these two important things on the lines below.

To *infer* a person must:

1. _____

_____

2. _____

_____

Emphasize the defining attributes of the concept by drawing the student's attention to them. Following the introduction, each defining attribute of the process concept was introduced. The presentation of a defining attribute of *inferring* is given next.

One of the things we must do to infer is:

Betty observed scientifically as Tom blew into a straw that was partly under water.

Betty knew that air takes up space and that Tom was blowing air into the water. She related her scientific observation to what she knew.

Provide a definition of the concept in terms of its defining attributes stated in vocabulary appropriate to the target population. In the next part of the lesson, the definition of *inferring* was presented as follows:

When we put together two important things about inferring, we make the *definition* of inferring.

Here is the definition of inferring. Read it carefully!

> *Inferring:* Relating a scientific observation to something which is known, and drawing a conclusion about what was observed.

Provide at least one rational set of examples and nonexamples of the concept. Rational sets of examples and nonexamples of *inferring* were provided. In each example, both of the defining attributes of *inferring* were present (they must be in order to serve as an example) as is indicated in the example which follows:

Example of *infer:*

Betty put two plants in a sunny spot on the same table. She watered Plant A every day for one week. She did not water Plant B at all. Plant A lived and grew. Plant B became dry and looked dead at the end of the week.

Betty did infer. You can tell by looking at the answers to these questions.

1. Did the person relate a scientific observation to something which is known?   (YES)   NO

2. Did the person draw a conclusion about what was observed?   (YES)   NO

   (Did the person infer?)   (YES)   NO

The answer to Questions 1 and 2 is "yes," so we know that Betty did infer.

Nonexamples of *infer:* (In a nonexample, either none or only one of the defining attributes was present.)

Betty put two plants in a sunny spot on the same table. She watered Plant A every day for one week. She did not water Plant B at all. Plant A lived and grew. Plant B became dry and looked dead at the end of the week.

Betty did *not* infer. You can tell by looking at the answers to these questions.

1. Did the person relate a scientific   YES   (NO)
   observation to something which
   is known?

2. Did the person draw a conclu-   YES   (NO)
   sion about what was observed?

   (Did the person infer?)   YES   (NO)

The answer to questions 1 and 2 is "*no,*" so we know that Betty did *not* infer.

Teach a strategy for evaluating examples and nonexamples of the concept. A strategy for evaluating examples and nonexamples of *inferring* was taught. The lesson presented a set of questions concerning the presence or absence of the defining attributes. The students were told that if they could answer "yes" to all of the questions, the instance was an example of the concept. If they answered "no" to one or more of the questions, the instance was not an example. The strategy for evaluating an example and a nonexample of the process-concept inferring is illustrated next:

Example of *inferring* showing use of a strategy:

Tom told Betty to look at the liquid in a beaker. Betty examined the liquid carefully.

Did Betty infer? Answer the questions below and decide.

1. Did the person relate a scientific   YES   NO
   observation to something which
   is known?
2. Did the person draw a conclu-   YES   NO
   sion about what was observed?

   (Did the person infer?)   YES   NO

Nonexample of *inferring* showing the use of strategy:

Early one morning, Tom looked out his bedroom window at the wet grass.

THE GRASS IS WET.

I KNOW THAT DEW MAKES GRASS WET.

Did Tom infer? Answer the questions below and decide.

1. Did the person relate a scientific   YES   NO
   observation to something which
   is known?
2. Did the person draw a conclu-   YES   NO
   sion about what was observed?

   (Did the person infer?)   YES   NO

As was shown in the preceding illustrations, questions to which the student responded were included in the PC lesson. Correct answers were provided for each set of questions to provide immediate feedback. An illustration follows of the feedback technique that was used in connection with teaching a strategy for evaluating instances as examples or nonexamples of inferring.

An illustration of immediate feedback from the *inferring* lesson:

> Answers provided in the lesson apply to the preceding story about Betty looking at the liquid in the beaker. (The questions and answers were placed on the next page of the lesson.)
>
> 1. Did the person relate a scientific observation to something which is known?   (YES)   NO
>
> 2. Did the person draw a conclusion about what was observed?   (YES)   NO
>
> (Did the person infer?)   (YES)   NO
>
> Answers provided in the lesson apply to the previous story about Tom looking out his bedroom window at the wet grass.
>
> 1. Did the person relate a scientific observation to something which is known?   (YES)   NO
>
> 2. Did the person draw a conclusion about what was observed?   ‹YES   (NO)
>
> (Did the person infer?)   YES   (NO)

In the final part of the lesson, the defining attributes and definition of *inferring* were reviewed and the student was asked to evaluate other examples and nonexamples. The last part of the lesson asked the student to make inferences from situations represented only pictorially, such as:

Look at the picture below:

Make an inference about what happened in the picture above.

_____

_____

_____

_____

_____

_____

The reader should properly infer that including the questions and exercises was designed to get the student to participate actively in learning the concept at the formal level of attainment. And although a meaningful reception process was predominant, some discovery learning was also included. You may wish to review the excerpts in the preceding pages to identify where the mental operations mentioned earlier were involved.

CONSTRUCTION OF THE PROCESS-CONCEPT TESTS

A test was constructed for each of the ten process concepts for which a PC lesson was prepared. Each test was designed to measure attainment of the concept at the formal level; however, items involving the classificatory level were also included.

Construction of the PC Tests

The PC tests were written in a paper-and-pencil, multiple-choice format. The first eight items of each test were designed to measure the ability to recognize activities in story format either as examples or nonexamples of the particular process concept. These items measure the student's attainment of the concept at the mature classificatory level, that is, the ability to classify examples correctly.

Other items were written to measure attainment at the formal level. Depending on the number of defining attributes of the process concept, an equal number of items was included to test the student's ability to discriminate the defining attributes of the concept. This is prerequisite for attaining the formal level. In all except one test, Controlling Variables, there were either two or three of these items. *Controlling Variables* was analyzed as having four defining attributes.

Other PC test items were constructed to measure the student's ability to evaluate examples and nonexamples of the process concept in terms of the presence or absence of the defining attributes. There were two of these items for each defining attribute of the various concepts. Each test also contained a single item to test knowledge of the definition of the process concept. Students who could do all three kinds of items correctly were presumed to be able to perform the operations at the formal level of concept attainment as given earlier in this chapter. The number of items in each of these tests ranged from 15 to 21. Six tests had 15 items each, three had 18 items, and one test contained 21 items.

From the preceding description of what was measured, it should be clear that the student who scored high on a test would understand the concept fully but might not be able to perform the process. Not clear, however, is the fact that no substantive content involving the science phenomena and events included in the SAPA exercise was included in the PC test. Therefore, even though study of the PC lesson might result in understanding the process concept and being able to classify examples and nonexamples, it could not be assumed that there would be transfer to improved performance of the SAPA lesson as measured by the SAPA test. For transfer to occur, the student would necessarily apply the understanding to phenomena included in the SAPA lesson and also to performing the process on SAPA content (see the earlier description of the SAPA test items in this chapter). Items from the PC test for inferring follow for illustrative purposes.

Items to measure the ability to recognize examples and nonexamples of *inferring:*

> Some of the following stories describe inferring. Some stories do not. You must read each story carefully and then decide whether or not the person inferred.
>
> If the story describes inferring, blacken in the space for "Yes" on your answer sheet; if the story does not, blacken in the space for "No."
>
> 1. Sandy observed many acorns underneath a tall tree. She knew that acorns fall from oak trees. Sandy concluded that the tall tree was an oak.
> 2. Don looked carefully at a slice of bread and saw

something green growing there. Don knew that bread mold was green.

3. Sam went to visit his uncle on the farm. He looked in the barn to see if his uncle was there, but he did not see his uncle. Sam did not see the cows either.

4. Joe baked a cake. The cake did not rise. Joe knew that baking powder makes cakes rise. He concluded that he had left the baking powder out of his cake.

Items to measure the ability to discriminate the defining attributes of *inferring:*

For the following questions, blacken in the letter of the correct answer on your answer sheet.

Which of the following tells about someone *relating a scientific observation to something which is known?*

a . Tom looked up information about African wildlife and gave a report on lions.

b. Mary drew pictures of three different types of clouds in the sky.

c. Bill saw some blue speckled eggs in a nest. He knew that robins lay blue speckled eggs.

d. Pam heard a noise in the dark room. She thought, "It must be a monster."

Which of the following tells about someone *drawing a conclusion about what was observed?*

a. Mike heard a noise. He thought, "There must be a squirrel walking on the roof."

b. Mary saw a duck sitting on a nest. She knew that ducks lay eggs. She observed that the nest was made of straw.

c. Tim ate five hamburgers and later got very sick. He had to go to the hospital.

d. Sally knew that birds leave tracks when they walk in the mud. She saw some tracks near the pond when she was fishing.

Items to measure the ability to evaluate examples and nonexamples of *inferring* in terms of defining attributes:

Look carefully at Cartoon A and Cartoon B.

Which of the following tells what is happening in Cartoon A but not in Cartoon B?

a. The girl in Cartoon A is *relating a scientific observation to something which is known,* but the girl in Cartoon B is not.

b. The girl is *making a scientific observation* in Cartoon A but not in B.

c. The girl is *making a prediction* in Cartoon A but not in B.

d. The girl in Cartoon A is *drawing a conclusion about what was observed,* but the girl in Cartoon B is not.

Look carefully at each of the following four cartoons.

Cartoon 1 is different from all the other cartoons in a certain way. How is it different?

a. Only Cartoon 1 shows someone *making a prediction.*

b. Only Cartoon 1 shows someone *relating a scientific observation to something which is known.*

c. Only Cartoon 1 shows someone *making a guess about something which is not known.*

d. Only Cartoon 1 shows someone *drawing a conclusion about what was observed.*

Item to measure knowledge of the definition of *inferring:*

Which of the following is the best definition of inferring?

a. Using one or more of the senses to examine things carefully and to draw a conclusion.

b. Relating a scientific observation to something which is known, and drawing a conclusion about what was observed.

c. Drawing a conclusion about what will happen without making a scientific observation.

d. Relating a scientific fact to something which is observed, and predicting the scientific outcome.

Reliability of the Tests

In the experiments 1–5 and 6–10, the PC lessons were used in the experimental schools only, but the corresponding tests were administered in both the experimental and control schools. The Hoyt reliability coefficients and standard errors of measurement of the PC tests for the 10 experiments are given in Table 5.2. In the second year, only two PC lessons, those for *observing scientifically* and *controlling variables,* were used in experiments 11 and 13. Table 5.2 also presents the technical character-

TABLE 5.2   Hoyt Reliability Coefficients and Standard Errors of Measurement for Students of the Experimental and Control Schools: Process-Concept Tests

Experiment	E1	C1	E2	C2
1: Classifying (18 items)				
Hoyt	.74	.75	.59	.69
SEM	1.48	1.56	1.55	1.52
2: Inferring (15 items)				
Hoyt	.60	.46	.51	.49
SEM	1.57	1.63	1.54	1.59
3: Predicting (15 items)				
Hoyt	.64	.17	.60	.18
SEM	1.50	1.69	1.53	1.60
4: Using numbers (15 items)				
Hoyt	.68	.56	.62	.39
SEM	1.47	1.70	1.50	1.65
5: Measuring (15 items)				
Hoyt	.79	.38	.64	.42
SEM	1.57	1.71	1.38	1.55
6: Observing (18 items)				
Hoyt	.78	.60	.59	.71
SEM	1.66	1.66	1.55	1.65
7: Inferring (15 items)				
Hoyt	.54	.45	.70	.33
SEM	1.65	1.70	1.52	1.68
8: Using space–time relationships (18 items)				
Hoyt	.67	.58	.76	.76
SEM	1.68	1.73	1.51	1.66
9: Controlling variables (21 items)				
Hoyt	.70	.70	.77	.66
SEM	2.01	2.03	1.87	2.02
10: Communicating (15 items)				
Hoyt	.72	.53	.66	.68
SEM	1.42	1.69	1.33	1.63
11: Observing (18 items)				
Hoyt	.58	.57	.85	.46
SEM	1.38	1.44	1.50	1.59
13: Controlling variables (21 items)				
Hoyt	.82	.48	.86	.52
SEM	1.81	2.13	1.74	2.07

istics of these two tests when used with Grade 5 students in experiments 11 and 13.

Inspection of Table 5.2 reveals that in E1 and E2 the coefficients ranged from .51 to .86, and in C1 and C2 from .17 to .76; however, only five were lower than .40 in C1 and C2. In 18 of 24 comparisons, the reliability coefficients were higher in an experimental school than in its paired control school. Five tests had coefficients above .50 for all four schools, namely, those used in experiments 1, 6, 8, 9, and 10. The only test with a coefficient less than .40 in more than one school was *predicting* (experiment 3), and the low coefficients were obtained for the two control schools only, .17 and .18 for C1 and C2 , respectively. Recall that the children of C1 and C2 did not receive any concept lessons; therefore, the lower reliability coefficients should be expected.

CONSTRUCTION OF TRANSFER TESTS

In the second year of the study, the design of each experiment 11 and 13 called for a test to measure the students' transfer of understanding the process concept. A 10-item transfer test for observing scientifically (experiment 11) and an 11-item transfer test for controlling variables (experiment 13) were constructed.

Each transfer test was constructed to measure the students' ability to apply understanding of the particular process concept to the scientific phenomena and events that were included in the SAPA lessons. As explained earlier in this chapter, neither the PC lessons nor the PC tests included science content that was also included in the SAPA exercises. Thus, the transfer tests were constructed because the PC tests by design did not contain examples, nonexamples, or other material included in the SAPA exercise, and the SAPA tests by design did not measure the student's understanding of the process as a concept.

Construction of the Tests

As with the PC tests, the first set of items in each transfer test was designed to measure the ability to recognize activities described in stories as examples or nonexamples of the particular process. There were six items of this type in each test. The content analyses of each of the two process concepts resulted in three defining attributes for *observing scientifically* and four for *controlling variables*. The same number of multiple-choice items were included in the transfer tests to measure discrimination of the defining attributes using content from the SAPA lesson. The last item in each test asked the student to identify the definition of the process concept among four choices. Items from the transfer test for *controlling variables* follow for illustrative purposes.

Item to measure recognizing examples and nonexamples of *controlling variables* using phenomena from the SAPA lesson on *controlling variables:*

> Some of the following stories describe *controlling variables.* Some stories do not. You must read each story carefully and then decide whether or not the person controlled variables.
>
> If the story describes *controlling variables,* blacken in the space for "Yes" on your answer sheet; if the story does not, blacken in the space for "No."

> *Story 1*
>
> > Jane tried to find out whether a solid cylinder or a hollow cylinder would roll down an inclined plane faster. She decided that the kind of cylinder (hollow or solid), the weight, length, and diameter of the cylinders, and the starting time and starting point of the cylinders would change the way the experiment came out. Jane manipulated just one variable: whether the cylinders were hollow or solid. She held all other variables constant. She chose the order in which the cylinders reached the bottom of the board as the responding variable.

Item to measure discriminating the defining attributes of *controlling variables:*

> For the following questions, blacken in the correct letter on your answer sheet.
>
> Which of the following tells about someone *manipulating just one variable?*
>
> a. Ted wanted to find out if a hollow cylinder would roll faster than a solid cylinder. He made this list: kind of cylinder (hollow or solid), the weight, length, and diameter of the cylinders, and the starting time and starting point.
> b. Ted decided to look at the order in which the cylinders reached the bottom of the board to see the results of the experiment.

c. Ted kept the following things the same for both cylinders: the weight, the length, and the diameter of the cylinders, and the starting time and starting point.
d. Ted changed only the kind of cylinders used (hollow or solid). He kept all the other things in the experiment exactly the same.

Item to measure identifying the definition of *controlling variables:*

Which of the following is the best definition of *controlling variables?*
a. Deciding which variables could keep the results of an experiment the same, choosing a variable to hold constant, and manipulating all the other variables.
b. Deciding which variables could make a difference in the way an experiment comes out, choosing a responding variable, manipulating just one variable, and holding all other variables constant.
c. Controlling an experiment by deciding which variables to use, manipulating two or more of those variables, holding one of the variables constant, and responding to all the other variables.
d. Deciding which two variables in an experiment to manipulate, which variables to hold constant, and which variables to control.

Reliability of the Tests

Table 5.3 gives the Hoyt reliability coefficients and standard errors of measurement for each of these transfer tests computed for each school. The coefficients obtained in the experimental schools ranged from .51 to .74 and were consistently higher than those in the control schools, which ranged from .24 to .46. Since the E1 and E2 students received the PC lessons on which these tests were based, whereas the students of C1 and C2 did not, the lower coefficients for C1 and C2 were anticipated.

We may conclude this chapter with a few evaluative comments regarding the reliability of the SAPA pretests and posttests, the process-concept tests, and the transfer tests. The reliability of the SAPA posttests used in E1, E2, C1, and C2, the PC tests in E1 and E2, and the transfer tests in E1 and E2 were sufficiently high that comparisons of group means based on these tests could be made with confidence. However, they were sufficiently low so that judgments regarding individual stu-

TABLE 5.3 Hoyt Reliability Coefficients and Standard Errors of Measurement for Students of the Experimental and Control Schools: Transfer Tests

Experiment	E1	C1	E2	C2
11: Observing scientifically (10 items)				
Hoyt	.51	.46	.69	.24
SEM	.91	1.02	1.05	1.25
13: Controlling variables (11 items)				
Hoyt	.74	.26	.63	.34
SEM	1.14	1.52	1.32	1.47

dent's performances, including mastery of a test, must be interpreted with caution.

The reliability coefficients of the SAPA pretests in E1, E2, C1, and C2, the PC tests in C1 and C2, and the transfer tests in C1 and C2 were quite low. We anticipated they would be because the students had not received instruction specifically directed toward enabling them to learn the content that was tested. Although we used all the tests in making group comparisons, we regard those with coefficients below .40 as not completely satisfactory for this purpose, particularly when a level of significance between the means was found to be nonsignificant.

We shall see in Chapters 6 and 7 that the SAPA pretest scores were used in initially placing the students of E1 and E2 for their SAPA instruction in high, middle, or low groups. We point out, however, that an instructional strategy that uses the entering cognitive achievement level of the student in this manner should take into account the possibility of low test reliability and related high measurement error. The pretests used in the present experiments, though adequate for the group comparisons that were made, have severe limitations for measuring reliably what each individual student had or had not achieved before starting each SAPA exercise.

REFERENCES

AAAS Commission on Science Education. *Science — A Process Approach*. Washington, D.C.: American Association for the Advancement of Science/Xerox, 1967.

Bull, K. S., & Klausmeier, H. J. *Lesson on the basic process concept of communicating scientific information intended for use in elementary science with fifth grade students*. Madison: Wisconsin Research and Development Center for Cognitive Learning, 1976(a).

Bull, K. S., & Klausmeier, H. J. *Lesson on the basic process concept of using numbers scientifically intended for use in elementary science with fourth grade students*. Madison: Wisconsin Research and Development Center for Cognitive Learning, 1976(b).

Schilling, J. M., & Klausmeier, H. J. *Lesson on the basic process concept of classifying intended for use in elementary science with fourth grade students*. Madison: Wisconsin Research and Development Center for Cognitive Learning, 1975(a).

Schilling, J. M., & Klausmeier, H. J. *Lesson on the basic process concept of* inferring *intended for use in elementary science with fifth grade students.* Madison: Wisconsin Research and Development Center for Cognitive Learning, 1975(b).

Schilling, J. M., & Klausmeier, H. J. *Lesson on the basic process concept of* inferring *intended for use in elementary science with fourth grade students.* Madison: Wisconsin Research and Development Center for Cognitive Learning, 1975(c).

Schilling, J. M., & Klausmeier, H. J. *Lesson on the basic process concept of* observing *scientifically intended for use with fifth grade students.* Madison: Wisconsin Research and Development Center for Cognitive Learning, 1975(d).

Schilling, J. M., & Klausmeier, H. J. *Lesson on the basic process concept of* controlling variables *intended for use in elementary science with fifth grade students.* Madison: Wisconsin Research and Development Center for Cognitive Learning, 1976.

Sipple, T. S., Katz, S. E., & Klausmeier, H. J. *Lesson on the basic process concept of* using space–time relationships *intended for use with fifth grade students.* Madison: Wisconsin Research and Development Center for Cognitive Learning, 1975.

Swanson, J. E., Schilling, J. M., & Klausmeier, H. J. *Lesson on the basic process concept of* measuring *scientifically intended for use in elementary science with fourth grade students.* Madison: Wisconsin Research and Development Center for Cognitive Learning, 1975.

Swanson, J. E., & Klausmeier, H. J. *Lesson on the basic process concept of* predicting *intended for use in elementary science with fourth grade students.* Madison: Wisconsin Research and Development Center for Cognitive Learning, 1975.

6

Experiments 1-10

Ten experiments were conducted during the first year of the project. Experiments 1-5 were conducted with Grade 4 children and experiments 6-10 with Grade 5 children. Experiments 1-3 and 6-8 were carried out during the first semester of the year and the other four during the second semester.

During the preparatory year before carrying out these experiments, SAPA tests were constructed and tried out in the two experimental schools (E1 and E2) and six process-concept (PC) lessons and the related PC tests were prepared, as has been described in Chapter 5. In the spring of the preparatory year, an experiment (Klausmeier, DiLuzio, & Brumet, 1976) was conducted in Grades 4 and 5 of E1 and E2 to ascertain the effectiveness of the PC lesson that had been prepared by project personnel (Schilling & Klausmeier, 1975) to teach the process concept *observing scientifically*. One sample of students in E1 and E2 received the lesson and the related test; the other sample received only the test. The teachers of both Grades 4 and 5 read the lesson and the test items to the children, and the children also read silently, following their teacher's reading.

Scores on the vocabulary and comprehension tests of the Gates–Mc-Ginitie Reading Test (1970) were combined and used as convariates in the analysis of covariance performed on the students' scores on the PC test. The means of the E1 and E2 students who received the PC lesson were significantly higher than of those not receiving it.

Teachers were given a six-item questionnaire to secure their reactions to the PC lesson and the test. All of the participating teachers felt the lesson met its objective of helping the students understand the concept, *observing scientifically.* However, one teacher indicated that it was too long, and another teacher felt that some of the vocabulary was too difficult.

The students completed a four-item questionnaire. On the interest item, 58–65% of the Grade 4 or the Grade 5 students of E1 or of E2 checked the "very interesting" category, and from 0–7% checked "not at all interesting." Thirteen and 30 percent of the Grade 4 students of E1 and E2, respectively, indicated that they did not know exactly what to do, based on the written directions within the lesson. Some Grade 4 students indicated that the lesson was hard to read, even though the teacher read it aloud. The Grade 5 students indicated no difficulty in following the directions or reading the lesson.

Based on these reactions of the teachers and the students, the directions to the students included in the PC lesson and the narrative were modified in an attempt to eliminate the problems cited by the teachers and the students. The decision was made to read the lessons and also the tests to the Grade 4 students when conducting the experiments but not to read them to the students of Grade 5.

EXPERIMENTS 1-5

Purposes

One purpose of each experiment was to ascertain the effects of using each PC lesson on the student's understanding of the process concept. Another was to ascertain the effects of the differentiated SAPA instruction on students' achievement of the SAPA objectives when the amount of time for the SAPA instruction was held constant in each paired set of experimental and control schools. Related to the second purpose, the experimental design did not allow for separating out the effects of the use of a PC lesson and of the differentiated SAPA instruction on the students' achievement of the SAPA objectives since all the students of E1 and E2 received the PC lessons, whereas the students of C1 and C2 did not. However, the PC tests were not constructed to measure SAPA information, and the SAPA tests did not measure non-SAPA information. As we shall see later, significant differences were found in some experiments related to the PC lessons, but not the SAPA exercises, whereas in other experiments, the opposite condition was found.

One secondary purpose was to ascertain whether or not aspects of CLD theory that had been applied successfully in developing lessons to help students learn other categories of concepts during short time intervals could be applied to developing lessons to help the present students learn the process concepts of science during extended time intervals. Another secondary purpose was to identify whether or not applications of the design of instructional programming for the individual student could be made successfully to science instruction as they had been to mathematics and reading instruction. Instruction in mathematics and reading does not require large numbers of students to use the same instructional space, equipment, and supplies; however, the teaching of science does. The instructional design takes into account interindividual differences and intraindividual variability in cognitive development as indicated in CLD principles of cognitive development; thus, the compatability of CLD theory with this aspect of the SAPA science instruction could be inferred from the results of the experiments.

Participating Students

The number of Grade 4 students participating in experiments 1–5 in each paired set of schools was as follows: E1 58 and C1 47, E2 59 and C2 51. These included all the students enrolled in the schools except those with serious handicapping conditions who were judged by their teachers to be incapable of learning the science processes and by those who were absent for one or more tests (SAPA, PC, attitude inventory) during the year.

The preceding numbers of E1, C1, E2, and C2 students include only those who took the SAPA pretest and posttest used in each experiment, the PC test used in each experiment, and the attitude inventory that was administered on three occasions during the year. The decision was made to analyze the SAPA, PC, and inventory scores of only the students who took all three sets of tests so that the results pertaining to all three categories of tests would be based on the performances of the same students in all five experiments. Thus, possible differences between the SAPA results and PC results in any experiment and possible differences in the results from one experiment to another would be due to the experimental treatments, not to different students taking the tests.

A considerble number of students who took the SAPA pretest and posttest in all five experiments did not take one or more of the PC tests because of the following conditions. The experimental design called for the students of each of the four schools not to start the first exercise of a set of SAPA exercises until after the PC lesson had been taught in the experimental schools and the PC test had been administered in each of the four schools. Furthermore, the experimentation was designed so as not to interfere in any way with the students' achievement of the objectives of the SAPA exercises or of the objectives in any other curricular area. Therefore, each set of SAPA exercises had to be started on a day scheduled well in advance of the actual start. If a student was absent from school or out of the classroom for any reason when the PC test was administered, the tendency was not to have the student miss the SAPA exercise, or any other lesson or school activity, in order to make up the PC test.

The means of the SAPA semester posttests of the students of each school who did not take all the PC tests or the science inventory during the year and who therefore were tentatively not included in the study were compared with the means of the students who took all the tests and were included. No differences between the means were found to be statistically significant. Therefore, only the students who took all the tests were included in all data analyses of experiments 1–5. As noted earlier, this assured that any differences obtained were due to the experimental treatments, not to differences in the particular students or the different numbers of students who took the particular categories of tests.

Separate analyses were not run for the boys and the girls in any experiment. Systematic sex differences in attaining concepts had not been found in the longitudinal descriptive study at any grade level, 1–12 (Klausmeier, Allen, Sipple, & White, 1976; Klausmeier, Sipple, & Allen, 1974).

Materials

The students studied eight SAPA lessons during the first semester of the school year and nine during the second semester, as shown in Table 6.1. A single SAPA exercise is defined as a set of activities involving a process of science and particular scientific phenomena or events. The usual SAPA exercise was started and completed in five instructional sessions of 25–30 minutes each. The 17 SAPA exercises required a total of 85–90 instructional sessions during the school year.

Three of the 17 SAPA exercises were not used in the experiments because they were single exercises, each dealing with a different science process. PC lessons were not developed for these single SAPA exercises because of the large amount of time required to teach a PC lesson and

TABLE 6.1   Titles and Sequence of SAPA Exercises, Experiments 1-5, Grade 4

Experiment	SAPA exercise title[a]	SAPA exercise classification
	Rate of change of position	Using space-time 14[b]
1	The color wheel-an order arrangement	Classifying 8
1	Separating materials from mixtures	Classifying 9
2	Observations and inferences	Inferring 3
2	Tracks and traces	Inferring 4
2	The displacement of water by air	Inferring 5
3	Surveying opinion	Predicting 2
3	Describing the motion of a bouncing ball	Predicting 3
4	Dividing to find rates and means	Using numbers 10
4	Metersticks, money & decimals	Using numbers 11
5	Temperature & thermometers	Measuring 11
5	Measuring volumes	Measuring 12
5	Describing the motion of a revolving phonograph record	Measuring 13
5	Measuring drop by drop	Measuring 14
5	Measuring evaporation of water	Measuring 15
	Observing animal responses to stimuli	Observing 15[b]
	Using maps	Communicating 10[b]

[a] A SAPA exercise extends for several class sessions of 25-30 minutes each.
[b] Single exercises not used in experiments.

to administer the accompanying PC test. As is shown in Table 6.1, each of the five sets of SAPA exercises included in the five experiments had two or more exercises. The numbers of SAPA exercises in the experiments were as follows: Experiment 1, *classifying,* two exercises; experiment 2, *inferring,* three exercises; experiment 3, *predicting,* two exercises; experiment 4, *using numbers,* two exercises; and experiment 5, *measuring,* five exercises.

All students in the four schools studied the five sets of exercises in the same sequence, but in C1 the exercises within each set were not taken by the students in the same sequence. (This does not violate the publisher's recommendations.) As we shall see later in this chapter, the teachers of C1 employed a "round robin" strategy in teaching the science exercises.

The same SAPA recommended materials and supplies were used in E1, E2, C1, and C2. Also, local materials were gathered by the teachers. For the classifying exercise dealing with separating materials from mixtures, marbles of different sizes and sieves with bottoms made of mesh of different sizes were supplied in the publishers's kit. Other materials recommended for the activities of this exercise but not in the publisher's kit, such as pebbles and coarse sand, were brought into the schools by either the teachers or the science coordinator. The SAPA program did not include any textbook or workbook to be read by the students. However, supplementary textbooks located in the instructional materials center of the schools were made available to the students in E1 and E2. These texts included materials judged to be appropriate for all the students, including those who were judged to master the SAPA content quickly and those who needed easy-to-read materials.

In each experiment a duplicated, illustrated PC lesson was used in E1 and E2. This lesson was prepared by the project staff to help the students understand the particular process concept, for example, *classifying, inferring,* etc. It was intended to serve as an advance organizer and, therefore, preceded the instruction on the first SAPA exercise dealing with the particular concept. The numbers of pages per PC lesson were as follows: *classifying* 61, *inferring* 50, *predicting* 52, *using numbers* 63, and *measuring* 63.

Patterns of and Time Spent on Instruction and Testing

In all four schools the students took the same pretest of 70 items at the beginning of the first semester and another pretest of 70 items at the beginning of the second semester. The items were constructed to measure the students' achievement of each of the three sets of SAPA exercises used in experiments 1-3 during the first semester of the school year and of the two sets of SAPA exercises in experiments 4 and 5 of the second semester. Based on the results of the pretest, the students in E1 and E2 were organized into three groups for instruction at the beginning of each set of SAPA exercises: the highest achieving one-third of the students, the middle achieving one-third, and the lowest achieving one-third. The teachers in C1 and C2 did not receive the pretest scores of their students. Their students were placed in heterogeneous groups at the beginning of the school year for their science instruction and remained in the same heterogeneous groups throughout the school year.

Before starting the first SAPA exercise of the set in each experiment, the teachers of E1 and E2 used the appropriate PC lesson. They read the lesson to the students as a group, and the students followed their teacher's oral reading. The students not only read the lesson and studied the visual illustrations, they also worked on the activities included within the lesson. As well as reading aloud, the teachers provided explanations and gave assistance to individual students in carrying out the activities as time was available.

Instruction with the PC lesson in each experiment was carried out during the same days of the semester in E1 and E2. After the PC instruction was completed and before instruction on the SAPA exercise began, the students of E1 and E2 and also of C1 and C2 were administered the PC test. The PC lessons required 4–7 instructional sessions of 20–35 minutes. The PC test required about 30 minutes.

The students of E1 and E2, upon completing each separate SAPA exercise, were administered a 10-item test on the exercise. Time was not available, however, for the teachers to use the test results in carrying out further instruction for any of the students, regardless of their scores on the test. The students of C1 and C2 were not tested at the end of the individual SAPA lessons.

At the end of experiment 3, which occurred toward the end of the first semester of the school year, the students of E1, C1, E2, and C2 received the same 70-item SAPA posttest on the exercises of experiments 1, 2, and 3. At the end of experiment 5, which occurred toward the end of the second semester, they received the same 70-item SAPA posttest on the exercises of experiments 4 and 5. These posttest scores were analyzed for each of the five sets of SAPA exercises used in the experiments.

The variation of the teaching arrangements in the paired sets of schools may now be considered. There were three teachers who taught the children science in each E1 and C1 and two in each E2 and C2. In E1, each teacher taught all the SAPA exercises of a given set to a high, middle, or low group of children. The three teachers agreed as to who would teach the high, middle, and low groups. They changed groups with each new set of exercises.

In C1, each teacher taught the same exercise of a given set to all three heterogeneous groups of children by a method called "round robin." Using this method, one teacher taught all three groups the *Inferring* 1 Exercise, another taught all three groups the *Inferring* 2 Exercise, and the third taught all three groups the *Inferring* 3 Exercise. The C1 teachers agreed as to which excercises of the various sets each would teach, so that the number of exercises taught was equal for the semester, regardless of how many exercises were in a set.

In E2 and C2, where two teachers taught the science, one teacher taught one of the three groups all the SAPA exercises of a given set, while the other taught all the exercises to two groups. They shifted both the number of groups and the level—high, middle, and low—for the next set of exercises. In all four schools, the teachers functioned as members of teaching teams in all curricular areas, including science. The allocation of the exercises and groups of children appeared to proceed very smoothly.

Much of the instruction in C1 and C2 was directed toward the heterogeneous class as a group although each teacher gave attention as time permitted to individual students. Furthermore, the teachers of C1 and C2 continued to follow the suggestions in the curriculum manual *Science: A Process Approach: Commentary for Teachers* (AAAS, 1968), as they had before starting Experiment 1. This manual outlines the SAPA curriculum; there are no texts or workbook for the students. Each of the seven parts of the curriculum package, also for use by the teacher, has the following sections for each set of exercises dealing with a particular process at a given point in the total sequence, for example, *Observing* 3 or *Classifying* 8: objectives, sequence, rationale, vocabulary, materials, instructional procedure, generalizing experience, appraisal, and competency measure. The Materials section lists all the equipment that is necessary for teaching each exercise. The Instructional Procedure is divided into an Introduction and Activities. Carrying out the Introduction as recommended should arouse interest and get the children involved. Completing the recommended activities in the recommended sequence using the materials and teaching procedures as outlined should enable the children to achieve the objectives. Alternative and optional activities are provided for some exercises. Not all the activities need be completed if the children appear to have attained the objectives. The Generalizing Experience is intended to enable the children to relate their newly acquired competency to a new situation in a different context. The Appraisal section provides a planned class activity to help the teacher assess whether or not the children have achieved the objectives.

The C1 and C2 teachers has used the *Commentary for Teachers* and also the other parts of the curriculum package for a number of years. In teaching their heterogeneous class-size group in experiments 1–5, they used these materials as they had before experiment 1. This was in accordance with the design of the experiments, namely, the control schools were to continue to teach the SAPA science as they had before the start of the experiments.

The E1 and E2 teachers also continued to use the *Commentary for Teachers* and the other teachers' materials; but they departed from many suggestions, particularly the whole-class introduction and other whole-class activities. They taught classes that were formed on the basis of pre-test scores. They organized these classes into small groups and pairs for many activities, in accordance with the design of instructional programming for the individual student. In general, the E1 and E2 teachers paced the instruction and used materials and methods in accordance with their perceptions of what would be best for the individual student. They had not done this before the start of the experiments; and in the beginning, this tended to reduce the amount of class time that the students actually spent on SAPA learning activities in some of the experimental teachers' classes.

In E1 and E2, the paper-and-pencil tests used in the experiments replaced the appraisal and competency measure provided in the SAPA curriculum package. The C1 and C2 teachers also did not carry out these two parts of the publishers' suggestions systematically.

The teachers of the four schools agreed as to the number of minutes to give to instruction of each SAPA exercise. The amount of time varied from one exercise to another, depending on the difficulty of the exercise. Each teacher was encouraged to give fewer minutes to an exercise if the judgment was that the students had achieved the content or if other activities were of higher priority, including continuation of a prior SAPA exercise or starting a new one. They were encouraged to give more than the allocated minutes if the students seemed not to have mastered the content or if difficulties arose with procuring equipment or materials according to schedule. In some experiments, an instructional session of approximately 30 minutes was taken from an exercise by one or more teachers; in other cases it was added.

In all four schools, scheduling the PC test administration before starting the first SAPA lesson dealing with the same science process, scheduling the science equipment and materials, school vacation days, and special school events were the main factors resulting in shortening or lengthening a SAPA exercise by as much as one period of instruction. Shifting the amount of time for the science instruction on a daily basis because of a conflict with other classes or school activities resulted in increasing or decreasing the amount of time for a SAPA instructional session by as much as 10 minutes.

Many of the same conditions that affected the length of the daily SAPA instruction and the total number of instructional sessions for a SAPA lesson in E1, E2, C1, or C2 also affected the amount of time given to the PC lessons in E1 and E2.

The mean number of minutes spent on the combined SAPA teaching and testing in E1 and E2, and the mean number of minutes spent in SAPA teaching only in C1 and C2 are given in the top part of Appendix Table A6.1. About 15 minutes was spent in testing at the end of each SAPA exercise in E1 and E2.

There was more variation in the amount of time for SAPA exercises in C2 than in any other school, and both C1 and C2 varied more from one exercise to another than did E1 and E2. The large variations in C1 and C2 generally occurred between the exercises of the same set of SAPA exercises dealing with a particular process; the average number of minutes for each total set of SAPA exercises did not vary greatly.

The teachers of E1 and E2 spent slightly more time on SAPA teaching than did the C1 and C2 teachers in experiments 1-3; about the same amount in experiments 4 and 5. The larger amount of time spent in E1 and E2 is not regarded as affecting the results in favor of the experimental students since the E1 and E2 teachers also had to do the additional testing (about 15 minutes for each exercise) and also used more class time, as inferred from the teacher logs, in noninstructional classroom management activities associated with the greater differentiation of instruction.

The amount of time given to the PC lessons in E1 and E2 is given in the lower part of Appendix Table A6.1. In experiments 2 and 3, respectively, E2 gave 30 minutes and 20 minutes less than E1.

Results

SAPA ACHIEVEMENTS

The results of tests of significance performed on the SAPA adjusted means for the Grade 4 students of E1 and C1 and of E2 and C2 for each experiment 1-5 are given in Appendix Table A 6.2. Analysis of covariance was used with the student's SAPA pretest score the covariate. The adjusted SAPA means are presented in Appendix Table A6.3. The difference between the *adjusted means* of the E1 and the C1 students was significant only in experiment 4; whereas the difference between the means for the E2 and the C2 students was significant in experiments 3, 4, and 5. In all cases the means of the experimental students were higher than the means of the control students. The results of Chi-square tests of significance for the frequencies of students who mastered the tests in E1-C1 and E2-C2 are given in Appendix Table A6.4; these results are now indicated.

To help the reader relate the results of the various data analyses, Table 6.2 gives the *unadjusted means* of the SAPA pretests and posttests for each experiment, the mean percentage correct for each SAPA test, and the percentage of students who mastered the test. The unadjusted means are given in this table because they served as the basis for determining the percentage correct. The percentage of students who mastered a test was also based on unadjusted scores. The asterisk in Table 6.2 indicates a difference between the *adjusted* means (see Table A6.2) that was statistically significant and also of a difference between the percentage of mastery by the E1-C1 and the E2-C2 students that was significant (see Table A6.4).

A significantly higher percentage of the students of E1 than of C1 demonstrated mastery of the SAPA posttests in experiments 1, 2, 3, and

TABLE 6.2 SAPA Pretest and Posttest Means, Standard Deviations, Mean Percentages Correct, and Percentages of Students Achieving Mastery, Experiments 1–5

	E1		C1		E2		C2	
	Pre	Post	Pre	Post	Pre	Post	Pre	Post
Experiment 1: Classifying (20 items)								
Mean	10.31	13.60	8.31	12.02	10.03	13.27	8.98	12.43
SD	2.66	3.51	2.17	3.04	2.75	2.55	1.86	2.24
Mean percentage correct	52	68	42	60	50	66	45	62
Percentage ach. mastery	0	29*	0	9	2	20*	0	6
Experiment 2: Inferring (30 items)								
Mean	16.17	21.24	12.06	18.11	14.14	21.32	14.78	20.73
SD	4.28	5.04	3.30	4.42	3.81	4.98	3.68	3.88
Mean percentage correct	54	71	40	60	47	71	49	69
Percentage ach. mastery	3	44*	0	17	0	37	0	24
Experiment 3: Predicting (20 items)								
Mean	11.93	16.00	9.33	13.42	11.00	16.53*	11.29	15.10
SD	3.83	3.45	3.11	3.45	3.35	3.07	2.73	2.66
Mean percentage correct	60	80	47	67	55	83	56	76
Percentage ach. mastery	21	69*	6	24	8	75*	4	49
Experiment 4: Using Numbers (20 items)								
Mean	8.71	12.05*	7.75	10.09	7.66	11.64*	8.63	11.06
SD	2.85	3.76	3.00	3.34	2.65	3.53	2.79	3.25
Mean percentage correct	44	60	39	50	38	58	43	55
Percentage ach. mastery	2	21	2	9	0	15	2	6
Experiment 5: Measuring (50 items)								
Mean	26.55	35.26	20.92	29.36	23.42	35.85*	23.84	32.12
SD	7.56	8.29	6.48	8.57	5.93	7.73	5.11	7.02
Mean percentage correct	53	71	42	58	47	72	48	64
Percentage ach. mastery	5	34*	2	17	0	36*	0	16

* $p < .05$

5. Similarly, a higher percentage of those of E2 than C2 did in experiments 1, 3, and 5. In every experiment the obtained percentages of mastery were higher in E1 than in C1 and in E2 than in C2.

The differences *between the SAPA exercises* in the percentages of students of any school achieving mastery were also large. For example, only 21% of the E1 students achieved mastery of *using numbers;* whereas 69% mastered *predicting.* The comparable percentages for the students of E2 were 15 for *using numbers* and 75 for *predicting;* for C1 they were 9 and 24 and for C2, 6 and 49.

We may now recapitulate the results of the two primary data analyses performed on the SAPA posttest data. All significant differences involving the means favored the experimental schools, and all significant differences involving percentages of mastery favored the experimental schools. In general, the students of E2, in comparison with those of C2, did not achieve mastery in more experiments than did those of E1 in comparison with C1; however, they did have higher adjusted means in more experiments. It is well to note also that the means for the students of both E1 and E2 were not significantly higher than those of C1 and C2 for the first two experiments. This lack of significance was attributed primarily to getting the new approach to the SAPA instruction started in E1 and E2, and also to a possible overload of information to the E1 and E2 students who received the PC lessons, whereas the C1 and C2 students did not. However, since all the significant differences favored the E1 and the E2 groups, we may infer the methods and materials that were used to adapt the SAPA instruction to the entering achievement levels of the students were equally or more effective in all experiments than were the methods that were continued in the control schools.

UNDERSTANDING THE PROCESS CONCEPTS

Appendix Table A6.5 presents a summary of the tests of significance for the PC tests for experiments 1-5. Analysis of variance was performed on the PC test scores. The differences between the means of E1 and C1 were significant ($p < .05$) in experiments 1-4 but not in experiment 5. The differences between E2 and C2 were significant in experiments 2, 4, and 5, but not in 1 and 3. The difference between E2 and C2 in experiment 3 was significant at the .15 level. All differences favored the experimental schools, and seven of them were at the .002 level of significance or beyond.

Appendix Table A6.6 gives the results of the tests of significance performed on the percentages of students of E1–C1 and E2–C2 who mastered the PC lessons in each of the five experiments. The difference in the frequency of mastery was statistically significant in experiments 1, 2,

3, and 4 favoring the students of E1 over C1, and in experiments 2, 4, and 5 favoring the students of E2 over C2.

The tabular summary of the preceding results (Table 6.3) gives the means, standard deviations, mean percentages correct, and the percentages of the Grade 4 students of experiments 1-5 attaining the mastery criterion. The asterisk indicates significant differences ($p < .05$). As indicated both by the significant differences in the means and in the percentages of mastery, we may conclude that the PC lessons helped the

TABLE 6.3 Process-Concept Means, Standard Deviations, Mean Percentages Correct, and Percentages of Students Achieving Mastery, Experiments 1-5

	E1	C1	E2	C2
Experiment 1:				
Classifying (18 items)				
Mean	13.98*	12.04	13.93	13.80
SD	3.01	3.20	2.50	2.79
Mean percentage correct	78	67	77	77
Percentage ach. mastery	64*	34	63	67
Experiment 2:				
Inferring (15 items)				
Mean	9.62*	8.00	9.69*	8.27
SD	2.57	2.29	2.27	2.28
Mean percentage correct	64	53	65	55
Percentage ach. mastery	24*	6	22*	2
Experiment 3:				
Predicting (15 items)				
Mean	9.38*	7.39	9.42	8.80
SD	2.60	1.92	2.50	1.82
Mean percentage correct	63	49	63	59
Percentage ach. mastery	22*	0	17	6
Experiment 4:				
Using numbers (15 items)				
Mean	10.69*	8.32	10.75*	8.75
SD	2.70	2.65	2.50	2.18
Mean percentage correct	71	55	72	58
Percentage ach. mastery	45*	11	44*	12
Experiment 5:				
Measuring (15 items)				
Mean	9.60	9.77	12.00*	10.51
SD	3.50	2.25	2.40	2.10
Mean percentage correct	64	65	80	70
Percentage ach. mastery	36	19	64*	35

* $p < .05$

students understand the process concepts of science. However, when we compare the pattern of the earlier significant differences involving the SAPA achievments and the present ones for the PC achievements, we do not find the significantly higher PC achievement to be associated with significantly higher SAPA achievement. Thus, although the E1 and the E2 students generally acquired a better understanding of the process concepts, this understanding did not appear to transfer systematically to achieving the SAPA objectives. We shall now see whether similar results were obtained for the older Grade 5 students using the different content allocated to Grade 5.

EXPERIMENTS 6-10

Purposes

The purposes of experiments 6-10 were the same as those given earlier for experiments 1-5. However, the participating students were enrolled in Grade 5 rather than in Grade 4, the science processes of the SAPA exercises and the process concepts of the PC lessons were for Grade 5 rather than for Grade 4, and no teachers of the Grade 5 students were also teachers of the students of Grade 4.

Participating Students

The number of Grade 5 students in each set of paired schools participating in the experiments was as follows: Experiments 6, 7, 8—E1 82 and C1 62; experiments 9 and 10—E1 60 and C1 46; experiments 6 through 10—E2 71 and C2 56. Notice that the numbers of students in E1 and C1 were larger in experiments 6, 7, and 8 than in experiments 9 and 10. This occurred because significant differences were found for experiments 6, 7, and 8 between the SAPA posttest means of the students of E1 and of C1, separately, who took all the SAPA and PC tests and the science inventory during the year and those who missed one or more PC tests or one or more science inventory administrations during the year. When this significant difference was found, all the students of both E1 and C1 who took the SAPA posttests of experiments 6, 7, and 8 were included in the comparison groups. Significant differences were not found for the same groups of E1 students and C1 students in experiments 9 and 10 nor for the two groups of E2 and the two groups of C2 students for any experiment, 6-10. Therefore, in all experiments involving Grade 5 students of all four schools, except in schools E1 and C1 in experiments 6, 7, and 8, the students who took all the tests during the year served as the basic comparison groups.

Recall that the Grade 4 comparison groups also included only the students who took all the tests. The rationale for including only the students who took all the tests was to assure that possible differences in an experiment between PC and SAPA results and also between experiments could not have occurred because of differences in the students who participated.

Materials

Five sets of SAPA exercises involving a total of 12 exercises were used. Three sets were used during the first semester in experiments 6, 7, and 8, and two sets were used during the second semester in experiments 9 and 10. Five single SAPA exercises, each dealing with a separate SAPA process, were not included in the experiments. The PC lessons and tests were not prepared for single lessons because of the large amount of time required to use them in the schools and also to administer the related tests. The number of SAPA exercises, their titles, and the experiments in which they were used are given in Table 6.4. The students in all schools

TABLE 6.4   Titles and Sequence of SAPA Exercises, Experiments 6-10, Grade 5

Experiment	SAPA exercise title	SAPA exercise classification
	Describing and representing forces	Measuring 16[a]
6	Magnetic poles	Observing 16
6	Observing growth from seeds	Observing 17
6	Observing falling objects	Observing 18
7	Loss of water from plants	Inferring 6
7	Inferring connection patterns in electrical circuits	Inferring 7
7	Shape of cut things	Inferring 8
8	2-D representations of 3-D figures	Using space–time 15
8	Relative position and motion	Using space–time 16
9	Rolling cylinders	Controlling variables 1
9	Upward movement of liquids	Controlling variables 2
	Guinea pigs in a maze	Interpreting data 1[a]
	Observations and hypotheses	Formulating hypotheses[a]
	Suffocating candle	Predicting 4[a]
	Using punch cards	Classifying 10[a]
10	Describing location	Communicating 11
10	Reporting an investigation in writing	Communicating 12

[a] Single exercises not included in experiments.

took the sets of exercises in the same sequence, but in E1 and C1, the exercises within the sets were not taken by the students in the same sequence because of the instructional technique used by the teachers. The recommended SAPA materials and local materials gathered by the teachers were used.

The materials included in the publisher's kit for the SAPA curriculum were used in both the experimental and the comparison schools. For example, prisms, cardboard shapes, and wire shapes were supplied for the exercise on 2-dimensional representations of 3-dimensional figures; this exercise involved the process, *using space-time relationships*. Other materials recommended for the activities of this exercise such as modeling clay and transparent cellophane were brought into the schools by either the teachers or the science coordinator.

A PC lesson was used in each experiment in E1 and E2 as an advance organizer in the same manner as in experiments 1–5. The number of pages per PC lesson were as follows: *observing* 47, *inferring* 50, *using space-time relationships* 63, *controlling variables* 66, and *communicating* 63.

Patterns of and Time Spent on Instruction and Testing

In E1 and E2, the same pattern of pretesting at the beginning of each semester, grouping the students, using the PC lesson, teaching the SAPA exercises, testing after each SAPA exercise, and SAPA posttesting at the end of the semester was followed in experiments 6–10 as described earlier for experiments 1–5. The sequence of testing and instruction was also the same in the control schools.

Different teachers from those of experiments 1–5 taught the science in experiments 6–10. There were three teachers who taught science to the children in each E1, C1, and E2, but only one teacher in C2. In E1 and E2, the students were placed in a high, middle, or low group based on SAPA pretesting done at the beginning of each semester. In C1 and C2, they remained in the same three heterogeneous class groups throughout the school year.

The teachers of both E1 and C1 followed the round robin technique as described earlier in this chapter. This involved each of three teachers teaching one of the three exercises of any SAPA set to all three groups of students. On the other hand, in E2 each of the three teachers started experiment 6 with a high, a middle, or a low entering achievement level group and taught all the exercises of the set of SAPA exercises to the particular group. These three teachers of E2 shifted from one achievement level group to another during the year. In C2, one teacher taught all the lessons to the three heterogeneous class-size groups.

In accordance with the project strategy and plan, the C1 and C2 teachers continued teaching science as individuals or as a team, and they also used the recommended SAPA procedures as they had before the start of experiment 6. Much of their instruction was directed toward the children as classroom groups; however, they tried to meet individual student needs as well as they could. In E1 and E2, the teachers departed from the SAPA suggestions to adapt instruction better to the characteristics of the students, in accordance with instructional programming for the individual student. We note in passing that the design of the experiments did not permit additional instructional time for the teachers to accomplish this; thus, they did not do it as well as they thought they might have.

The teachers in experiments 6-10, as described earlier for experiments 1-5, agreed on the total amount of time to be used for each set of SAPA exercises. As we shall see, the actual amount of time spent varied somewhat from school to school because of unavoidable events that occurred in the usual operation of each school's instructional and other activities and also teacher judgments.

The mean number of minutes spent in SAPA teaching only in C1 and C2, and the mean number of minutes spent both in SAPA teaching and in SAPA testing in E1 and E2 are given in the top part of Appendix Table A6.7. Some differences occurred between the schools of the paired sets in the amount of time spent in teaching individual SAPA exercises and in teaching the total set of SAPA lessons of an experiment.

The differences resulted from one or a combination of the following: scheduling of the school's science laboratory and equipment, conflicts with school activities such as those that occur at Thanksgiving and Christmas, variations between schools in the amount of the daily time of a larger block of time assigned to science instruction, and differences among the teachers regarding the amount of time that they judged should be spent on an exercise. We note that relatively little time was given in E1 and E2 to the last SAPA exercise in experiment 8. This was the last experiment of the first semester. Three PC lessons had been used throughout the semester, and no more time could be found for the SAPA instruction.

The amount of time given to the PC lessons in experiments 6-10 is given in the lower part of Table A6.7. Differences between E1 and E2 of 30, 15, and 20 minutes occurred in experiments 6, 8, and 9, respectively.

These minor differences were due to the same conditions as those mentioned earlier that resulted in differences between schools for the sets of SAPA lessons.

Results

SAPA ACHIEVEMENTS

The results of tests of significance between the SAPA means of E1–C1 and E2–C2 for experiments 6–10 using analysis of covariance, with the SAPA pretest score the covariate, are given in Appendix Table A6.8. The *adjusted means* are reported in Appendix Table A6.9. The results of the Chi-square tests of significance involving the mastery data are given in Appendix Table A6.10. The summary results of these tests of significance are reported in Table 6.5, as well as the SAPA *unadjusted* pretest and posttest means, the standard deviations, the mean percentages correct, and the percentages of the students who achieved mastery.

The adjusted means of the Grade 5 students of E1 were not significantly different from those of C1 in any experiment; whereas the students of E2 achieved significantly higher (.001) than those of C2 in all five experiments. The pretest means for the students of the two paired sets of schools did not differ greatly. The percentage of students who achieved mastery was significantly higher in E1 than in C1 in experiments 6 and 10. The percentage of students of E2 who achieved mastery was significantly higher than that of C2 in all five experiments. The consistency in the superior achievements of the E2 students over the C2 students is noteworthy. The percentage of SAPA posttest mastery in E2 ranged from 32 to 72%, whereas in C2 it ranged from 4 to 39%.

Based on a visual inspection of the adjusted means (Table A6.9), we see that E2 consistently had the highest SAPA posttest mean in each experiment, whereas the means for E1, C1 and C2 did not differ greatly from one another. These results and the fact that the differences between the adjusted SAPA means of E2 and C2 were significant in all five experiments, whereas none of E1 and C1 were, suggests that the teachers of E1 and E2 and the procedures they used may have been a primary factor contributing to the results of the five experiments. It is of interest that the one-teacher arrangement of C2 achieved about the same results as did the three-person team arrangements of both E1 and C1.

Based on the results related to the SAPA mean achievements and the percentages of students who achieved the SAPA mastery criterion, we may infer that the applications of the design of instructional programming for the individual were highly effective in E2, but in E1 they were no more effective than the adaptations to individual differences made under the heterogeneous classroom conditions in C1 and C2.

TABLE 6.5 SAPA Pretest and Posttest Means, Standard Deviations, Mean Percentages Correct, and Percentages of Students Achieving Mastery, Experiments 6-10

	E1		C1		E2		C2	
	Pre	Post	Pre	Post	Pre	Post	Pre	Post
Experiment 6:								
Observing scientifically (30 items)								
Mean	15.90	21.15	15.06	20.24	16.19	23.99*	15.04	21.20
SD	4.54	6.22	3.62	3.81	4.38	4.03	2.95	3.71
Mean percentage correct	53	71	50	68	54	80	50	71
Percentage ach. mastery	6	48*	2	19	8	63*	2	32
Experiment 7:								
Inferring (30 items)								
Mean	13.32	18.96	13.92	18.66	14.57	21.38*	13.67	17.68
SD	3.25	5.11	2.80	4.05	3.08	3.91	3.36	3.58
Mean percentage correct	44	63	46	62	49	71	46	59
Percentage ach. mastery	0	18	0	10	1	32*	0	4
Experiment 8:								
Using space-time relationships (20 items)								
Mean	9.13	11.82	9.47	11.39	9.39	15.70*	9.69	11.04
SD	2.34	3.70	2.34	2.11	3.04	2.91	2.71	3.24
Mean percentage correct	46	59	47	57	47	78	48	55
Percentage ach. mastery	0	20*	0	0	4	61*	0	9
Experiment 9:								
Controlling Variables (20 items)								
Mean	10.17	13.45	10.16	14.17	11.03	15.99*	10.75	13.54
SD	3.41	4.04	3.12	3.06	3.38	3.25	3.62	3.90
Mean percentage correct	51	67	51	71	55	80	54	68
Percentage ach. mastery	5	45	4	35	8	72*	5	39
Experiment 10:								
Communicating (20 items)								
Mean	9.75	12.77	10.16	12.22	10.81	16.00*	9.51	11.82
SD	3.31	3.86	3.07	3.96	3.30	3.28	3.44	3.77
Mean percentage correct	46	61	48	59	51	76	45	56
Percentage ach. mastery	2	28	7	22	10	66*	4	14

* $p < .05$

UNDERSTANDING THE PROCESS CONCEPTS

The tests of significance based on the means of the PC tests used in experiments 6-10 are reported in Appendix Table A6.11. The Chi-square tests of the significance of the differences between the paired sets of frequencies of mastery are found in Appendix Table A6.12. The PC results are based on the following numbers of students: E1 60, C1 46, E2 71, and C2 56. The E2 and C2 students are the same upon which the SAPA analyses for experiments 6-10 were performed. The E1 and C1 students are the same students included in the prior SAPA analyses for experiments 9 and 10, and are part of the larger numbers included in experiments 6-8. Recall that in experiments 6-8, the numbers were larger for the SAPA analyses because in these schools a number of students who took the SAPA pretests and posttests did not take all five PC tests; thus, those students were not included in the PC analyses.

The PC means, standard deviations, mean percentages correct, the percentages achieving mastery, and the indications of significant differences are given in Table 6.6. In experiments 6, 7, and 8, the students of E1 achieved about the same as those of C1; however, they achieved significantly higher in experiments 9 and 10. The PC means for the students of E2 were significantly higher than the means for the students of C2 in all five experiments. In all except experiment 7, the probability level was .001 or beyond.

The pattern of the significant differences in the percentages of students achieving the mastery criterion on the PC tests is similar to that of the PC means. The percentage of students in E1 who achieved mastery was significantly greater than in C1 in experiment 10 only, whereas in experiments 8, 9, and 10, the percentage of E2 students was significantly higher than that of C2.

Study of the teacher logs and post hoc questioning of the teachers gave no indication as to why the students' PC performances in E1 were relatively low in experiments 6, 7, and 8. The most probable factor is how the teachers handled the PC lessons. In experiments 6, 7, and 8, the means of the students of C1 and C2 who did not receive the lessons were about the same as the means of the students of E1. Recall that a similar pattern was found for the adjusted means of the SAPA tests.

We may conclude that the use of the PC lessons achieved the predicted results in E2 in all five experiments and in the last two of the five experiments in E1. Apparently the teachers of E1 were unable to use the PC lessons to secure the desired results in the early experiments. The high PC achievements in E2 were accompanied with parallel high SAPA achievements; however, this did not occur in experiments 9 and 10 in E1. Thus, it is recognized that the PC lessons must be used properly to pro-

TABLE 6.6   Process-Concept Means, Standard Deviations, Mean Percentages Correct, and Percentages of Students Achieving Mastery, Experiments 6–10

	E1	C1	E2	C2
Experiment 6:				
Observing Scientifically				
(18 items)				
Mean	12.52	12.84	14.01*	12.36
SD	3.61	2.70	2.50	3.15
Mean percentage correct	70	71	78	69
Percentage ach. mastery	47	46	61	46
Experiment 7:				
Inferring (15 items)				
Mean	8.20	8.53	9.39*	8.47
SD	2.53	2.36	2.88	2.13
Mean percentage correct	55	57	63	56
Percentage ach. mastery	12	11	18	7
Experiment 8:				
Using space–time relationships				
(18 items)				
Mean	12.47	12.18	13.76*	11.45
SD	3.03	2.77	3.16	3.47
Mean percentage correct	69	68	76	64
Percentage ach. mastery	40	33	63*	32
Experiment 9:				
Controlling variables (21 items)				
Mean	11.93*	10.20	13.79*	10.73
SD	3.76	3.76	4.03	3.55
Mean percentage correct	57	49	66	51
Percentage ach. mastery	12	7	24*	9
Experiment 10:				
Communicating (15 items)				
Mean	11.40*	9.30	12.13*	9.20
SD	2.77	2.55	2.36	2.98
Mean percentage correct	76	62	81	61
Percentage ach. mastery	58*	26	70*	23

* $p < .05$

duce better understanding of the process concepts of science. Similarly, it cannot be inferred from these five experiments, as was also true for the first five presented in this chapter, that understanding of the process concept gained through the use of the PC lessons transfers consistently to higher achievement of the objectives of the SAPA science curriculum. However, in 6 of the 7 comparisons where the SAPA adjusted mean of the students of an experimental school was higher than that of a control school, the PC mean was also signficantly higher.

ATTITUDES TOWARD SCIENCE

The same locally constructed science attitude inventory (SAI) was administered in September, December, and May to all the students participating in experiments 1-10. The items were not related to any one set of SAPA exercises or PC lessons but to the science instruction generally. The test scores of September were used as the covariate in analyzing the test results in December and May. The results of the tests of significance are given in Appendix Table A6.13.

The SAI results for Grade 4 are based on the following numbers of students: E1, 58; C1, 47; E2, 59; and C2, 51. These are the same students who were included in the SAPA and PC analyses for experiments 1-5. The students included in the SAI analyses for experiments 6-10 were also the same as those whose PC data were analyzed. The numbers of these Grade 5 students from each school were as follows: E1, 60; C1, 46; E2, 71; and C2, 56. As may be seen in Table 6.7, the means of the Grade 4 students of E1, C1, E2, and C2 participating in experiments 1-5 were about the same in September. They were higher in December than in September but lower in May than in either December or September. In experiments 1-5, the means of the Grade 4 E1 students were significantly higher than those of C1 in December and May, but those of E2 were not significantly higher than those of C2.

The only difference between the means of the paired groups of Grade 5 students involved in experiments 6-10 occurred in December; the C2 students had the higher mean. (Recall that in C2 the three groups of students were taught science by one teacher.) The SAI means of the students of both E2 and C2 dropped quite sharply from December to May, and in May they were lower than the means of both E1 and C1.

In summary, the attitudes of the Grade 4 and the Grade 5 students at

TABLE 6.7 Science Attitudes Means for Grade 4 and Grade 5: Experiments 1-10

	E1	C1	E2	C2
Grade 4				
September	45.47	44.38	45.36	44.08
December	49.60*	45.65	46.29	47.90
May	48.12*	43.10	45.58	43.67
Grade 5				
September	44.67	42.16	44.30	44.65
December	42.97	44.53	42.89	46.45*
May	43.00	43.29	41.17	40.18

*$p < .05$

the different times of measurement during the school year apparently were influenced by many variables and cannot be accounted for by any specific one. For example, the effects of taking the inventory in the week before the Christmas recess and late in the school year, in May, may have been different in the different schools. In this regard, the more favorable attitudes of the Grade 5 students of C2 in December (mean 46.45 and the highest of the four groups) did not continue into May when they were the least favorable of the four groups (40.18).

CORRELATIONS AMONG MEASURES USED IN EXPERIMENTS 1-10

The Grade 4 students of experiments 1-5 and the Grade 5 students of experiments 6-10 in each E1 and E2 were organized for their SAPA instruction into a high, middle, and low group based on their pretest SAPA scores. This method for grouping was based on the assumption that starting the SAPA instruction for each group at the students' entering achievement level and then adapting instruction appropriately for each group would yield higher mean SAPA achievement. A second assumption was that in each experiment, positive and significant correlations would be found between the SAPA pretest scores and the SAPA pottest scores in both the experimental and comparison schools, but that they might be higher in E1 and E2 than in C1 and C2 unless the posttests were too easy for some of the students, particularly those of E1 and E2. Another assumption was that the SAPA pretest-posttest correlations would be higher than the SAPA pretest-PC correlations in all four schools and that the SAPA pretest-PC correlations would be higher in E1 and E2 than in C1 and C2, since the students of C1 and C2 did not receive PC instruction.

As we saw earlier in Table A6.2, in 4 of 10 comparisons involving experiments 1-5, the adjusted means of the E1 and E2 Grade 4 students were higher than those of the Grade 4 students of C1 and C2, respectively, at or beyond the .02 level. Were the correlations also higher between the SAPA pretests and posttests in E1 and E2 than in C1 and C2 in experiments 1-5? As shown in Table A6.14, 19 of the 20 correlations involving E1, C1, E2, and C2 were significant at or beyond the .05 level. Thus, the SAPA pretest-posttest correlations were about the same for the experimental and comparison schools. We may conclude that the differentiated instruction generally did not lead to lower SAPA pretest -posttest correlations in the experimental schools.

Earlier in Table A6.5 dealing with experiments 1-5 we saw that in

7 of 10 comparisons, the PC means were significantly higher for the students of E1 and E2 than for those of C1 and C2, respectively. Table A6.14 shows that 7 of 20 correlations between the SAPA pretests and PC tests were not significant, 4 for C2, 2 for C1, and 1 for E1. Thus, the SAPA pretest achievements and PC achievements tended to be less closely related in the schools where the students did not receive PC instruction. We may infer that the use of the PC lessons tends to promote PC achievement in accordance with the entering SAPA achievement levels of the Grade 4 students.

Turning now to experiments 6-10, we saw earlier that the SAPA means were not significantly different between E1 and C1 in any experiment, but they were between E2 and C2 in all five experiments (Table A6.8). As indicated in Table A6.14, all the correlations between the SAPA pretests and posttests were statistically significant at or beyond the .01 level, except for E1 in experiment 7 and for C1 in experiment 8. Based on these findings, we may infer that the Grade 5 students continued to achieve the SAPA science in accordance with their entering achievement levels to about the same extent in the experimental and comparison schools.

The differences between the PC means for E1 and C1 were significant in experiments 9 and 10, and for E2 and C2 in all five experiments (Table A6.11). The correlations of the PC scores with the SAPA pretest scores were not significant at or beyond the .05 level for C1 or C2 in experiments 7, 8, and 10, but they were in E1 and E2 in all five experiments. Thus, how well the Grade 5 students had achieved the SAPA content before the start of the experiment was more highly related to their PC achievements when the PC lessons were used than when they were not used.

In summarizing the correlational analyses conducted in experiments 1-10, we find that the differentiated instruction as carried out in E1 and E2 under the experimental conditions, including the equal amount of time for SAPA instruction, did not yield higher SAPA pretest–posttest correlations than did the less differentiated instruction of C1 and C2. On the other hand, receiving the PC lessons in E1 and E2 fostered understanding of the process concepts in accordance with the entering SAPA achievement levels of the students.

DISCUSSION OF EXPERIMENTS 1-10

It may be convenient to deal with experiments 1-5 first, and then experiments 6-10. New information will then be presented based on post hoc analyses of the achievements of the students who were in the highest one-third, the middle one-third, and the lowest one-third, based on the SAPA pretest scores. Observation of Table 6.8 indicates that in experiments 1–5, the students of E1 had a significantly higher SAPA mean than those of C1 in one of the five comparisons and a significantly higher PC mean in four of five comparisons. In the same experiments, the students of E2 had a higher SAPA mean than C2 in all five comparisons and a higher PC mean in three of five comparisons. The differentiated instruction achieved much better results in E2 relatively than in E1, whereas the PC instruction had about equally effective results in E1 and E2. These results are now related to the pattern of teaching in the four schools, to the amount of time spent in SAPA instruction in the four schools, and in PC instruction in E1 and E2, and to the SAPA and PC means of the students of each school.

In each experiment 1–5, more time was spent in E1 in combined SAPA instruction and testing than was spent in C1 in instruction alone; however, in only one experiment was a significant difference between the adjusted SAPA means obtained. More time was used in combined SAPA instruction and testing in E2 than in C2 in four of five experiments and an equal amount in the other. One of the three significant differences occurred when the amount of time was equal. Thus, the fact that better results were achieved in E2 than in E1 appears not to be related to relatively small differences in the amount of time spent in SAPA instruction.

Inspection of Appendix Table A6.3 shows that E2 had the highest SAPA mean of all four schools in every experiment 1–5. Apparently, the E2 teachers were able to differentiate the SAPA instruction more effectively than those of E1. The teacher logs indicate that the E1 teachers made more changes than E2 teachers in their attempts to differentiate the instruction. It is possible that the children of E1 may not have been able to use the time assigned to SAPA science instruction equally effectively as those of E2. (Recall that the E1 students had unusually high SAPA pretest scores and this may have influenced their adjusted post-test means negatively.)

In experiments 1, 4, and 5, the same amount of time was spent on the PC lesson in E1 and E2, namely, 150 minutes; in the other two experiments, slightly more time was spent in E1. However, any difference in the amount of time between E1 and E2 appeared to be unrelated to whether or not the students of E1 and E2 achieved significantly higher than the comparison students of C1 and C2. The PC means for E1 and E2 were very much alike, except in experiment 5 where the means of E1 were much lower than those of E2. The PC means of C1 and C2 were much alike in three experiments; however, in experiment 1, C2 had a very

TABLE 6.8 Summary of Significant Differences between Paired Sets of SAPA and PC Means and Total Minutes of Instruction: Experiments 1–10

Experiment number	School	Minutes	
		SAPA	PC
1	E1	275	150*
	C1	225	—
	E2	320	150
	C2	240	—
2	E1	415	150*
	C1	355	—
	E2	445	120*
	C2	360	—
3	E1	280	120*
	C1	210	—
	E2	310*	100
	C2	225	—
4	E1	300*	150*
	C1	260	—
	E2	300*	150*
	C2	300	—
5	E1	730	150
	C1	630	—
	E2	730*	150*
	C2	630	—
6	E1	50	180
	C1	375	—
	E2	450*	150*
	C2	450	—
7	E1	500	120
	C1	515	—
	E2	480*	120*
	C2	540	—
8	E1	220	120
	C1	180	—
	E2	240*	135*
	C2	300	—
9	E1	360	180*
	C1	300	—
	E2	480*	200*
	C2	315	—
10	E1	300	120*
	C1	330	—
	E2	300*	120*
	C2	315	—

* Indicates a significant difference between SAPA adjusted means and PC means which, in all cases, favored E1 or E2.

high mean, 13.80 vesus 12.04 for C1; and in experiment 3, the means for C2 and C1 were 8.80 versus 7.39. These unaccountably high means for C2 are probably the cause of the lack of significance of E2 over C2 in these two experiments. Recall that the PC lessons were not used in C1 and C2; only the PC tests were administered.

Returning to Table 6.8 and experiments 6–10, we see that the adjusted SAPA means for the Grade 5 students of E1 were not significantly higher than those for the Grade 5 students of C1 in any experiment, whereas those for the Grade 5 students of E2 were higher than those of the Grade 5 students of C2 in all five experiments. The differentiated instruction was more effective in E2 than in E1. However, in three of five experiments *more* time was spent in E1 than in C1 in SAPA instruction and testing combined; in the other two experiments, slightly less. In three of five experiments *less* time was spent in E2 than in C2 and in another, an equal amount. Clearly, the amount of time spent in SAPA instruction was not a contributing factor to the differential results.

In experiments 6–10, there were three teachers in each E1 and C1, and in both schools the round robin method was followed; in E2 and C2, there were three teachers and one teacher, respectively. The adjusted means for E2 were the highest of the four schools in all five experiments, ranging from about 10% to 40% higher, whereas the adjusted means for C1 and C2 were much alike in the five experiments; thus, it seems the three teachers versus one teacher made no difference. It may be concluded that the differentiated instruction for the SAPA adjusted means was carried out more effectively in E2 than in E1 (see Appendix Table A6.9).

The PC means of the Grade 5 students of E1 were higher than those of the Grade 5 students of C1 in two of the five experiments, whereas those of the Grade 5 students of E2 were higher than those of the Grade 5 students of C2 all five experiments. Differences in the amount of time spent in PC instruction in the two schools did not appear to be a contributing factor to the differential results. The PC means of the students of E2 were the highest of all four schools in all five experiments; whereas those of C1 and C2 were much alike. Thus, the conditions of instruction in E2 appear to have produced the higher PC achievements.

We are now ready to examine whether or not the students of high, medium, or low entering SAPA achievement were differentially affected by receiving the differentiated instruction in E1 and E2 and also the PC lessons. To make this determination, post hoc analyses were conducted on the data on which significant differences were obtained between the SAPA means and the PC means of E1–C1 and E2–C2. High, middle, and low groups not only of E1 and E2, but also of C1 and C2 were identified for the post hoc analyses. The reader is forewarned that the high, middle, and low groups used for the post hoc analyses were identified in the same way for all four schools and therefore are not the same as those into which the students of E1 and E2 were arranged for their SAPA instruction. We shall now examine how the post hoc groups of Grade 4 students were formed; the same strategy was used for the Grade 5 students of experiments 6-10.

The SAPA pretest scores of the students of both E1 and C1 combined were ranked from lowest to highest, regardless of the school attended by the students. Those of E2 and C2 were ordered in the same way. Different groups were formed on the basis of the pretest scores of experiments 1 and 2 combined, experiment 3 alone, and experiments 4 and 5 combined.

The low group of each paired set of schools included students whose pretest scores were lower than the scores of two-thirds of the students of that pair of schools. The high group was composed of the students whose pretest scores were higher than the scores of two-thirds of the students. Students in the middle group had scores between the low and high groups. The cut-off scores are given in Appendix Table A6.15. The rankings based on the SAPA pretest scores that were done separately for each pair of schools resulted in cut-off points for the three groups of students of E1-C1 that were slightly different than those for the three groups of E2-C2. In experiments 4 and 5, for example, 35 students from E1 and C1 combined had pretest scores of 26 or lower and formed the low group, whereas 35 students who comprised the low group for E2 and C2 had pretest scores of 27 or lower. Furthermore, because the scores of each paired experimental and control school were ranked together, the numbers of students in each of the three groups from the experimental school and the control school were not necessarily equal. The only large differences in the Ns occurred for experiments 1 and 2 where, as reported earlier, the pretest scores of E1 were unexpectedly much higher than those of C1.

For each of the three post hoc groups based on pretest scores, t-tests were performed between the SAPA posttest means and between the PC means of the students of each E1-C1 and E2-C2, provided a significant difference had been found between the means of the total E1-C1 and E2-C2 groups in the earlier experiments. The probability values are reported in Table 6.9.

Only one difference between the adjusted SAPA posttest means of the Grade 4 students of E1 and C1, experiments 1-5, and not any difference between the Grade 5 students, experiments 6-10, were significant; therefore, only one post hoc analysis was performed. In this analysis, no difference between the SAPA posttest means of the high, the middle, and the low post hoc groups of E1-C1 was significant.

TABLE 6.9 Summary of Significant Differences for Total Groups of Students of E1–C1 and E2–C2 and for Low, Middle, and High Pretest-Based Groups of E1–C1 and E2–C2 Using SAPA Posttest Scores and PC Test Scores: Experiments 1–10

Experiment Number	SAPA								PC							
	E1–C1				E2–C2				E1–C1				E2–C2			
	Total	Low	Mid	High	Total	Low	Mid	High	Total	Low	Mid	High	Total	Low	Mid	High
1	–[a]	NC[b]	NC	NC	–	NC	NC	NC	–	–	–	–	NC	NC	NC	NC
2	–	NC	NC	NC	–	NC	NC	NC	.002	–	–	–	.002	–	.02	.001
3	–	NC	NC	NC	.001	–	.009	.002	–	–	–	–	–	NC	NC	NC
4	.02	–	–	–	.01	–	.012	.02	.001	–	.002	–	.001	.007	.04	.001
5	–	NC	NC	NC	.001	–	.002	.001	.001	NC	NC	NC	.001	–	.002	.001
6	–	NC	NC	NC	.001	.002	.002	.001	.001	NC	NC	NC	.001	–	–	.04
7	–	NC	NC	NC	.001	.001	.001	.001	.05	NC	NC	NC	.05	–	.02	–
8	–	NC	NC	NC	.001	.02	–	.001	.001	NC	NC	NC	.001	.04[c]	.002	.02
9	–	NC	NC	NC	.02	.001	.001	.001	.001	–	–	–	.001	.004	.03	.02
10	–	NC	NC	NC	.001	.001	.001	.001	.001	–	.02	.001	.001	.001	.02	.001

[a] Dash denotes insignificant differences.
[b] NC means "not computed."
[c] Denotes difference favoring the comparison school

Turning to the PC results for E1–C1, we see that in 6 of the 10 experiments, the PC means were significantly higher for E1 than C1. In the post hoc analyses, only 3 of 18 possible differences between the means of the post hoc high, middle, and low groups were found to be significantly different. Two were for the middle group and one for the high group. Thus, the PC lessons did not appear to have a differential effect on acquiring an understanding of the science process concepts by the students of any particular entering achievement level.

We may now observe the results for the E2–C2 post hoc comparisons of the SAPA posttest and PC test data. The SAPA means of the high post hoc groups of students from E2 were significantly higher than those of the high C2 groups in eight of eight cases; the means of the middle E2 group were higher than those of the C2 middle group in six of eight cases; and the means of the E2 low groups were higher than those of the C2 low groups in four of eight cases. We may interpret this as a tendency for the high and middle groups of E2 to achieve relatively higher than the low group in comparison with the same groups in C2. We see in Table 6.9 that this same tendency was found for the PC test means. Post hoc discussion with the teachers of E1 and E2 indicted that some of the E1 teachers made a relatively larger effort than did some of the E2 teachers to enable the lower-achieving students to achieve both the SAPA objectives and to understand the process concepts.

REFERENCES

American Association for the Advancement of Science. *Science: A process approach: Commentary for teachers.* Washington, D.C.: American Association for the Advancement of Science/Xerox, 1968.

Gates, A. L., & MacGinitie, W. H. *Gates–MacGinitie Reading Tests.* New York: Teachers College Press, 1970.

Klausmeier, H. J., DiLuzio, G. L. & Brumet, M. L. *First Year of intervention study to facilitate children's concept learning* (Technical Report No. 424). Madison: Wisconsin Research and Development Center for Cognitive Learning, 1976.

Klausmeier, H. J., Sipple, T. S., & Allen, P. S. *First cross-sectional study of attainment of the concepts equilateral triangle, cutting tool, and noun by children age 5 to 16 of city A* (Technical Report No.287). Madison: Wisconsin Research and Development Center for Cognitive Learning, 1974.

Klausmeier, H. J., Sipple, T. S., Allen, P. S., & White, K. M. *Second cross-sectional study of attainment of the concepts* equilateral triangle, cutting tool, noun, *and tree by children age 6 to 16 of city A* (Technical Report No. 367). Madison: Wisconsin Research and Development Center for Cognitive Learning, 1976.

Schilling, J. M., & Klausmeier, H. J. *Lesson on the basic process concept of observing scientifically intended for use with fifth-grade students.* Madison: Wisconsin Research and Development Center for Cognitive Learning, 1975.

7

Experiments 11-13 and Cumulative Effects of Participation in the Experiments

Experiments 1-10 were carried out with quite severe time constraints placed on the teachers and the students of E1 and E2. The amount of time required in E1 and E2 in each experiment for teaching the process-concept (PC) lesson and for the SAPA testing at the end of each SAPA exercise was substantial. In addition to the time factor, the students of E1 and E2 received a large amount of information in the five PC lessons; the students of C1 and C2 did not receive the PC lessons. It was difficult for the E1 and E2 students to process this added information within the same number of weeks of science instruction as the C1 and C2 students received.

At the end of the year, both the participating teachers and the project personnel felt that it had not been possible to use the PC lessons as effectively as was possible or to carry out the SAPA instruction in accordance with the theory of instructional programming for the individual student as well as the teachers were capable of doing. Therefore, the number of experiments was reduced from five to four the ensuing year, two each semester. Also, the amount of time for instruction in E1 and E2 for a PC lesson, the set of SAPA exercises, or both was permitted to be increased above that for C1 and C2. Other experimental conditions also were varied in the successive experiments.

Data for a doctoral dissertation were gathered by one of the project assistants (Swanson, 1977) that included four single SAPA exercises as well as the set of two exercises on communicating that were planned for use in the fourth experiment. A rearranged sequencing of these six exercises and other changes in the planned instructional conditions resulted in not being able to carry out this last experiment on *communicating* as had been planned initially.

EXPERIMENT 11: OBSERVING SCIENTIFICALLY

Purpose

Two questions regarding the PC lessons prepared by the project staff remained unanswered after experiments 1–10 were completed. Experiment 11 was directed toward answering them.

One question was whether or not a process concept would be understood better by the students if the teachers were free to give as much time to teaching the PC lesson as they thought would be effective. Only a fixed and limited amount of time was used in experiments 1–10 in accordance with the design of the experiments.

Another question was whether or not students' comprehension of a process concept gained from studying a PC lesson would transfer to understanding the concept when applied to the scientific phenomena and events included in the SAPA exercises. Recall that, in accordance with the experimental design, the items of the SAPA tests used in experiments 1–10 were constructed to measure the student's ability to carry out the SAPA process on the content included in the SAPA curriculum, not to measure understanding of the process as a concept or to apply the process to phenomena and events not included in the SAPA lessons. On the other hand, neither the PC lessons nor the PC tests of experiments 1–10 or of experiment 11 included any content drawn from the SAPA curriculum.

A third question, the same one as addressed in experiments 1–10, dealt with determining the effects of adapting the SAPA instruction to the entering achievement levels of the students in accordance with instructional programming for the individual student when the amount of time for the SAPA instruction was held constant in the experimental and control schools as was done in experiments 1–10.

Before proceeding to more details of this experiment, we should be aware that the Grade 5 students participating in this experiment were the Grade 4 students of experiments 1–5. However, the Grade 5 teachers of E1–C1 and E2–C2 in this experiment were those who had participated in experiments 6–10. The PC lessons and the set of SAPA exercises dealing with observing scientifically used in this experiment were those used in experiment 6.

Materials

A set of three SAPA exercises on *observing scientifically* was used in experiment 11. They dealt with the following topics: observing magnetic poles, observing growth from seeds, and observing falling objects. The materials included in the instruction in both the experimental and comparison schools were those in the publisher's kit. For example, bar magnets, iron filings, copper, aluminum and steel nails, and dry-cell batteries were included for the exercise on observing magnetic poles. Other materials suggested by the publisher were brought into the schools by either the teachers or the science coordinator of the district, for example, corn, wheat, and blue grass seeds for the exercise on observing growth from seeds.

A 47-page printed PC lesson was used in E1 and E2 to teach understanding of the process *observing scientifically* before teaching the SAPA exercises dealing with the process of *observing scientifically*. The teachers in E1 and E2 had supplementary science texts to use in their instruction. These texts included material appropriate for students who were judged by the teachers to master the SAPA content quickly as well as for those who were evaluated as needing easy-to-read material to supplement the classroom–laboratory science instruction.

Participating Students

The number of Grade 5 students participating in experiment 11 in each school was as follows: E1—61, C1—48, E2—66, C2—55. This included all the students enrolled in Grade 5 of the four schools who took all the tests during the first semester of the school year. Most of these students participated the year before in experiments 1–5 as Grade 4 students. Students with severe learning handicaps did not take the tests and some students who were absent did not make up one or more tests that they missed.

Let us digress briefly to see how the students who did not take all the tests were dealt with in experiments 11, 12, and 13. For each experiment, the SAPA posttest means of the students of each school who received all the tests were compared with the means of those who took the SAPA pretests and posttests but only some of the other tests. The results of t-tests showed no statistically significant differences between the means of the two groups of any school for any experiment. Therefore, the results reported in this chapter for experiments 11, 12, and 13 are based on the groups that took all the tests.

Patterns of and Time Spent on Instruction and Testing

Three teachers in C1 taught the students science, whereas one teacher did all the science teaching in C2. The three teachers in C1 organized their teaching in a "round robin" pattern. In this pattern, each of the three teachers was responsible for preparing and teaching one of the three exercises on *observing scientifically*. Each teacher taught the same exercise to each of the three groups of approximately 25 students. This resulted in the three groups of students taking the three exercises in difference sequence, that is, $1 \rightarrow 2 \rightarrow 3$; $2 \rightarrow 3 \rightarrow 1$; $3 \rightarrow 1 \rightarrow 2$. (The exercises are not hierarchially organized within a set.) The teachers in both C1 and C2 followed the publisher's recommendations for teaching science to heterogeneous, classroom-size groups of about 25 students.

In accordance with the experimental design, the students in C1 and C2 were pretested with the SAPA tests for *observing scientifically* (and also *inferring*) at the beginning of the semester and were posttested at the end of the semester using the same tests. They did not receive the PC lesson, but they were administered the PC test on *observing scientifically* in the same week as the students of E1 and E2 and before instruction started on the first of the three SAPA exercises on *observing scientifically*. The 10-item transfer test on *observing scientifically* was administered to them at the end of the semester along with the regular SAPA posttest. The students in E1 and E2 were administered the SAPA, PC, and transfer tests at the same times as the C1 and C2 students.

Based on the SAPA pretest scores for *observing scientifically*, the teachers formed three groups of students with about 25 students in a high group, a middle group, and a low group. Three teachers in each E1 and E2 taught these students science. Each teacher took the low, middle, or high group and taught all the SAPA exercises of experiment 11 to that group. The teachers changed groups from one set of exercises to the next.

According to the design of experiment 11, the students of E1 and E2, organized into high, middle, and low groups, received the PC lesson on *observing scientifically* as an advance organizer. The teachers of E1 and E2 used as much time as they judged necessary for the majority of the students to comprehend the concept. After taking the PC test, the students of E1 and E2 started the first SAPA exercise. An equal amount of time was allocated for teaching the three SAPA exercises in E1, E2, C1, and C2, when planning the experiment.

The main procedures used in E1 and E2 to adapt SAPA instruction to the individual student's characteristics were to introduce the same content somewhat differently to the high, middle, and low groups as groups, to pace the instruction somewhat differently for these groups, and to arrange more activities for small groups, pairs, and individuals and fewer for the class as a whole. Some of the students of E1 and E2 also studied other science texts that contained information dealing with the same SAPA content. For example, students who appeared to demonstrate mastery of the SAPA exercises early either worked on individual science experiments, read supplementary science texts, or both.

The amount of time actually spent in experiment 11 in SAPA instruction and in SAPA testing at the end of each set of exercises in E1 and E2, in SAPA instruction only in C1 and C2, and in PC instruction and testing in E1 and E2, and in PC testing only in C1 and C2 was as follows:

	E1	C1	E2	C2
SAPA exercises	450	420	450	480
PC lesson	150	30 (testing)	150	30 (testing)

Results

The levels of significance between the adjusted means of E1–C1 and between E2–C2 and between the frequencies of mastery for the SAPA posttest, transfer test, and PC test are provided in Appendix Table A7.1. Analysis of variance was used in determining the level of significance for the PC means and Chi-Square for the frequencies. Analysis of covariance, with the pretest score the covariate, was used in obtaining the level of significance for the SAPA posttest means and also for the transfer means. The adjusted SAPA posttest means and transfer means are given in Appendix Table A7.2.

The unadjusted means for the pretests and posttests, the standard deviations, the mean percentages correct, and the percentages of the students achieving mastery of the SAPA tests, the transfer test, and the PC test are given in Table 7.1. A difference between the achievements of the students of E1-C1 and E2-C2 significant at the .05 level or beyond is indicated with an asterisk.

The students in E1 scored significantly higher on the SAPA tests than did the students in C1 (Table 7.1). The mean for the students in E2 was

TABLE 7.1 Experiment 11: Pretest and Posttest Means, Standard Deviations, Mean Percentages Correct, and Percentages Achieving Mastery for Grade 5 Students of E1, C1, E2, and C2: SAPA Test, Transfer Test, and Process-Concept Test

	E1 (N = 61)		C1 (N = 48)		E2 (N = 66)		C2 (N = 55)	
	Pre	Post	Pre	Post	Pre	Post	Pre	Post
Observing scientifically								
SAPA test (30 items)								
Mean	17.26	23.52*	15.67	20.29	16.17	23.38	16.15	21.59
SD	4.15	3.80	3.47	4.13	4.69	4.89	3.60	3.39
Mean percentage correct	58	78	52	68	54	78	54	72
Percentage ach. mastery	7	57*	4	27	8	61*	4	30
Transfer test (10 items)								
Mean		8.70		8.44		7.97*		7.18
SD		1.37		1.46		1.98		1.50
Mean percentage correct		87		84		80		72
Percentage ach. mastery		79		73		68*		38
Process-Concept test (18 items)								
Mean		15.13		14.48		13.47		13.42
SD		2.19		2.26		3.96		2.23
Mean percentage correct		84		80		75		75
Percentage ach. mastery		77		73		67*		44

*$p < .05$

higher than in C2, but the difference was significant at the .13 level, not at the .05 level. The percentage of students achieving mastery (57 and 27 respectively) was significantly higher in E1 than in C1; it was also significantly higher in E2 than in C2 (61 and 30, respectively).

The students in E2 had a significantly higher mean than did the students of C2 on the transfer test. Also, the percentage mastering the transfer test (68 versus 38) was significantly higher. The mean on the transfer test for the students of E1 was higher than for C1 but not significantly so. Similarly, the percentage of E1 students achieving mastery of the transfer test was higher but not significantly higher.

On the PC test, the means for E1 and E2 were slightly higher than for C1 and C2, respectively; however, the differences were not statistically significant at the .05 level. A significantly higher percentage of the students of E2 than of C2 achieved the PC mastery criterion.

Discussion

It is instructive to compare the adjusted SAPA means and the PC means of the prior Grade 5 groups of students of E1, C1, E2, and C2 who participated in experiment 6 and those of the present experiment 11. In experiment 11, the same SAPA materials and PC lesson were used as in experiment 6. Also the same teachers taught the different groups of Grade 5 students who participated in the two experiments. The adjusted SAPA means and the PC means for the students of the four schools for experiments 6 and 11 follow:

	E1	C1	E2	C2
Experiment 6 SAPA	20.88	20.60	23.96*	21.59
Experiment 11 SAPA	23.57*	21.71	23.40	22.44
Experiment 6 PC	12.52	12.84	14.01*	12.36
Experiment 11 PC	15.13	14.48	13.47	13.42

*Statistically significant

We see that the means of both the SAPA test and the PC test for E1, C1, and C2 were higher in experiment 11 than in experiment 6, but both were lower for E2. Examination of the teachers' logs, the pretest scores of the students, and the amount of time spent in instruction provides no clues to account for the relatively low means of the E2 students in experiment 11. However, the lower means of the students of E2 in experiment 11 probably account for the lack of significance at the .05 level between E2 and C2 on both the SAPA posttest and the PC test.

The fact that the SAPA means for E1 and E2 were higher than for C1 and C2 at the .001 and .13 levels, respectively, and that the percentages of mastery were also significant enable us to conclude that the differentiation of the SAPA instruction carried out in the experimental schools was effective, more so in E1 than in E2, however.

Despite the fact that the teachers of E1 and E2 were free to give more time to the PC lesson, the means for the students of E1 and E2 were not significantly higher than those for the students of C1 and C2.

How may this be accounted for? We have observed that the students of E2 in experiment 11 scored lower on the PC test than did the students of E2 in experiment 6. On the other hand, the students of C1 scored much higher in experiment 11 than did the students of experiment 6. In fact, the PC mean of the students of C1 is considerably higher than that of the students of both E2 and C2 in experiment 11. Thus, the relatively low PC mean of the E2 students and the very high PC mean of the C1 students probably account for the lack of significance between both paired sets of schools. However, post hoc examination of the teacher logs and discussion with the E2 teachers gave no clue to account for the low scores of E2 or the high scores of C1.

The mean for the E2 students on the transfer test was significantly higher than that for the C2 students, whereas the transfer mean for the E1 students was not significantly higher than that of the C1 students (see Table 7.1). Thus, in E2, understanding *observing scientifically* as a process concept transferred to understanding it when applied to the objects and events included in the SAPA curriculum, but it did not in E1.

EXPERIMENT 12: INFERRING

Purpose

In experiments 1 through 11, a PC lesson was used in E1 and in E2 and, except for unanticipated minor departures from the experimental design, the same total amount of time was used in instruction for the 11 sets of SAPA exercises in all four schools. Use of the PC lesson in E1 and E2 took a substantial amount of instructional time and also required the students of E1 and E2 to deal with a large body of information that was not required of the students of C1 and C2.

The purpose of experiment 12 was to determine the effects of greater differentiation of SAPA instruction in E1 and E2 without the use of an accompanying PC lesson. Also, the amount of time for SAPA instruction in E1 and E2 was permitted to be greater than in C1 and C2 to carry out the greater differentiation of instruction.

Participating Students

The identical students indicated earlier for experiment 11 participated in experiment 12.

Patterns of and Time Spent on Instruction and Testing

The three teachers in C1 and the one teacher in C2 proceeded as they had in experiment 11. Recall that the C1 teachers employed a round robin instructional arrangement by which each teacher taught all three groups of students the same SAPA exercise. In E1 and E2, the teachers proceeded with the SAPA instruction in the same manner as in experiment 11 except for the last part of the instructional sequence of each exercise as is now explained.

In E1 and E2, the students were organized for their initial SAPA instruction into a high, a middle, and a low group based on their pretest scores on *inferring*. Regardless of the difference in their entering achievement levels, each group received about the same number of minutes of initial instruction on each SAPA exercise, for example, 180 minutes, on the exercise dealing with loss of water from plants. After this initial instruction, a 10-item posttest was administered and scored immediately by an instructional aide. Results of this posttest were used diagnostically as follows.

Based on the rank order of the students' scores, three new groups were formed. The group that mastered the content (had 8–10 items correct) spent a few minutes reviewing the content included in the test items which two or more of the students had missed; and after this review, they either helped other students who had not mastered the test, or they worked on enrichment activities.

The group of students who were near mastery (six to seven items correct) were retaught the particular content that most of them had not yet mastered. Here, the reteaching was directed toward the content represented by the test items most frequently missed by the middle group.

The group that scored five or lower was also taught the content of the exercise that they had missed. These students generally were given the same amount of time for reteaching as the middle group.

Two or three class sessions of about 25–30 minutes each were used in this manner for each of the three groups for each of three SAPA exercises of the set. In this way, all three groups of students of each E1 and E2 used the same amount of time in SAPA instruction but they used it differently.

Testing of the students in experiment 12 proceeded as follows. Students in E1, E2, C1, and C2 received the same 30-item pretest on *inferring* in September and the same 30-item posttest in December. The students in E1 and E2, as noted earlier, also received the 10-item diagnostic post-test following the initial instruction for each exercise. About 15 minutes was used in E1 and E2 for this testing. The number of minutes spent on instruction and testing combined in E1 and E2 and on instruction only in C1 and C2 was as follows:

	E1	C1	E2	C2
Exercise 1	270	225	270	225
Exercise 2	300	225	320	225
Exercise 3	270	225	270	225
Total	840	675	860	675

See that combined time for instruction and testing was greater in E1 and E2 than in C1 and C2 for each exercise. Since the results of the testing were used for regrouping the students and differentiating the instruction of the groups, the additional time for testing is included as part of the total time for instruction.

Materials

Three SAPA exercises on *inferring* were used in experiment 12. They dealt with inferring loss of water from plants, inferring connection patterns in electrical circuits, and inferring the shape of cut things. The same materials provided in the publisher's standard kit were used in E1, E2, C1, and C2. For example, circuit boards and insulated wire were used for the SAPA lesson dealing with inferring connection patterns in electrical circuits. Other materials recommended but not supplied in the publisher's standard kit were brought into the schools by either the teachers or the science coordinator. For example, geranium plants and celery stalks were used in the lesson on inferring loss of water from plants.

As part of the pattern of greater differentiation of the SAPA instruction, the students of E1 and E2 were reorganized into high, middle, and low achievement level groups based on their posttest scores, and various materials in addition to those of the SAPA kit were provided for enrichment and relearning. For example, the students in E1 and E2 who scored eight or higher on the SAPA diagnostic posttest for any of the three exercises were provided enrichment activities. One enrichment activity for the high achieving students on the exercise dealing with inferring the shape of cut things was to construct a balanced, hanging mobile from wooden strips, construction paper, string, and masking tape, such that four different shapes would be represented.

Supplementary textbooks and other printed material were made available for students of all three groups in E1 and E2. For example, students in E1 and E2 who scored low on the SAPA test were provided easy-to-read materials that dealt with *inferring*.

Results

The levels of statistical significance between the means of E1–C1 and F2–C2 obtained by analysis of covariance and between the frequencies of mastery obtained by Chi-square testing are given in Appendix Table A7.3. The adjusted means are provided in Appendix Table A7.4. The means for the unadjusted pretest and posttest, the standard deviations, the mean percentages correct, and the percentages of the students achieving the mastery criterion on the SAPA tests are given in Table 7.2. A difference between the achievements of each paired set of schools significant at or beyond the .05 level is indicated with an asterisk.

The posttest means were significantly higher for the students of E1 than C1 and of E2 than C2, and the difference in each case was significant at the .001 level. The percentage of students achieving mastery was much higher in E1 and E2 than in C1 and C2, 61 versus 17 and 47 versus 9, respectively. These differences were statistically significant.

Approximately 30% more time was spent on instruction and testing combined in E1 and E2 than in C1 and C2, 165 minutes more in E1, and 185 minutes more in E2. The substantially larger percentage of students achieving mastery is undoubtedly related to the combined effects of the larger amount of time spent on instruction and the related differentiated instruction that followed the diagnostic posttesting. Being administered the test once more may also have contributed to the higher percentage achieving mastery.

Recall that other groups of Grade 5 students of E1–C1 and E2–C2 participated in experiment 7. In experiment 7, the same set of SAPA exercises on *inferring* was taught by the same teachers as in experiment 12; however, there was less differentiation of instruction and less time spent in instruction in E1 and E2 in experiment 7. The adjusted means of the Grade 5 students of experiment 7 and the adjusted means of Grade 5 students of the present experiment 12, and also the minutes spent in instruction follow:

	E1	C1	E2	C2
Experiment 7	19.15 – 500	18.42 – 515	21.21 – 480	17.97 – 540
Experiment 12	23.39 – 840	19.48 – 675	22.09 – 860	18.86 – 675

TABLE 7.2 Experiment 12: Pretest and Posttest Means, Standard Deviations, Mean Percentages Correct, and Percentages Achieving Mastery for Grade 5 Students of E1, C1, E2, C2: SAPA Test

	E1 (N = 61)		C1 (N = 48)		E2 (N = 66)		C2 (N = 55)	
	Pre	Post	Pre	Post	Pre	Post	Pre	Post
Inferring (30 items)								
Mean	14.39	23.64*	13.16	19.40	14.50	22.41*	13.32	18.65
SD	3.27	4.14	3.45	3.79	4.02	4.96	2.92	3.31
Mean percentage correct	48	79	44	64	48	75	44	61
Percentage ach. mastery	2	61*	0	17	3	47*	0	9

$*p < .05$

Each of the four schools had a higher mean in experiment 12 than in experiment 7. Both C1 and C2 used more time for instruction in experiment 12 than in experiment 7 but not as much more as did E1 and E2.

The percentages of the students who achieved the mastery criterion for the two experiments were as follows:

	E1	C1	E2	C2
Experiment 7	18	10	32	4
Experiment 12	61	17	47	9

The percentage of the E1 students achieving the mastery criterion of the SAPA test in experiment 7 was 18, whereas in experiment 12 it was 61. As noted earlier in Chapter 6 when discussing the results of experiments 6–10, the E1 students did not achieve well on either the SAPA or the PC tests in experiments 6, 7, and 8. A substantially larger percentage of the E2 students also achieved the mastery criterion in experiment 12 than in experiment 7.

How may the significantly higher means for E1 and E2 than for C1 and C2 in experiment 12 and also the significantly higher percentages of mastery be accounted for? It appears that the differentiation of the SAPA instruction combined with the larger amount of time spent directly on the SAPA instruction and testing in E1 and E2 yielded higher achievement, including greater mastery. Apparently, the additional time was needed for the differentiated instruction to be sufficiently effective so that the same type of results were obtained in both pairs of schools.

EXPERIMENT 13: CONTROLLING VARIABLES

Purpose

In experiment 11, the teachers of E1 and E2 gave as much time to the PC lesson as they judged necessary to be effective. Despite this, the students of E1 and E2 did not perform significantly better on the PC test than did the students of C1 and C2. In experiment 12, the PC lesson was not used, and more time was given to differentiate the SAPA instruction more fully in E1 and E2. The E1 and E2 students achieved significantly higher on the SAPA tests than did those of C1 and C2.

One purpose of experiment 13 was to determine the combined effects of giving more time to the PC lesson as was done in experiment 11 and giving more time to the differentiation of the SAPA instruction as was done in experiment 12. The other purpose was to ascertain whether or not understanding the process concept, *controlling variables,* transferred to applying the process to the SAPA content as measured by a transfer test.

Participating Students

The number of participating students was 56 in E1, 49 in C1, 64 in E2, and 53 in C2. Except for students with pronounced learning handicaps and others who were absent for one or more tests during the school year, this was the total number of Grade 5 students enrolled in each school.

Patterns of and Time Spent on Instruction and Testing

In C1 and C2, instruction was carried out in the same manner as in earlier experiments. In E1 and E2, the PC lesson on *controlling variables* was used as an advance organizer in the same manner as in experiment 11 whereas the SAPA instruction proceeded in the same manner as in experiment 12.

In accordance with the experimental design, the students of Grade 5 in all four schools were administered a SAPA pretest at the beginning of the second semester consisting of 20 items dealing with the two exercises on controlling variables and a posttest at the end of the semester. A transfer test was constructed to measure the ability to apply understanding of the concept to the content used in the two SAPA exercises on *controlling variables.* This test was administered to the students of E1, E2, C1, and C2 at the end of the semester. In this experiment, as in all other experiments, SAPA pretesting and SAPA posttesting of all the experimental lessons was done only at the beginning and end of the semester because of time constraints related to scheduling of the science laboratory and equipment for use by all the students of the schools and also to enable the C1 and C2 teachers to use instructional time effectively when they were not teaching science, while the E1 and E2 teachers were using the PC lessons.

The students of E1 and E2 also received a 10-item diagnostic SAPA posttest at the end of each of the two SAPA exercises as was done in experiment 12. The results of this testing were used in regrouping for more highly differentiated instruction. The PC test to measure students' understanding of the process concept, *controlling variables,* was also administered in all four schools before teaching the first SAPA exercise on *controlling variables.*

The time spent in instruction and diagnostic testing in E1 and E2 and in instruction only in C1 and C2 follows:

	E1	C1	E2	C2
SAPA Lesson 1	220	180	240	180
SAPA Lesson 2	220	180	240	180
Total:	440	360	480	360
Process Concept	180	30 (testing)	180	30 (testing)

Materials

A printed lesson of 66 pages dealing with the process concept *controlling variables* was used in E1 and E2 to teach understanding of this process concept before teaching the SAPA exercises dealing with *controlling variables*. The two SAPA lessons on *controlling variables* dealt with rolling cylinders and upward movement of liquids.

The science materials included in the publisher's kit for the SAPA curriculum were used in E1, E2, C1, and C2. Equal arm balances and spheres of different diameters are examples of the materials that were used with the exercise dealing with rolling cylinders.

The students in E1 and E2 who mastered each of the SAPA diagnostic posttests on *controlling variables* used textbooks, other printed material, and some three-dimensional material as part of their enrichment activities. Students of the middle and low achieving groups in E1 and E2 also used various printed material and some three-dimensional material as part of the reteaching and relearning process.

Results

The levels of significance between the means of E1–C1 and E2–C2 and between the frequencies of mastery are found in Appendix Table A7.5. The adjusted SAPA posttest means and transfer test means for E1, C1, E2, and C2 may be found in Appendix Table A7.6.

The means for the pretest and posttest, the standard deviations, the mean percentages correct, and the percentages of the students achieving mastery on the SAPA tests, the transfer test, and the PC test are given in Table 7.3.

The students in E1 and E2 scored significantly higher on the SAPA test, the transfer test, and the PC test than the students of C1 and C2. The differences between each pair of schools on each test was significant at or beyond the .002 level.

The percentage of students who achieved mastery of the SAPA mate-

TABLE 7.3 Experiment 13: Pretest and Posttest Means, Standard Deviations, Mean Percentages Correct, and Percentages Achieving Mastery for Grade 5 Students of E1, C1, E2, and C2: SAPA Test, Transfer Test, and Process-Concept Test

	E1 (N=56)		C1 (N=49)		E2 (N=64)		C2 (N=53)	
	Pre	Post	Pre	Post	Pre	Post	Pre	Post
Controlling variables								
SAPA test (20 items)								
Mean	10.95	16.57*	9.53	14.33	10.12	15.56*	11.20	13.11
SD	3.49	2.95	2.99	3.05	3.51	4.10	2.72	3.30
Mean percentage correct	55	83	48	72	51	78	56	66
Percentage ach. mastery	14	71*	2	43	6	64*	4	23
Transfer test (11 items)								
Mean		8.18*		5.12		7.61*		4.86
SD		2.36		1.86		2.27		1.89
Mean percentage correct		74		47		69		44
Percentage ach. mastery		48*		4		41*		2
Process-Concept test (21 items)								
Mean		14.37*		9.35		14.78*		9.64
SD		4.37		3.03		4.84		3.07
Mean percentage correct		68		45		70		46
Percentage ach. mastery		45*		2		42*		2

*$p < .05$

rial increased from 14% on the pretest to 71% on the posttest in E1, and from 6 to 64% in E2. The corresponding percentages for the students of the control schools were from 2 to 43 in C1, and from 4 to 23 in C2. The percentages achieving mastery of the transfer test were even more pronounced: 48 in E1 versus 4 in C1, and 41 in E2 versus 2 in C2. The differences in the percentages achieving the mastery criterion for the PC test were also large: 45 in E1 versus 2 in E2, and 42 in E2 versus 2 in C2. These results are of great practical significance considering the goal of getting as many students as possible to a mastery criterion.

Discussion

The adjusted means for the SAPA posttest and the means for the PC test for the Grade 5 students of experiment 9 and those for the Grade 5 students of the present experiment 13, and also the minutes spent in the PC teaching and testing combined in E1 and E2 and in PC testing only in C1 and C2 follow.

	E1	C1	E2	C2
Experiment 9: SAPA	13.45 — 360	14.20 — 300	15.90 — 480*	13.63 — 315
Experiment 13: SAPA	16.30 — 440*	14.70 — 360	15.90 — 480*	12.82 — 360
Experiment 9: PC	11.93 — 180*	10.20 — 30	13.79 — 200*	10.73 — 30
Experiment 13: PC	14.37 — 180*	9.35 — 30	14.78 — 180*	9.64 — 30

*$P < .05$

The adjusted SAPA mean for E1 was substantially higher in experiment 13 than it was in experiment 9; in the other schools the means were not greatly different. The higher SAPA mean for E1 in experiment 13 accounts for the significantly higher achievement for E1 than C1 in experiment 13; conversely, the relatively low mean for E1 in experiment 9 accounted for the lack of significance in experiment 9.

The students of E1 and E2 achieved higher on the PC lesson in experiment 13 than did those of experiment 9; the means were lower in C1 and C2. In experiment 13, study of the PC lesson was accompanied with greater understanding of the concept, *controlling variables,* and also with transfer to the SAPA content measured by the transfer test. It is possible also that the higher achievements of the SAPA content as measured by the SAPA posttest may have contributed to the higher transfer. Clearly the combined effects of the PC lesson and the differentiated SAPA instruction were high SAPA achievement and high transfer.

In summary, the differentiated SAPA instruction combined with the PC lesson in experiment 13 produced statistically significant and practically important results; however, the amount of time for the combined PC and SAPA instruction was considerably greater in E1 and E2 than in C1 and C2.

PERFORMANCES OF HIGH, MIDDLE, AND LOW
ONE-THIRD OF STUDENTS

To determine whether high, medium, or low entering SAPA achievement groups profited more or less from the interventions, post hoc analyses like those carried out in experiments 1–10 and reported in detail in Chapter 6 were also performed on the data from experiments 11, 12, and 13. The cutoffs based on the SAPA pretest scores that were used to identify the three groups are given in Appendix Table A7.7. Table 7.4 presents a summary of the significant differences for the SAPA, transfer, and PC posttests. All significant differences favored the groups of E1 or E2.

As in experiments 1–10 involving E1 and C1, no pattern emerges that would indicate that any one of the three achievement groups consistently profited more than another from the experimentation. Also, similar to the results of experiments 1–10 for E2–C2, the high and middle E2 groups scored significantly higher than the C2 groups in each experiment 11, 12, and 13; whereas the low one-third did not.

The post hoc treatment of the transfer and PC test data of experiments 11 and 13 revealed no clear pattern favoring any one group. Essentially no differences were found for any group except in experiment 13, and in it all three groups of E1 and E2 scored significantly higher than those of C1 and C2 on the transfer and the PC tests.

We may conclude, then, that the effects of the experimentation were essentially the same for the highest, middle, and lowest one-third of the students in experiments 11, 12, and 13. On exception was the tendency for the lowest one-third of the E2 students not to achieve higher on the SAPA test than the lowest one-third of the C2 students.

RELATIONSHIPS AMONG VARIOUS MEASURES
USED IN EXPERIMENTS 11, 12, AND 13

In experiments 11, 12, and 13, a SAPA pretest on each set of SAPA exercises was administered at the beginning of each semester. This served as the basis for dividing the students of E1 and E2 into high, middle, and low instructional groups in each experiment. The students' SAPA pretest

TABLE 7.4   Experiments 11, 12, and 13: Summary of Significant Differences in SAPA Post-test Scores, Transfer Test Scores, and PC Test Scores for Total Groups and for Low, Middle, and High Pretest-Based Groups of Students of E1-C1 and E2-C2

	SAPA							
	E1–C1				E2–C2			
Experiment	Total	Low	Mid	High	Total	Low	Mid	High
11	.008	.02	.04	—	—	—	.007	.003
12	.001	.04	.001	.01	.001	—	.001	.001
13	.002	—	—	.001	.001	—	.001	.001

	Transfer							
	E1–C1				E2–C2			
Experiment	Total	Low	Mid	High	Total	Low	Mid	High
11	—	—	—	—	.011	—	—	.001
12	[a]							
13	.001	.05	.001	.001	.001	.003	.002	.001

	PC							
	E1–C1				E2–C2			
Experiment	Total	Low	Mid	High	Total	Low	Mid	High
11	—	—	—	—	—	—	—	—
12	[a]							
13	.001	.04	.001	.001	.001	.02	.001	.001

[a] Transfer and PC tests were not used in Experiment 12.

scores on each set of SAPA exercises were also used as the covariate in the analysis of covariance performed on the SAPA posttest means. The assumption was that the entering SAPA achievement level of the students would correlate positively and significantly with the posttest SAPA achievement. A further assumption was that the correlations would be about the same for the E1, E2, C1, and C2 groups.

In experiments 11 and 13, a PC lesson was used in E1 and E2. The lesson was prepared and used to enable students to attain the particular process concept at the formal level. Recall that the SAPA items measured recognition, comprehension, and analysis of the science information that appeared in the SAPA exercises and also performing the process on the scientific phenomena and events included in the exercises. On the other hand, the PC test measured understanding of the process concept, and the test did not include information from the SAPA exercise. Therefore, a transfer test was constructed to measure understanding of the process concept using substantive material drawn from the SAPA exercise.

Two predictions were made regarding the correlations between the SAPA pretests and the SAPA posttests, the transfer tests, and the PC tests. The first prediction was that the SAPA pretests would correlate higher with the SAPA posttests than with the PC tests and the transfer tests. This prediction was upheld. As shown in Appendix Table A7.8, 10 of the 12 SAPA pretest–SAPA posttest correlations were significant at or beyond the .001 level; and the other 2 were significant at the .01 and .05 level. Six of the 8 correlations between the SAPA pretests and PC tests were significant at or beyond the .05 level, and 5 of 8 between the SAPA pretests and transfer tests were significant.

The second prediction was that the SAPA pretest–transfer correlations would be higher for E1 and E2 than for C1 and C2, respectively. This prediction follows from the fact that the E1 and E2 students received the PC lessons and those of C1 and C2 did not. This prediction also was upheld. Furthermore, the correlations of the SAPA pretests with the PC tests and with the SAPA posttests, with minor exceptions, were also higher in E1 and E2 than in C1 and C2, respectively. From this we may infer that the differentiated instruction in E1 and E2 both with the SAPA and the PC lessons resulted in students' final achievements being more in line with their initial SAPA achievement than was the case in C1 and C2 where the instruction was not differentiated and the students did not receive the PC lessons.

Other predictions were made regarding the correlations between the transfer tests and the other two posttests. One prediction was that the transfer–PC correlations would be higher than the transfer–SAPA posttest and the PC–SAPA posttest correlations. The second was that the transfer–PC correlations would be higher for E1 and E2 than for C1 and C2. Both predictions were upheld. All eight correlations between the transfer and PC tests were significant at or beyond the .01 level, with seven being at or beyond the .001 level; five of eight between the transfer tests and the SAPA posttests were significant at or beyond the .05 level, and three were not significant; seven of eight between the PC–SAPA posttests were significant and one was not significant. Only one of the 12 correlations involving these three sets of correlations was higher in a C school; in the other 11, the correlations were higher in E1 or E2.

Clearly, students who received the PC lessons were able to apply their understanding of the process concepts to the scientific phenomena and events included in the SAPA lessons as measured by the transfer tests. It is perhaps of more interest that the students of E1 and E2 who received differentiated SAPA and PC instruction in accord with the theory of instructional programming for the individual student performed more in line with their entering SAPA science achievement levels than did the students of C1 and C2.

ATTITUDES TOWARD SCIENCE

The students of the four schools took a science attitude inventory in September, December, and May. The mean was higher in December than in May for all schools except E2. In May, the means were lower than in September in all four schools. It was only slightly higher in E1 and E2 in May than in C1 and C2, respectively.

Since there was a substantial difference in the mean for E1 and the other three schools in September, analysis of covariance was used in testing the significance of the difference between the means of E1–C1 and E2–C2. The difference between E2 and C2 was significant at the .13 level in May. Differences in the other set of means were not significant. The adjusted means are reported in Appendix Table A7.9. The reader may be interested in comparing the adjusted means given in Appendix Table A7.9 with the unadjusted means in Table 7.5. The considerably higher mean in September for E1 had the effect of substantially reducing the adjusted means for both December and May.

TABLE 7.5   **Means for Grade 5 Students of E1, C1, E2, and C2: SAI**

	E1	C1	E2	C2
September	48.98	43.60	43.55	44.34
December	47.72	44.22	41.58	43.60
May	44.40	41.32	43.26	41.34

CUMULATIVE EFFECTS OF PARTICIPATING IN THE EXPERIMENTS

The design of the study made it possible to ascertain the cumulative effects of receiving the PC lessons and the differentiated SAPA instruction in the experimental schools and of being the comparison groups in the two control schools. It is noted that the effects may not be merely cumulative for the E1 and E2 students, inasmuch as changes were made in both the amount of time given for instruction and also in the methods of instruction in Year 2 of the study.

Recall that the Grade 5 students of E1, E2, C1, and C2 in experiments 11, 12, and 13 participated in the study for two years; they were the Grade 4 students who participated in experiments 1–5. On the other hand, the Grade 5 E1, E2, C1, and C2 students of experiments 6 through 10 during Year 1 of the study participated only during that year. Three identical sets of SAPA exercises were used, one in experiment 6 and 11, another in 7 and 12, and the third in 9 and 13. Two identical PC lessons were used, one in experiments 6 and 11, and the other in 9 and 13.

Two comparisons of the means for the paired sets of schools are of particular interest:

1. Grade 5 students of E1 and E2, experiments 6, 7, and 9, Year 1 versus Grade 5 students of E1 and E2, experiments 11, 12, and 13, Year 2, to determine the effects of receiving the differentiated SAPA instruction for one year and for two years. The PC lessons were used only in experiments 6 and 9, and 11 and 13.

2. Grade 5 students of C1 and C2, experiments 6, 7, and 9, Year 1 versus Grade 5 students of C1 and C2, experiments 11, 12, and 13, Year 2, to determine the effects of serving as comparison groups for one year and for two years. Three SAPA lessons and two PC lessons as described earlier were involved in these comparisons.

Table 7.6 presents the adjusted SAPA means, the PC means, and the levels of statistical significance between the means of the groups of students who participated in the experimental treatments for one and two years and for those who were enrolled in the control schools for one and two years. The number of students in each treatment, also given in Table 7.6, was less in the second year than in the first year. To be included in the first year, the student had to have taken all the tests administered throughout the year. To be included in Year 2, the student had to have taken all of the tests administered both years. The lower number of students of Year 2 is accounted for by three conditions. Some students who were enrolled in Year 1 were not enrolled in the same school in Year 2. Some students who were enrolled in semester 1 of the second year did not come back in the second semester. Finally, some students who did return for the second year did not take all of the tests during either the first or the second semester of Year 2.

The SAPA means of the E1 students who were in their second year of receiving differentiated instruction were significantly higher at or

TABLE 7.6 Cumulative Effects: Adjusted SAPA Means, PC Means, and Levels of Statistical Significance between Means of the Groups That Participated in Experimental Treatments and That Were Enrolled in Comparison Schools

	Experiments 6, 11 SAPA Observing scientifically		Experiments 7, 12 SAPA Inferring		Experiments 9, 13 SAPA Controlling variables		Experiment 6, 11 PC Observing		Experiment 9, 13 PC Controlling variables		N
E1 Yr. 1	22.83		20.01		13.46		12.52		11.93		60
		.78		.0001		.0001		.0001		.008	
E1 Yr. 2	23.03		23.71		16.38		15.37		14.02		43
E2 Yr. 1	24.11		21.52		15.81		13.96		13.79		71
		.38		.17		.32		.79		.039	
E2 Yr. 2	23.58		22.51		16.38		13.79		15.48		42
C1 Yr. 1	19.86		18.19		14.11		12.78		10.20		46
		.62		.042		.94		.002		.41	
C1 Yr. 2	20.25		19.77		14.15		14.64		9.52		33
C2 Yr. 1	21.34		17.68		13.62		12.39		10.73		56
		.78		.10		.22		.09		.086	
C2 Yr. 2	21.57		18.67		12.78		13.38		9.51		39

beyond the .05 level on two of the three SAPA tests than were the means of the E1 students who were in their first year of receiving the differentiated instruction. However, none of the three SAPA means of the E2 students in their second year was higher than those of the E2 students in their first year. Thus, the cumulative effect of the differentiated SAPA instruction for the students of E2 was to maintain the same level of SAPA achievement and for the students of E1 to raise the level.

Being in the second year of participation as a control group in C1 or C2 resulted in higher SAPA mean achievements on one of the six sets of SAPA tests in comparison with being in the first year. Thus, the effect of cumulative participation in a control school also was to maintain SAPA achievement.

On three of four process-concept test administrations, the means of the E1 and E2 students who were in their second year of receiving the PC lessons on *observing* and *controlling variables* were significantly higher than the means of E1 and E2 students in their first year of receiving the PC lessons. The cumulative effect of receiving PC lessons was to increase achievement.

Unaccountably, the PC mean of the C1 students in Year 2 for *observing* was significantly higher at the .002 level than that of the C1 students of Year 1. The mean for the other concept, *controlling variables,* was not significantly different for Years 1 and 2. The PC mean of the C2 students in Year 2 for *observing* was higher at the .09 level than in Year 1, whereas the PC mean for *controlling variables* was lower in Year 2 than in Year 1. Thus, the effects of the different concepts, being enrolled in different schools, and having different teachers appeared to be more powerful than the cumulative effects of participating as a comparison group. Recall that the PC lessons were not taught to the C1 or C2 students; therefore, no changes in either direction were expected.

REFERENCES

Swanson, J. E. *The effects of adapting elementary science instruction to students' entering achievement levels* (Technical Report No. 417). Madison: Wisconsin Research and Development Center for Cognitive Learning, 1977.

8

Summary and Reflections

Throughout this book we have had three major interests. Our first has been to get a better understanding of the internal and external conditions that facilitate students' attainment of concepts at the formal level. The particular interest here is with process concepts; that is, concepts such as *observing* and *inferring* that may be experienced or performed as well as understood. A second interest has been the adaptation of instruction to individual differences, particularly to the differing entering achievement levels of the students. Each of the preceding areas is important in its own right. However, the lessons that were prepared to teach students to understand the process concepts and the method that was employed to provide for individual differences are applications of a theory of cognitive learning and development (CLD). CLD theory specifies the internal conditions necessary for learning concepts at successively higher levels, including the mental operations that are necessary at each level, the external conditions that facilitate the learning of concepts at each level, and both interindividual differences and intraindividual variability in the rate of learning concepts from different subject fields throughout the school years. From the standpoint of methodology, the third interest, namely, testing the applications of CLD theory, is of substantial significance inasmuch as this kind of research has rarely been conducted previously.

We may pause to consider why applications of learning theories are tested so infrequently in real-world learning environments, namely in the schools. One obstacle is that, with few exceptions, the theories ignore both differences among individuals of the same age in the processes and rates of learning and also within-individual variability in learning different outcomes. Furthermore, learning theories generally have not taken into account obvious *developmental* differences in either the internal or the external conditions of learning, as for example, between college students and children of primary school age. In this regard, CLD theory specifies the four successive levels at which the same concept is learned and also the mental operations that are necessary for learning each level. Individual differences in the rate of learning have been delineated also.

Glaser (1967) summarized the situation regarding learning theory as follows: "The widespread inattention to individual differences seems to indicate that psychologists have been uniquely optimistic in their expectations for the generality for behavioral laws. In the pursuit of these laws, the assessment of ranges of generalization and of limiting conditions have been by-passsed [p. 13]." Glaser further indicated that individual differences in learning should be delineated and should form a significant part of a learning theory so that the limiting conditions for each principle may be specified. Without this knowledge the principle cannot be used reliably in describing and predicting events in the many situations to which the principle purportedly can be applied.

In a similar vein, Snow (1976) indicated that some of the same mental processes very likely underlie measures of aptitude and measures of learning. He indicated that learning processes and aptitude constructs cannot be understood fully independently of one another. The concept of aptitude–treatment interactions suggests that general principles of learning cannot be applied to all individuals because of their different aptitudes for learning (Snow, 1976, p. 50).

Developmental theories suffer from the same deficiency as learning theories. They seek to identify normative patterns of development but do not take fully into account interindividual differences in rate of learning and intraindividual variability in attaining various outcomes, such as mathematical concepts, English-language concepts, and science concepts. Piaget's structural theory of intellectual development is illustrative.

Siegel and Brainerd (1978) point out that Piaget's theory of development has dominated the study of children's intelligence for several decades. They indicated that with such a massive amount of Piaget-oriented research already completed, it was only a matter of time before major inconsistencies would appear between what the theory says about the way intelligence develops and what the research actually shows. They reported very serious inconsistencies between empirical data and predictions based on the theory and recommended that Piagetian theory should be accepted as hypotheses for testing rather than as proven theory.

Consistent with this view, Klausmeier and Associates (1979), in their longitudinal study, found no empirical support for the construct of stage as a reliable descriptor of actual cognitive development of children and youth during the school years, Grades 1–12. The variability within the individual that we found in the attainment of concepts, principles, and other outcomes drawn from the fields of English, mathematics, and science is in direct opposition to the Piagetian stage construct that indicates that there is concurrent and synchronous development of all the items of each stage, such as the concepts from all subject fields. Furthermore, the amount of variability that we found cannot be explained adequately by the Piagetian construct of horizontal décalage. We also found concurrent, but not necessarily synchronous, development of many of the Piagetian items of the stage of concrete operational thought and the stage of formal operational thought. This finding contradicts Piaget's stage construct regarding the nature of development between two adjacent stages. The Piagetian construct of vertical décalage does not appear to take into account this phenomenon of concurrent development adequately. Finally, the fact that some normally developing children of age 9 were found to be as advanced in certain areas of cognitive development as some normally developing adolescents at age 18 suggests that the stage construct as a description of actual development is relatively meaningless when applied to the most rapid and the least rapid developers. Clearly, it would be helpful if structural stage theory could specify the percentage of the population of each year of chronological age to which the description of a given stage does and does not apply. Intelligent applications of the stage construct to education at any level, preschool through high school, would seem to benefit from knowledge about these limitations.

Before turning to the main conclusions of the present project, we may review the main features of the research strategy so that they may be related to the three areas of interest. The main part of the project was carried out during two years as a series of 13 experiments in two paired sets of elementary schools. In the two experimental schools (E1 and E2), the students received a process-concept (PC) lesson before receiving the SAPA instruction (AAAS Commission on Science Education, 1967) dealing with the same process. The SAPA instruction was adapted to the students' entering achievement levels. In the two control schools (C1 and C2), the SAPA instruction proceeded as before the study started, and the students did not receive the PC lessons. Thus, the first part of each experiment was directed toward gaining knowledge concerning students' learning to understand the process concepts of science. The second part was directed toward gaining knowledge about adapting science instruction to the entering achievement levels of the students.

Another purpose was to test the applications of CLD theory that were incorporated in the PC lessons and in the method of adapting the SAPA instruction to the entering achievement levels of the students. Finally, post hoc analyses were made to ascertain whether or not the results of each experiment in which a significant difference was found were the same for the highest one-third, the middle one-third, and the lowest one-third of the students. These one-thirds were based on the SAPA pretest scores of all the students of E1, E2, C1, and C2 and not on the instructional groups arranged in E1 and E2. These post-hoc analyses made it possible to identify possible limitations of the generalizability of the results.

Each of the 13 experiments was carried out during the same time period in the two paired sets of experimental and control schools, E1-C1 and E2-C2. This made possible a simultaneous replication of each experiment. Replication made it possible to determine whether or not the results were the same for the children and their teachers of E1-C1 and E2-C2, and thereby to avoid drawing incorrect conclusions when the same results were not obtained in both sets of schools.

The SAPA objectives of instruction in each experiment were the same for the students of all four schools. However, a different SAPA science process was taught in each experiment 1-10 except that in one experiment the same process was taught but at a higher level of sophistication. In this way, application of CLD theory to nine different science processes and to a more sophisticated level of one process was tested. Similarly, a different PC lesson to help the students understand the science process as a concept was used in each experiment. This permitted determining whether or not the results of using the PC lessons and of the method of the SAPA instruction were the same for all 10 concepts. This strategy ensured the avoidance of drawing incorrect conclusions when the results varied for the different concepts.

The Grade 4 students in experiments 1-5 were the Grade 5 students of experiments 11-13 during the next year. This made it possible to study the cumulative effects of the second year of the experimentation with that of the first year.

The experimental treatments, or instructional processes, were carried out by the participating school teachers of E1 and E2, not by the project personnel. Thus, the results were obtained under fairly typical conditions for teaching science. It would appear that other teachers could learn to carry out the same procedures.

LEARNING AND TEACHING PROCESS CONCEPTS

Let us first review the results of the tests of significance performed on the PC data in all the experiments and consider how departing from the present strategy of simultaneous replication and use of several concepts might have affected the results and conclusions. Then it may be instructive to consider the applications of CLD theory to students' learning process concepts at a mature classificatory level and the formal level.

Results of Use of Process-Concept Lessons

Table 8.1 summarizes the results of the tests of significance performed on the PC means and also on the percentage of students who mastered the PC tests in each experiment. (The detailed information on which this summary table is based is given in tables of Chapters 6 and 7 and in the appendix tables for these chapters.) Analysis of variance was performed on the obtained PC means; a Chi-square test was performed on the percentages of mastery.

Another phenomenon merits attention. In certain experiments the mean of the students of one control school was about as high or higher than was the mean of both experimental schools. Similarly, in certain experiments the mean of an experimental school was about as low or as low as that of both control schools. These are regarded as anomalies in that the students of the experimental schools received the PC lessons, whereas the students of the control schools did not. Where an anomaly occurred (see Table 8.1), the difference between the particular paired set of experimental and control schools was not significant. We may account for the low performance of the students of an experimental school tentatively in terms of possible testing conditions and other conditions associated with their receiving the PC lessons. The high scores of the control schools cannot be accounted for except on a chance basis. One possibility is that substantial numbers of the control students guessed correctly. We noted earlier in Chapter 5 that the reliability estimates for the PC tests were consistently lower in the control schools than in the experimental schools.

As indicated in Table 8.1 for experiments 1–5, the PC means of the Grade 4 students of E1 were significantly higher than the means of the

TABLE 8.1 Summary of Significant Differences: Process Concepts

Exp. no.	Grade	Name of process concept	E1-C1 Significant?	Anomaly	E2-C2 Significant?	Anomaly	E1-C1 Transfer	Anomaly	E2-C2 Transfer
1	4	Classifying							
		Mean	Yes		—				
		% Mastery	Yes		—	C2			
2	4	Inferring							
		Mean	Yes		Yes				
		% Mastery	Yes		Yes				
3	4	Predicting							
		Mean	Yes		—				
		% Mastery	Yes		—				
4	4	Using numbers							
		Mean	Yes		Yes				
		% Mastery	Yes		Yes				
5	4	Measuring							
		Mean	—		Yes				
		% Mastery	—		Yes				
6	5	Observing							
		Mean	—	E1	Yes				
		% Mastery	—		—				

			C1	E1
7	5	Inferring		
		Mean	—	Yes
		% Mastery	—	—
8	5	Using space–time relationships		
		Mean	—	Yes
		% Mastery	—	Yes
9	5	Controlling variables		
		Mean	Yes	Yes
		% Mastery	—	Yes
10	5	Communicating		
		Mean	Yes	Yes
		% Mastery	Yes	Yes

			C1	E2	C1
11	5	Observing			
		Mean	—	—	Yes
		% Mastery	—	Yes	Yes
12	5	Inferring			
		Mean	NA[a]	NA	NA
		% Mastery	NA	NA	NA
13	5	Controlling variables			
		Mean	Yes	Yes	Yes
		% Mastery	Yes	—	Yes

[a] NA means not administered

197

C1 students in four of the five experiments, and the means of the students of E2 were higher than those of C2 in three of the five experiments. In experiment 1, the mean of the students of C2 was about the same as that of both E1 and E2. This unaccountably high mean of the students of C2 led to a lack of significance between E2 and C2.

Returning to Table 8.1 and moving to experiments 6–10, we note that the PC means of the Grade 5 students of E1 were not significantly different from those of C1 in experiments 6, 7, and 8, but they were in experiments 9 and 10. On the other hand, the PC means for the Grade 5 students of E2 were significantly higher than those for the students of C2 in all five experiments. Based on examination of the teacher logs and post-hoc discussion with the teachers, it appears that the teachers of E1 during the first semester of the experimentation were unable to use the PC lessons in such a way as to help their students understand the three process concepts. However, in the second semester when experiments 9 and 10 were conducted, they were successful in using the lessons.

We now turn to experiments 11–13. The same Grade 5 teachers of experiments 6–10 were responsible for the instruction in experiments 11, 12, and 13. The PC lesson was not used in experiment 12. In experiment 11, the mean of the students in C1 was about as high as that of either E1 or E2, whereas the mean of E2 was about as low or lower than that of both C1 and C2. Thus, the results were not significant for either pair of schools in experiment 11. In experiment 13, however, the means of the students in E1 and E2 were significantly higher than those of C1 and C2, respectively.

In experiments 11 and 13, transfer tests were administered. The means for the students of E2 were significantly higher than those for the students of C2 in both experiments; the mean for the students of E1 was significantly higher only in experiment 13. In experiment 11, the mean for the students of C1 was about the same as that for the students for both E1 and E2. This relatively high mean for the students of C1 is associated with the lack of significance between E1 and C1.

The merits of the strategy with respect to simultaneous replication of each experiment, carrying out the experiments with different concepts, and carrying out the experiments with students at different grades and with different teachers may be inferred from analyzing the preceding results in various ways. Let us start with the simultaneous replication of each experiment.

In every experiment 1–10, a significant difference was found favoring one or both of the experimental schools and no difference was found favoring a control school. Based on this result, we may conclude that use of the PC lessons achieved desirable results with each process concept although the conclusion is most straightforward for the concepts of the experiments in which both E1 and E2 had significantly higher means. We also observed that in 6 of the 10 experiments, nonsignificant effects were found in one of the paired sets of schools, whereas significant effects were found in the other paired sets. Thus, had only six experiments been performed as single experiments in the set of schools showing the nonsignificant effects, a totally different and incorrect conclusion undoubtedly would have been drawn.

Experiments 1–5 were carried out with students of Grade 4 and experiments 6–10 with students of Grade 5. At both grade levels, 7 of the 10 differences between the means of the students of the paired sets of schools were significant. We may conclude from this that the PC lessons were equally effective at both grades. It is worth noting, however, that had only two experiments been run, namely experiment 1 with the Grade 4 students of E2–C2 and experiment 6 with the Grade 5 students of E1–C1, the probable conclusion would have been that the PC lessons were not effective at either grade. Furthermore, the unusually high mean of the C2 students of experiment 1 and the unusually low mean of the E1 students in experiment 6 would not have been identified.

Experiments 11 and 13 dealt with the same concepts as experiments 6 and 9; the identical PC lessons were used; and the same teachers of the four schools were involved in the two experiments. However, none of the students were the same, and the amount of time given to the PC lessons was greater in experiments 11 and 13. Recognizing these differences, we note that in experiments 6 and 11 dealing with the concept *observing,* only one of the four differences between the means of the paired set of schools was significant, whereas all of the four were for *controlling variables* in experiments 9 and 13. Shall we conclude that the PC lessons were less effective for *observing?* Possibly, but there were differences in conditions that may account for the lower achievements of the E1 and E2 students related to *observing.* Experiments 6 and 11 were conducted in the first weeks of the first semester, and these PC lessons were the first science instruction that the E1 and E2 students received during the school year. The teachers and the students were probably still getting adjusted to the opening of the school term. And as was pointed out earlier, anamalous findings were identified for E1 in experiment 6 and for both C1 and E2 in experiment 11. Nonetheless, one cannot rule out the possibility that the PC lesson was less effective for *observing.* Another matter regarding this concept merits attention. The project personnel, the participating teachers, and the experts in science education who reviewed the PC lesson for observing had difficulty in accepting the SAPA definition of *observing* because it included as one of three defining attributes, "accurately reporting the results of the observation." Logically, reporting in oral or written form what was observed does not appear to be part of the observing process itself.

Applications of Theory Regarding Cognitive Learning and Development

In Chapter 3, we saw that CLD theory provided the substantive basis for the content analysis, behavioral analysis, and instructional analysis that were performed on the science processes used in the SAPA curriculum. The results of these three analyses were incorporated in the PC lessons used in experiments 1–10 and in experiments 11 and 13.

In the preceding section of this chapter, we saw that the large majority of the PC means of the students of E1 and E2 were significantly higher than those of C1 and C2 and that in no experiment was any mean of C1 or C2 significantly higher than that of E1 or E2. We may now summarize the more specific CLD constructs and principles regarding the internal conditions of learning and the external conditions of learning that were supported by these results.

INTERNAL CONDITIONS OF CONCEPT LEARNING AND DEVELOPMENT

One principle is that the cognitive structure of the individual continues to increase as the individual learns and that learning concepts and organizing them into increasingly comprehensive conceptual cores is a major contributor to the growth of the cognitive structure. To learn a concept and to relate it to other concepts as part of a conceptual core implies knowledge of the defining attributes of the various concepts that comprise the conceptual core. In the present content analysis, the process concepts were organized into a hierarchy, and the attributes of each concept were identified as the subprocesses necessary to perform it, the prerequisite process, or both. These defining attributes of each process concept were taught to the students as part of each PC lesson. The positive results of the experimentation are in accordance with this view regarding the cognitive structure and its growth.

Another principle is that the four successively higher levels of the same concepts are attained in an invariant sequence. The internal conditions of learning regarded as necessary and possibly sufficient for attaining the successively higher levels of a concept are as follows: (a) mastery of the prior level; (b) functioning of at least one new mental operation in combination with the continuing operations of the prior level; (c) functioning of the operations of the prior level with content of increasing quantity and complexity experienced in a greater variety of contexts; (d) intending to attain the next higher level; and (e) persisting until it is attained. In addition, being able to discriminate the defining attributes of the concept and to name the concept and its defining attributes are necessary for carrying out the new operations at the formal level.

The mental operations necessary for attaining concepts at each of four successively higher levels were identified initially through a behavioral analysis of concept learning tasks and a review and synthesis of research related to the learning of concepts (Klausmeier, Ghatala, & Frayer, 1974). Results from subsequent controlled experiments and from a longitudinal study confirm the results of the behavioral analysis (Klausmeier & Allen, 1978).

The 10 PC lessons of the present project were prepared to help the students attain each of 10 process concepts at the formal level. It was presumed that the students would employ the meaningful reception operations specified for this level and also the mental operations at the preceding levels. The necessary operations of the prior level are discriminating, generalizing, and remembering, and those of the formal level are discriminating the defining attributes of the concept, acquiring and remembering the attribute names and the concept name, assimilating the information that is presented, remembering the information, and evaluating examples and nonexamples of the concept on the basis of the presence or absence of the defining attributes.

As noted earlier, controlled experimentation and longitudinal research were carried out in which tests were used that were designed to measure these operations. From the results of the earlier work, we inferred that these are the necessary operations. Based on these earlier results and the results of the present experiments, we may infer that the same mental operations are necessary for learning process concepts, namely, the process concepts of science.

Besides the mental operations necessary for learning the formal level, another internal condition is motivational, namely the individual must intend to learn and persist until the concept is attained. Activation of mental and motor acts, their direction, and continuing them until goal achievement are regarded as controlled by intentions. An individual's intending, like other operations such as discriminating and remembering, are controlled by a mechanism called executive control. The results of the present experiments are consistent with this view of motivation inasmuch as each PC lesson incorporated specific information designed to encourage the learner to attempt to learn the concept.

The preceding conclusions and discussion result from analysis of only the mean scores. In Table 8.1, the significant differences in the percentages of the students who achieved the mastery criteria are given. In general, these followed the means quite closely. Thus, the merits of simultaneous replication of each experiment and the use of the different concepts in the various experiments are about the same using this kind of analysis as they were when using the mean scores.

EXTERNAL CONDITIONS OF CONCEPT LEARNING

We may now turn to the external conditions of concept learning, all of which were incorporated in each PC lesson as was explained and illustrated in Chapter 5. The facilitative external conditions may be inferred from the following guidelines used in preparing the PC lessons.

1. Elicit student verbalization of the name of the concept and the defining attributes.
2. Establish an intention to learn the concept.
3. Emphasize the defining attributes of the concept.
4. Provide a definition of the concept in terms of its defining attributes.
5. Provide at least one rational set of examples and nonexamples of the concept.
6. Teach a strategy for evaluating examples and nonexamples of the concept.
7. Provide for feedback.

The results of the experiments are regarded as verifying these applications of CLD theory to learning the process concepts of science. But this is not to be construed as meaning the application of each principle might not have been made more effectively or that each principle was applied equally well. It is true that each PC lesson was prepared to guide the learning process precisely and to make it possible for the student to employ the necessary mental operations effectively. Despite this, writing and illustrating lessons to teach concepts is partly an art. We cannot be sure that all lesson developers will apply the guidelines equally well.

Of special interest when preparing a lesson is determining the number of examples and nonexamples to include. Klausmeier and Feldman (1975) found that three rational sets of examples and nonexamples produced better results than did one or two sets. Tennyson and Rothen (1977) and Rothen and Tennyson (1978) report that the most effective way to handle this matter is not to provide the same number of sets to all students. Rather, each student should determine the desired number. Their experimental students were found to be able to do this when computer-assisted instructional arrangements were provided.

In the schools of the present project, computer-assisted instructional arrangements were not available for teaching concepts, so we provided a fixed number of sets in each lesson. Our assumption was that the observant teacher could determine whether particular students needed more examples and nonexamples that the teacher might provide, or whether the students might profit from further study and review of the examples and nonexamples provided in the lesson. Given sufficient time and other instructional conditions, teachers probably can make these adjustments.

TRANSFER OF UNDERSTANDING CONCEPTS

One purpose of experiments 11 and 13 was to determine whether or not there was transfer of understanding the concept, gained from study of the PC lesson, to understanding it and performing it as a process on the phenomena and content included in the SAPA curriculum. Three of the four means of the E1 and E2 students in experiments 11 and 13 were significantly higher than those of the C1 and C2 students; and in experiment 11 where the mean of E1 was not, C1 had an unusually high mean. Thus, we may conclude with considerable confidence that understanding a process as a concept, gained from study of a PC lesson, transfers to understanding the process when performed on phenomena included in the SAPA exercise dealing with the same process. (It will be recalled that, by design, the PC tests did not include SAPA phenomena and content and the SAPA tests did not measure experiencing or performing the process except with SAPA content.) Returning to the merits of simultaneous replication of each experiment and testing the same hypothesis with more than one concept, we see that had only experiment 11 been conducted with the students of E1 and C1, we would probably have concluded that transfer of concept understanding did not occur.

In the preceding pages, conclusions have been presented regarding the learning and transfer of process concepts, based on the analyses of mean scores. Do these conclusions apply to all the students of E1 and E2 as individuals, or are they limited to a portion of the students? This question was not answered directly through an analysis of each individual student's PC performances. However, post-hoc analyses were made, comparing the performances of the highest one-third, the middle one-third, and the lowest one-third of the E1-C1 and E2-C2 students. The one-thirds were based on the students' SAPA pretest scores. Statistically significant differences were not found between the PC means that favored one or another group of the E1 or E2 students. We may conclude, then, that the PC lessons, and the applications of CLD theory tested through use of the lessons, were the same for students of these different entering achievement levels.

ADAPTING INSTRUCTION TO INDIVIDUAL
DIFFERENCES

As with the results regarding the PC lessons, we shall first review the results of the tests of significance performed on the SAPA data in the 13 experiments and consider how departures from the present strategy of replication and use of several concepts might have affected the results. Then we shall consider CLD theory and its applications to adapting instruction to individual differences.

Results of Adapting Science Instruction
to Students Entering Achievement Levels

Table 8.2 gives the results of tests of significance performed on the adjusted means of the SAPA posttests and on the percentage of the students who mastered the SAPA posttests. (The detailed information on which this summary table is based is given in tables of Chapters 6 and 7 and in related appendix tables.) Analysis of covariance was performed on the adjusted means. Chi-square tests were computed for the mastery percentages based on the observed data rather than the adjusted data.

The SAPA adjusted means for the students of E2 were significantly higher than those for C2 in experiments 3, 4, and 5. The adjusted means for the Grade 4 students of E1 were higher than those of the students of C1 only in experiment 4. Recall that the SAPA pretest score was used as the covariate in the analysis of covariance. The students of E1 had much higher SAPA pretest scores in experiments 1–5 than did the students of any other school. Having higher pretest scores tended to lower the adjusted posttest means; thus, the adjusted means for the students of E1 were about as low or lower than those of C1 and C2 in experiments 2 and 5. Even though the difference in the adjusted means between E1 and C1 was not significant in four of the five experiments, the difference in the percentage of mastery in four of the five experiments was. One may infer, based on all of the data gathered, that the students of E1 achieved as high as could be expected and that their high pretest scores contributed to the lack of significance when the analysis of covariance was performed. It is interesting to note, however, that the differences between the adjusted means were not significant in either experiment 1 or 2 in either set of paired schools. This suggests that starting the new method of adapting the SAPA instruction to the entering achievement levels of the students was probably not accomplished as successfully during the first two experiments as it was during the last three experiments that were carried out later during the same school year.

Turning to experiments 6–10 in Table 8.2, we observe that the adjusted means for the Grade 5 students of E2 were significantly higher than those for the Grade 5 students of C2 in all experiments 6–10. On the other hand, the adjusted means for the Grade 5 students of E1 were not significantly different from those of C1 in any experiment 6–10. The students of E1 had an adjusted mean that was about as low or lower than that of both C1 and C2 in four of the five experiments. This lower mean cannot be attributed to higher pretest scores. Rather, the students of E1 simply did not achieve higher than did those of C1 or C2. We observed earlier in this chapter that the differences between the PC means of E1 and C1 were also not significant in experiments 6, 7, and 8. Examination of the teacher logs, observations during workshops and in the classrooms, and post-hoc discussions suggest that during the first year of the experimentation the teachers of E1 were not able to change their instructional procedures in such a way as to use the PC lessons effectively or to adapt their SAPA instruction to the entering achievement levels of the students.

In experiments 11, 12, and 13, the adjusted SAPA means of the Grade 5 students of E1 were significantly higher than those of C1; the means for the students of E2 were significantly higher in experiments 12 and 13 but not in experiment 11. However, in experiment 11, significance approached the .05 level and the percentage of students mastering the SAPA posttest was significantly higher for the students of E2 than of C2.

We may conclude, based on the experiments 5–13, that the teachers of E1 were not successful in adapting SAPA instruction to the entering achievement levels of the students during their first year, but they were highly successful in the second year; whereas the teachers of E2 were successful during both years.

We may relate the preceding results to the research strategy that included simultaneous replication of each experiment, carrying out the separate experiments for the different SAPA processes, and carrying out the experiments with students of two grades and with different teachers. The merits of this strategy are readily apparent from examining Table 8.2 and are similar to those for the PC lesson presented in the preceding section. For example, in the seven of eight experiments of the first year that the adjusted SAPA means of the E2 students were higher than those of the C2 students, the means of the E1 students were not higher than those of C1. Had any of these seven experiments involving only the E1–C1 students been conducted separately, an incorrect conclusion would probably have been drawn. Furthermore, had only the E1–C1 Grade 4 students participated, the fact that the pretest scores of the E1 students were unusually high could not have been established. (Ap-

TABLE 8.2 Summary of Significant Differences: Adapting SAPA to Students' Entering Achievement Levels

Exp. no.	Grade	Name of process concept	E1–C1		E2–C2	
			Significant?	Anomaly	Significant?	Anomaly
1	4	Classifying				
		Mean	—		—	
		% Mastery	Yes		Yes	
2	4	Inferring				
		Mean	—	E1	—	
		% Mastery	Yes		—	
3	4	Predicting				
		Mean	—		Yes	
		% Mastery	Yes		Yes	
4	4	Using numbers				
		Mean	Yes		Yes	
		% Mastery	—		—	
5	4	Measuring				
		Mean	—	E1	Yes	
		% Mastery	Yes		Yes	
6	5	Observing				
		Mean	—	E1	Yes	
		% Mastery	Yes		Yes	

No.	n	Skill / Measure			
7	5	Inferring			
		Mean	—		Yes
		% Mastery	—		Yes
8	5	Using space–time relationships			
		Mean	—	E1	Yes
		% Mastery	Yes		Yes
9	5	Controlling variables			
		Mean	Yes	E1	Yes
		% Mastery	—		Yes
10	5	Communicating			
		Mean	—	E1	Yes
		% Mastery	—		Yes
11	5	Observing			
		Mean	Yes		—
		% Mastery	Yes		Yes
12	5	Inferring			
		Mean	Yes		Yes
		% Mastery	Yes		Yes
13	5	Controlling variables			
		Mean	Yes		Yes
		% Mastery	Yes		Yes

parently, these E1 students had achieved higher than the E2, C1, or C2 students on earlier SAPA exercises dealing with the same processes.)

The simultaneous replication of the experiments, the use of different concepts, and the follow-up of the Grade 4 students of experiments 1–5 into Grade 5 also yielded interesting results. For example, the same teachers of E1 whose Grade 5 students did not achieve higher than the students of C1 in experiments 6–10 taught the Grade 5 students of experiments 11–13. In each of these experiments, their students achieved signficantly higher than those of C1. Thus, these teachers also were able to adapt the SAPA instruction to the entering achievement levels of the students. As a matter of fact, in experiments 6–13, the SAPA mean of the students of the E1 or E2 teacher in at least one experiment was higher than that of the C1 or C2 students. Therefore, it appears that the method of adapting the SAPA science instruction is equally effective with all concepts rather than only with some of them.

Applications of Theory Regarding Individual Differences

We may consider the prior results in relation to applications made of the theoretical design dealing with instructional programming for the individual student. This generic seven-step design takes into account the wide differences that Klausmeier and Allen (1978) found among students in attaining concepts; for example, some individuals at age 9 were as advanced as others at age 18. It also takes into account within-individual variability in achieving concepts from different subject fields, including science. A better application of this design was made to the SAPA instruction in the experimental schools in experiments 11, 12, and 13 when more time was given to the SAPA instruction than in experiments 1–10. Recall that in experiments 11–13 the first part of the instruction on each SAPA exercise was adapted to the entering achievement levels of the students. After all the students received about the same amount of instruction, a posttest was given. Based on the posttest results, further differentiation of instruction was carried out. In these experiments, the adjusted means of the E1 and E2 students were generally much higher than those of C1 and C2 and the percentages of the students achieving the mastery criterion were even more favorable for the students of E1 and E2.

As noted earlier, post-hoc analyses were performed on the SAPA data of the highest one-third, the middle one-third, and the lowest one-third of the students, the groups being based on the students' SAPA entering achievement levels. Statistically significant differences were not found that consistently favored one or another of these three groups and it appears that this method of adapting the SAPA science instruction to the entering achievement levels of the students was equally effective for these different groups.

Despite these excellent results, the generic model was not applied fully, even in experiment 13. All the students of E1 and E2 were still progressing through the same number of SAPA exercises each year. The rapid learners were not proceeding through more exercises even though they probably could have been without experiencing any difficulty. Similarly, the slower learners were not taking fewer exercises. During the project, it became clear to the project personnel and teachers that some of the slower learners were unable to deal effectively with these abstract science processes either as concepts to be understood or as processes to be performed.

It was our judgment that requiring these students to spend more school time receiving SAPA instruction would not yield higher science achievement. We also felt that the students who learned very little, as inferred from their very low SAPA posttest scores, should not proceed from one set of SAPA exercises to another with the students who achieved high. At the same time, requiring all the students to meet a mastery criterion before proceeding to the next set of exercises of a SAPA hierarchy would not be wise, particularly if the same science process would be encountered at a higher level of sophistication in a later set of exercises. Needed instead was further differentiation of the science instruction, starting in Grade 1, that would permit the rapid learners either to complete more sets of SAPA exercises than the slow learners or to complete other science or other curricular activities.

A final word may be in order regarding the advisability of researchers in the behavioral sciences, and particularly in education and psychology, to relate their experimentation to a theoretical framework. This appears to be necessary for the refinement and revision of theory and also to advance knowledge in a field systematically and cumulatively. Replication of the experiments is also critical. It would seem wise to carry out both simultaneous replication, in which the identical experiment is carried out in two different situations, and successive near-replications, in which only a single aspect of the experiment is changed.

One unresolved problem related to replication is that the M.S. or Ph.D. candidate purportedly must do an "original" study. Another is that monetary support is more readily available for funding an original study than a replication. A third is the additional cost involved. However, it does not increase costs greatly to conduct a simultaneous replication. And retrospectively, in examining the results of the 13 experiments, we see that simultaneous replication proved to be beneficial. In many instances, had only one experiment been conducted without simultaneous replication, an incorrect conclusion probably would have been drawn concerning the internal or external conditions of concept learning, adapting science instruction to the entering achievement levels of the students, or the applicability of CLD theory to learning process concepts.

REFERENCES

AAAS Commission on Science Education. *Science — A process approach.* Washington, D.C.: American Association for the Advancement of Science/Xerox, 1967.

Glaser, R. G. Some implications of previous work on learning and individual differences. In R. M. Gagné (Ed.), *Learning and individual differences.* Columbus, Oh.: Charles E. Merrill, 1967, 1–18.

Klausmeier, H. J., & Allen, P. S. *Cognitive development of children and youth: A longitudinal study.* New York: Academic Press, 1978.

Klausmeier, H. J., & Associates. *Cognitive learning and development: Information-processing and Piagetian perspectives.* Cambridge, Mass.: Ballinger, 1979.

Klausmeier, H. J., & Feldman, K. V. Effects of a definition and a varying number of examples and nonexamples on concept attainment. *Journal of Educational Psychology,* 1975, 67(2), 174–178.

Klausmeier, H. J., Ghatala, E. S., & Frayer, D. A. *Conceptual learning and development: A cognitive view.* New York: Academic Press, 1974.

Rothen, W., & Tennyson, R. D. Application of Bayes' theory in designing computer-based adaptive instructional strategies. *Educational Psychologist,* 1978, 12(3), 317–323.

Siegel, L. S., & Brainerd, C. J. (Eds.), *Alternatives to Piaget: Critical essays on the theory.* New York: Academic Press, 1978.

Snow, R. E. Research on aptitude for learning: A progress report. In L. S. Shulman (Ed.), *Review of research in education* (Vol. 4). Itasca, Il.: F. E. Peacock, 1976, 50–105.

Tennyson, R. D., & Rothen, W. Pretask and on-task adaptive design strategies for selecting number of instances in concept acquisition. *Journal of Educational Psychology,* 1977, 69(5), 586–592.

Appendix

TABLE A6.1 Mean Number of Minutes Spent on Sets of SAPA Exercises, Including Time for Posttest Administration in Experimental Schools, and on Process-Concept Lessons, Experiments 1–5

Experiment	Lesson	E1	C1	E2	C2
1	SAPA classifying 8	135	115	150	150
1	SAPA classifying 9	140	110	170	90
1	Total	275	225	320	240
2	SAPA inferring 3	140	115	145	120
2	SAPA inferring 4	140	120	150	120
2	SAPA inferring 5	135	120	150	120
2	Total	415	355	445	360
3	SAPA predicting 2	140	105	150	120
3	SAPA predicting 3	140	105	160	135
3	Total	280	210	310	255
4	SAPA using numbers 10	150	130	150	150
4	SAPA using numbers 11	150	130	150	150
4	Total	300	260	300	300
5	SAPA measuring 11	130	120	130	120
5	SAPA measuring 12	150	140	150	120
5	SAPA measuring 13	150	90	150	90
5	SAPA measuring 14	150	160	150	180
5	SAPA measuring 15	150	120	150	120
5	Total	730	630	730	630
1	Classifying PC lesson	150	0	150	0
2	Inferring PC lesson	150	0	120	0
3	Predicting PC lesson	120	0	100	0
4	Using numbers PC lesson	150	0	150	0
5	Measuring PC lesson	150	0	150	0

TABLE A6.2 Results of Tests of Significance between Adjusted Means of E1–C1 and E2–C2, SAPA Tests, Experiments 1–5

Experiment	E1–C1	E2–C2
1	.57	.33
2	.86	.29
3	.10	.001
4	.01	.01
5	.54	.001

TABLE A6.3 Adjusted Means, E1, C1, E2, C2, SAPA Tests, Experiments 1–5

Experiments	E1	C1	E2	C2
1	13.03	12.67	13.08	12.65
2	19.84	19.70	21.45	20.58
3	15.46	14.38	16.61	15.00
4	11.77	10.35	12.00	10.65
5	32.79	32.15	36.03	31.91

TABLE A6.4 Results of Chi-Square Tests of Significance between Frequencies of Mastery of SAPA Tests, E1–C1 and E2–C2, Experiments 1–5

Experiment	E1–C1	E2–C2
1	.01	.05
2	.05	NS[a]
3	.001	.01
4	NS	NS
5	.05	.05

[a] NS means "not significant."

TABLE A6.5 Results of Tests of Significance between Means of E1–C1 and E2–C2, PC Tests, Experiments 1–5

Experiment	E1–C1	E2–C2
1	.002	.80
2	.001	.002
3	.001	.15
4	.001	.001
5	.78	.001

TABLE A6.6 Results of Chi-Square Tests of Significance between Frequencies of Mastery of Process-Concept Tests, E1–C1 and E2–C2, Experiments 1–5

Experiment	E1–C1	E2–C2
1	.001	NS[a]
2	.05	.001
3	.001	NS
4	.001	.001
5	NS	.001

[a] NS means "not significant."

TABLE A6.7 Mean Number of Minutes Spent on Sets of SAPA Exercises, Including Time for Posttest Administration in Experimental Schools, and on Process-Concept Lessons, Experiments 6–10

Experiment	Lesson	E1	C1	E2	C2
6	SAPA observing 16	180	120	150	135
6	SAPA observing 17	220	135	150	135
6	SAPA observing 18	120	120	150	180
6	Total	520	375	450	450
7	SAPA inferring 6	140	180	150	180
7	SAPA inferring 7	160	135	185	180
7	SAPA inferring 8	200	180	145	180
7	Total	500	515	480	540
8	SAPA using space-time 15	160	120	150	120
8	SAPA using space-time 16	60	60	90	180
8	Total	220	180	240	300
9	SAPA controlling variables 1	180	150	240	135
9	SAPA controlling variables 2	180	150	240	180
9	Total	360	300	480	315
10	SAPA communicating 11	160	180	150	180
10	SAPA communicating 12	140	150	150	135
10	Total	300	330	300	315
6	Observing PC lesson	180	0	150	0
7	Inferring PC lesson	120	0	120	0
8	Using space-time PC lesson	120	0	135	0
9	Controlling variables PC lesson	180	0	200	0
10	Communicating PC lesson	120	0	120	0

TABLE A6.8   Results of Tests of Significance between Adjusted
Means of E1-C1 and E2-C2, SAPA Tests, Experiments 6-10

Experiment	E1-C1	E2-C2
6	.70	.001
7	.30	.001
8	.25	.001
9	.22	.001
10	.27	.001

TABLE A6.9   Adjusted Means, E1, C1, E2, C2, SAPA Tests,
Experiments 6-10

Experiments	E1	C1	E2	C2
6	20.88	20.60	23.96	21.59
7	19.15	18.42	21.21	17.97
8	11.88	11.30	15.72	11.00
9	13.45	14.20	15.90	13.63
10	12.89	12.19	15.65	12.31

TABLE A6.10   Results of Chi-Square Tests of Significance between
Frequencies of Mastery of SAPA Tests, E1-C1 and E2-C2,
Experiments 6-10

Experiment	E1-C1	E2-C2
6	.001	.001
7	NS[a]	.001
8	.001	.001
9	NS	.001
10	NS	.001

[a] NS means "not significant."

TABLE A6.11 Results of Tests of Significance between Means of E1–C1 and E2–C2, PC Tests, Experiments 6–10

Experiment	E1–C1	E2–C2
6	.61	.001
7	.50	.05
8	.62	.001
9	.02	.001
10	.001	.001

TABLE A6.12 Results of Chi-Square Tests of Significance between Frequencies of Mastery of Process-Concept Tests, E1–C1 and E2–C2, Experiments 6–10

Experiment	E1–C1	E2–C2
6	NS[a]	NS
7	NS	NS
8	NS	.001
9	NS	.05
10	.001	.001

[a] NS means "not significant."

TABLE A6.13 Summary of Significant Differences for Total Groups of Students of E1–C1 and E2–C2 and for Low, Middle, and High Pretest-Based Groups of E1–C1 and E2–C2: SAI

Grade		E1–C1 Total	Low	Middle	High
4	Dec	.02	—	—	.03
	May	.006	—	—	—
5	Dec	—	—	—	—
	May	—	—	—	—

Grade		E2–C2 Total	Low	Middle	High
4	Dec	—	—	—	.02[a]
	May	—	—	—	—
5	Dec	.02[a]	.04[a]	—	—
	May	—	—	—	—

[a] Difference favoring a control school.

TABLE A6.14 Correlations of SAPA Pretest with SAPA Posttest and PC Test, Experiments 1–10

Experiment	School	N	SAPA pretest with	
			SAPA post	PC post
1: Classifying	E1	58	.58 (.001)	.50 (.001)
	C1	47	.24 (–)	.08 (–)
	E2	59	.40 (.001)	.30 (.05)
	C2	51	.37 (.01)	.27 (–)
2: Inferring	E1	58	.72 (.001)	.47 (.001)
	C1	47	.53 (.001)	.43 (.001)
	E2	59	.34 (.01)	.51 (.001)
	C2	51	.37 (.01)	.12 (–)
3: Predicting	E1	58	.61 (.001)	.50 (.001)
	C1	47	.59 (.001)	.26 (–)
	E2	59	.59 (.001)	.39 (.01)
	C2	51	.71 (.001)	.06 (–)
4: Using numbers	E1	58	.49 (.001)	.10 (–)
	C1	47	.61 (.001)	.33 (.05)
	E2	59	.70 (.001)	.36 (.01)
	C2	51	.54 (.001)	.39 (.01)
5: Measuring	E1	58	.81 (.001)	.53 (.001)
	C1	47	.82 (.001)	.50 (.001)
	E2	59	.74 (.001)	.39 (.01)
	C2	51	.65 (.001)	.22 (–)

Experiment	School	N	SAPA pretest with	
			SAPA post	PC post
6: Observing	E1	60	.65 (.01)	.33 (.01)
	C1	46	.51 (.001)	.47 (.001)
	E2	71	.67 (.001)	.52 (.001)
	C2	56	.61 (.001)	.47 (.001)
7: Inferring	E1	60	.27 (.05)	.35 (.01)
	C1	46	.61 (.001)	.28 (–)
	E2	71	.37 (.001)	.42 (.001)
	C2	56	.68 (.001)	.23 (–)
8: Using space–time relations	E1	60	.33 (.01)	.44 (.001)
	C1	46	.04 (–)	.46 (.001)
	E2	71	.34 (.01)	.62 (.001)
	C2	56	.53 (.001)	.26 (–)
9: Controlling variables	E1	60	.44 (.001)	.34 (.01)
	C1	46	.69 (.001)	.54 (.001)
	E2	71	.45 (.001)	.46 (.001)
	C2	56	.59 (.001)	.65 (.001)
10: Communicating	E1	60	.68 (.001)	.53 (.001)
	C1	46	.47 (.001)	.25 (–)
	E2	71	.58 (.001)	.46 (.001)
	C2	56	.64 (.001)	.39 (.001)

TABLE A6.15 Cutoff SAPA Pretest Scores and Corresponding Numbers of Students with Low, Middle, and High SAPA Pretest Scores in E1, C1, E2, and C2: Experiments 1-2, 3, 4-5, 6-7-8, and 9-10

School	Group						Experiments					
		N	1, 2	N	3	N	4, 5	N	6, 7, 8	N	9, 10
E1	Low	14		13		12		22		20	
	Middle	17	21	16	31	22	27	14	35	20	18
	High	27	28	29	40	24	38	24	42	20	23
C1	Low	24		19		23		15		18	
	Middle	20	21	12	31	13	27	20	35	14	19
	High	3	28	2	45	11	38	11	42	14	23
E2	Low	22		21		21		20		23	
	Middle	17	23	18	33	22	28	25	36	25	20
	High	20	27	20	39	16	36	26	43	23	25
C2	Low	14		13		14		20		24	
	Middle	23	23	22	33	17	28	19	36	20	20
	High	14	27	16	39	20	36	17	43	12	25

TABLE A7.1 Experiment 11: Levels of Significance between Adjusted Means for E1-C1 and E2-C2 and between Frequencies of Mastery of SAPA Posttest, Transfer Test, and PC Test

Test	Differences Adjusted Means		Differences Mastery Frequencies	
	E1-C1	E2-C2	E1-C1	E2-C2
SAPA	.008	.13	.001	.001
Transfer	.19	.001	—	.001
PC	.13	.93	—	.01

TABLE A7.2 Experiment 11: Adjusted SAPA Posttest Means and Transfer Test Means for E1, C1, E2, and C2

Test	E1	C1	E2	C2
SAPA	23.57	21.71	23.40	22.44
Transfer	8.62	8.55	7.97	7.18

TABLE A7.3 Experiment 12: Levels of Significance between Adjusted Means of E1-C1 and E2-C2 and between Frequencies of Mastery for SAPA Posttest

Test	Differences Adjusted Means		Differences Mastery Frequencies	
	E1-C1	E2-C2	E1-C1	E2-C2
SAPA	.001	.001	.001	.001

TABLE A7.4 Experiment 12: Adjusted SAPA Posttest Means for E1, C1, E2, and C2

Test	E1	C1	E2	C2
SAPA	23.39	19.48	22.09	18.86

TABLE A7.5   Experiment 13: Levels of Significance between Adjusted Means of E1–C1 and E2–C2 and between Frequencies of Mastery for SAPA Posttest, Transfer Test, and PC Test

Test	Differences Adjusted Means		Differences Mastery Frequencies	
	E1–C1	E2–C2	E1–C1	E2–C2
SAPA	.002	.001	001	.001
Transfer	.001	.001	.001	.001
PC	.001	.001	.001	.001

TABLE A7.6   Experiment 13: Adjusted SAPA Posttest Means and Transfer Test Means for E1, C1, E2, and C2

Test	E1	C1	E2	C2
SAPA	16.30	14.70	15.90	12.82
Transfer	7.99	5.35	7.73	4.71

TABLE A7.7   Experiments 11–12 and 13: Cutoff SAPA Pretest Scores and Corresponding Numbers of Students with Low, Middle, and High SAPA Pretest Scores in E1, C1, E2, and C2

School	Group			Experiments		
		N	11–12	N	13	
E1	Low	17		15		
	Middle	22	36	19	17	
	High	22	44	22	24	
C1	Low	21		21		
	Middle	17	36	18	17	
	High	10	44	10	24	
E2	Low	23		23		
	Middle	18	37	16	19	
	High	25	43	25	23	
C2	Low	19		10		
	Middle	22	37	25	19	
	High	14	43	18	23	

TABLE A7.8   Experiments 11, 12, and 13: Correlations and Levels of Significance among SAPA Pretests, SAPA Posttests, Transfer Tests, and PC Tests

Experiment	School	N	SAPA Pretest with			SAPA posttest with		PC with
			SAPA post	PC	Transfer	PC	Transfer	Transfer
11: Observing	E1	61	.50 (.001)	.50 (.001)	.40 (.001)	.47 (.001)	.28 (.05)	.59 (.001)
	C1	48	.60 (.001)	.28 (.05)	.18 (—)	.40 (.001)	.21 (—)	.63 (.001)
	E2	66	.61 (.001)	.52 (.001)	.46 (.001)	.51 (.001)	.68 (.001)	.54 (.001)
	C2	55	.37 (.01)	.50 (.001)	.14 (—)	.35 (.05)	.29 (.05)	.37 (.01)
12: Inferring	E1	61	.39 (.001)					
	C1	48	.52 (.001)					
	E2	66	.61 (.001)					
	C2	55	.33 (.05)					
13: Controlling variables	E1	56	.55 (.001)	.61 (.001)	.51 (.001)	.77 (.001)	.65 (.001)	.72 (.001)
	C1	49	.46 (.001)	.24 (—)	.32 (.05)	.22 (—)	.21 (—)	.39 (.001)
	E2	64	.63 (.001)	.58 (.001)	.46 (.001)	.69 (.001)	.61 (.001)	.67 (.001)
	C2	53	.47 (.001)	.08 (—)	.19 (—)	.43 (.001)	.26 (—)	.38 (.001)

TABLE A7.9   Adjusted Means for Grade 5 Students of E1, C1, E2, and C2: SAI

	E1	C1	E2	C2
December	45.91	46.09	41.81	43.34
May	42.97	42.81	43.45	41.12

Index

EDUCATIONAL PSYCHOLOGY

continued from page ii

Harvey Lesser. Television and the Preschool Child: A Psychological Theory of Instruction and Curriculum Development

Donald J. Treffinger, J. Kent Davis, and Richard E. Ripple (eds.). Handbook on Teaching Educational Psychology

Harry L. Hom, Jr. and Paul A. Robinson (eds.). Psychological Processes in Early Education

J. Nina Lieberman. Playfulness: Its Relationship to Imagination and Creativity

Samuel Ball (ed.). Motivation in Education

Erness Bright Brody and Nathan Brody. Intelligence: Nature, Determinants, and Consequences

António Simões (ed.). The Bilingual Child: Research and Analysis of Existing Educational Themes

Gilbert R. Austin. Early Childhood Education: An International Perspective

Vernon L. Allen (ed.). Children as Teachers: Theory and Research on Tutoring

Joel R. Levin and Vernon L. Allen (eds.). Cognitive Learning in Children: Theories and Strategies

Donald E. P. Smith and others. A Technology of Reading and Writing (in four volumes).

> Vol. 1. *Learning to Read and Write: A Task Analysis (by Donald E. P. Smith)*
> Vol. 2. *Criterion-Referenced Tests for Reading and Writing (by Judith M. Smith, Donald E. P. Smith, and James R. Brink)*
> Vol. 3. *The Adaptive Classroom (by Donald E. P. Smith)*
> Vol. 4. *Designing Instructional Tasks (by Judith M. Smith)*

Phillip S. Strain, Thomas P. Cooke, and Tony Apolloni. Teaching Exceptional Children: Assessing and Modifying Social Behavior